The Price of Independence

A REALISTIC VIEW OF THE
AMERICAN REVOLUTION

Broadus Mitchell

New York
Oxford University Press
1974

Affectionately dedicated to
Sarah Otis Mitchell and Jacob Alexander Dyer
who were not available last time

Foreword

THIS IS A BOOK OF MISFORTUNES AND DISCOURAGEMENTS, THE DISCONCERTING BYPRODUCTS OF WAR. SOME WERE HUMAN FAILURES, OF FAITHLESSNESS, GREED, ANGER. OTHERS were cruelties, not deliberately perpetrated, but inescapable in crowded prisons and pestilential, starving camps. Persecution of loyalists by patriots and retaliatory raids by King's men were not innocent, though surpassed by murder and arson on the frontiers. More mischiefs were political and economic. These were not ascribable to individuals, but resulted from inexperience and unpreparedness of a people suddenly plunged into military contest. Years were necessary to repair the defects of public law and provide for payment of neglected debt. Certain hurtful dislocations could not have been avoided with the best intent and knowledge. Included were the breakdown of the credit of the Continental Congress and the lyrical inflation of prices. These were accompaniments of war that have plagued nations far better established than the erstwhile American colonies.

Actually, the undeveloped character of the country eased the social privations and injustices. America was almost wholly agricultural, with a sparse population in a large area. Forces that would have had violent impact in a tight-knit, sophisticated economy were weakened and diffused. Local self-sufficiency subtracted from the authority of the central government, but by the same token reduced wartime restraints of an advanced community.

It would be agreeable to say that the moral fervor of the people for the War of Independence was high. Such devotion would have made sufferings bearable as the badges of partiotism. Unhappily, such praise must be qualified. In the first place, more of the people were opposed or indifferent to the cause than espoused it. This internal conflict drew off energies from fighting the foreign foe. Moreover, at times lassitude settled on those who before had been active in supporting the national effort. Enlistment dragged, drafts were resisted, militia downed their arms at the end of short terms of service. This reluctance was especially discreditable when a French army arrived to co-operate with American troops who did not report to camp. The sloth of states in taxing themselves in order to forward money and supplies was the counterpart of lagging recruitment of the ranks.

Fortunately, the frequent unresponsiveness of Americans was balanced by lack of ardor of the enemy. The Howe brothers—Lord Richard the Admiral and General Sir William—were on the whole half-hearted in pressing the war. They hoped that after moderate chastisement the colonies would abandon the demand for separation and return to the protection of the mother country. Sir Henry Clinton, when he succeeded to command, was more committed to his responsibility, but his confirmed caution saved the Americans from worse punishment. Burgoyne boasted and blundered. Of the principal British Generals, Lord Cornwallis was the most in earnest, but he came to grief by following the orders of Clinton and waiting in vain for the promised rescue.

In contrast to the faltering of the enemy was the excellence of the ally in financial, military, and naval assistance. It is doubtful whether the American Revolution could have succeeded without the help of France. Practically, it made no difference that the motive of the French was ulterior to the American aim, that it was to be revenged on Britain for defeat in 1763.

What has been said of divided loyalties in this country, and of lukewarm patriots, must not obscure the fidelity of many leaders and bodies of citizens and soldiers. The chief of these, in fact as well as in name, was George Washington. The dark shadows in these pages cast his heroism into brighter light. Attempts have been made by critics, in several ways, to diminish his merit. As a General, it is said, he avoided battles and, when all-out fights were forced on him, he lost more than he won. His deliberation betokened a slowness of mind. Most erroneous of all, he has been pictured as a bronze statue, admirable but insensitive, the mold of nobility devoid of the common human failings. The truth is he was modest, confessed to costly mistakes, and suffered unfair censure in silence rather than reply and injure the cause in which he was embarked. His patriotic sacrifice knew no limits. In spite of stateliness, he had his lighter moments. He did not underestimate the dangers that he set himself to overcome.

Washington's prevailing optimism, which did much to keep up the spirits of the country, was encouraged by the realization, if one may judge, that America would be hard to subdue. The enemy had to send armies and supplies across three thousand miles of ocean. Capture of principal coast cities, including the capital, did not severely impede the life of the country. He persevered in the confidence that all would come right in the end. The more one inquires into his qualities and actions, the greater the admiration in which one must hold him. Of those who disparaged him, numbers later repented of their lapses. If a man is to be known by his friends, a remarkable company of partiots, military and civil, stood around the Commander in Chief. Their contributions worthily appear in the story that follows.

As always in trying to describe a period in history, more evidence of the opinions of the general run of people would be welcome. Literacy during the Revolution was far rarer than since, so that revealing records, reflecting common approval or complaint, are correspondingly scarce. Where kept at all, or where they have survived, diaries of soldiers in the ranks are apt to note daily doings, not attitudes toward public policy. With the poor transport and communications existing, parts of the country were little touched by the war. Where enemy armies passed, many Americans were said to have taken British protection. Desertions from patriot forces offer some indication, though often induced by crops to be harvested or by dislike of subordinate officers. The most eager enlistment for war service seems to have been on privateers; here recruiting was intensive, with the promise of adventure and booty. On the whole, the soldiers appear to have borne their lot with characteristically sardonic humor.

B.M.

New York City
November 1, 1973

Contents

Rash Incursion

A T DEERFIELD, MASSACHUSETTS, IS PRESERVED AN OLD DOOR WHICH, IN FRONTIER DAYS, GUARDED THE STRONGEST HOUSE IN THE VILLAGE. GASHED BY TOMAHAWKS, IT IS a souvenir of the massacre of 1704, in which fifty of Deerfield's inhabitants, men, women, and children, were killed and most of the rest carried off into cruel captivity. That was only one of many murderous raids on the American frontiersmen, for the Indians, and, later, the French, struck time and time again across the Canadian border.

When Canada was annexed by Britain in 1763, the colonists of New England and New York relaxed, but only briefly, for the Quebec Act of 1774 revived their fears. By that Act, the whole region north of the Ohio and between the Appalachians and the Mississippi was assigned to the Canadian province, and several of the American colonies had land claims in that area. Moreover, the new Act fed the fur trade to Montreal, to the injury of Albany. It also reinstated the Catholic establishment, and the American Protestants were intolerant of "Popery." Accustomed to a large measure of self-government, and demanding more, the Americans were suspicious of royal rule in Canada. They were also wary, for the St. Lawrence gave easy access to Lake Champlain, Lake George, and the Hudson River as an invasion route.

Now, at the start of the American Revolution, volunteers from New England and New York, men who had bitter memories of Canadian incursions, were gathering in Washington's ill-organized camp at Cambridge. Among the armed assemblage were two patriots whose excessive physical and emotional vitality was not matched by prudent judgment. Ethan Allen, leader of the Green Mountain Boys, and Benedict Arnold, far-ranging enterpriser of the Connecticut coast, had recently surprised and captured Ticonderoga, the natural jumping-off place for an assault upon Canada. But the Continental Congress had no mind to improve upon this exploit; Ticonderoga was ordered abandoned and any expedition against Canada was flatly forbidden.

Allen and Arnold resented the forfeit of their bold stroke. They urged, with ebullient rhetoric, that Montreal and Quebec were weakly held, and that they now had a God-sent opportunity to conquer that desirable region. And, with minimum knowledge, they argued that the Canadian people were eager to be liberated, and that the Indians would become allies, or at least remain neutral.

Congress had already embraced this ambition, and ordered General Philip Schuyler to command an expedition through Lake Champlain against Montreal. Washington authorized Arnold's assault by the eastward route against Quebec. This first American offensive, and one of few in the American Revolution, was the attack on Canada in 1775–76. It was ill-conceived and ill-executed, both politically and militarily, for which Washington must bear a share of blame. We remember the vigor with which Benedict Arnold pursued the enterprise, in spite of miserable hardships, but we forget the utter failure of the undertaking.

[4]

The idea was that the French Canadians would be drawn into a continental colonial revolt. Actually, they were content under British rule, for their civil law and Catholic religion were preserved. The population was sparse and peasant-minded. The only aid given the invading forces was that of individual farmers, in petty trade at high prices. The small Canadian military contingent that sided with the Americans ran away from the attack on Quebec. Following the expulsion of the Americans, Canadians who had in any way assisted the invasion trembled lest they suffer British reprisals, and were more than ever quiescent.

The campaign was planned in two thrusts, one, by way of Lake Champlain, against Montreal as the first objective, the other, from the Atlantic seaboard through the wilds of Maine, against Quebec. The former was with difficulty accomplished, while the exhaustions of the latter foredoomed any military success. As communication between Montreal and Quebec by means of the St. Lawrence River, a distance of 150 miles, was easy, it is hard to understand why the separate approach to Quebec was attempted. The misdirected enthusiasm of Arnold in the camp at Cambridge must be the explanation. Always vain, he was irked because Ethan Allen got the credit for the capture of Ticonderoga, while his own role was ignored. The investment of Boston was tedious, and Arnold was eager for action, as were others.

At the end of June 1775, General Philip Schuyler, commanding in the Northern Department, was ordered to Lake Champlain with a view to taking possession of Canada. His second in command was the admirable Brigadier General Richard Montgomery, who, three years before, had resigned from the British army, settled in New York, and espoused the patriot cause. On reaching Ticonderoga in mid-July of 1775, they found the fort sadly in need of troops, supplies, and equipment. Discipline was bad: the citizen-soldiers defied their officers' authority, while those from New England were at odds with the New Yorkers and their hostility was to grow worse. While waiting for reinforcements, Schuyler constructed a couple of rigged vessels and sufficient bateaux to move against the British at the other end of Champlain. There General Carleton, the Canadian governor, had small forts on the Richelieu River, at St. John's and Chambly, and he was building two vessels and the necessary bateaux. Believing it was the moment to strike before Carleton could come against them, 1200 Americans sailed down the lake and encamped on Ile aux Noix in the Richelieu, September 4. In the next fortnight they made abortive approaches to the fort at St. John's. It was mimic warfare, with reluctant, almost rebellious troops who each time scampered back to their temporary base on the island. Schuyler fell ill and turned over command to Montgomery.

Finally the fort at St. John's was besieged. Montgomery now had 2000 men; the garrison was little more than a third as numerous. A party of Americans moved past St. John's and readily compelled the surrender of the weak fort at Chambly. The enemy's armed vessels in the river were sunk. After holding out for nearly two months, the St. John's garrison surrendered.

Having downed Montreal's outer defenses, Montgomery quickly captured that town. The place was not defensible, certainly not by the few score of troops Carleton had there. Carleton put his garrison and stores aboard his little fleet in the St. Lawrence. The population, thus deserted, attempted no resistance. Carleton's vessels and all they contained fell into American hands. Carleton himself escaped to Quebec in disguise.

Every feature of the expedition from Cambridge appears to have been impromptu and characterized by a light-hearted ignorance of the conditions to be encountered. In late August of 1775, a Kennebec boatbuilder, Reuben Colburn, was queried on the construction of 200 "Battoos" (bateaux); a fortnight later the order was given, and by September 13 Arnold's entire corps of something more than 1100 had marched from Cambridge to Newburyport.

[6]

Only 250 frontier riflemen, those from Virginia under Captain Daniel Morgan, could be called woodsmen, though that term was supposed to apply to the whole force of volunteers. The others, except for a few unattached youngsters (Aaron Burr among them), were New England farmers. The bateaux, which had been hastily built of unseasoned pine, and were supposed to convey supplies and five or six men each, proved to be the chief impediment. Each bateau, which was shaped like a breadtray, weighed 400 pounds when empty. This would not have been so bad except that navigation on the waterways to be traversed was more dangerous and the portages more numerous than had been guessed. The score of carrying-places ranged in length from a few rods to eight miles. The most nearly exact knowledge of the route they had was from the map and journal of Lieutenant John Montresor, an English engineer, who had traveled it in June and July of 1761. His description of the terrain was imperfect in important respects, but particularly in that he could not have told of the floods, freezes, and snows of the autumn season in which Arnold's men embarked. Also, Montresor had had the judgment to use Indian canoes, each light enough to be carried, if necessary, by a single man, while one bateau required four men, and even then their shoulders were painfully rubbed by the rough gunwales. The frail canoe was more easily maneuvered in rough water and less apt to be swamped or smashed than the unwieldy bateau.

Arnold thought the journey, or amphibious "march," would take twenty days; it took forty-five. The distance covered from Fort Western on the Kennebec (Augusta, Maine) was 350 miles, not the 180 expected. The route embraced tolerable going up the Kennebec, with portages around successive falls. Next was a roughly equal distance that included the "Great Carrying Place" that separated the Kennebec from the Dead River, which led into Lake Megantic. The third and longest stage was through the Chaudière River, which emptied into the St. Lawrence near Quebec.

The middle portion brought the worst trials. The populated banks had been left behind. This was an untouched wilderness of rushing current, rocky rapids, extensive bogs, and stretches of fallen timber. Boats were wrecked and food supplies lost. At the last point where it was possible to turn back, one division, a fourth of the whole corps, deliberately abandoned the march and took with them more than their share of the dwindling pork and flour. Often the loyal men who pressed forward had to wade waist deep to guide the bateaux through rock-strewn rips. Those who did not labor at the oars and setting-poles had their own troubles in tramping through rough bordering country. All were obliged to struggle boats and baggage over the "carries," making several trips at each portage, with barrels and bales slung beneath poles. The burdens were heavier if the way lay through ice-glazed swamps, where a man sank half up to his knees. Deluges of wind-driven rain—it may have been a wandering hurricane—produced special discomfort and danger. The stream no longer revealed its course, for adjacent lands were flooded. The marching parties were compelled to go miles out of the way to find fordable depths. One group almost perished as the result of taking a wrong direction in the waste of waters.

Before the first French settlements were reached, each soldier's daily ration was reduced to a cupful of flour and two ounces of pork; the men boiled scraps of moose hide and swallowed the glutinous mess, perhaps with the addition of hair-powder for thickening. Tallow candles were eaten, and a couple of dogs were completely devoured. Some trudged forward in six inches of snow, though they had not eaten for forty-eight hours. To fall was to be left to die. Increasing numbers of sick were sent back over the trail or were left in brush shelters in the care of a few companions. The intense cold bit through summer clothing. More than once a party could not make camp until late at night, then renewed the march at dawn.

Colonel Arnold, with inexhaustible energy, ranged backward and forward over the twenty-mile straggling line of troops, constantly encouraging, betraying no doubts of success of the enterprise.

It was November 9 when 600 tatterdemalions, a few more than half of the 1150 who had set out from Cambridge, reached the bank of the St. Lawrence. They assembled at Point Levi, directly opposite Quebec; crossing the mile-wide river presented difficulties. Distant shores had to be scoured for canoes and dugouts; the British had removed those that had been on shore. In the stream lay a frigate and a sloop of war from which guard boats passed on patrol. Ladders for scaling the thirty-foot walls of the fortress had to be prepared. A three-day storm made the river impassable, but on the night of November 13 Arnold got 500 of his men across to a cove below the cliff. They climbed to the fields west of the town (the Plains of Abraham) and quartered in deserted houses.

In spite of the reports of some that Arnold was eager for an immediate attack, he was not that rash. The garrison—a few regulars, more British and Canadian militia and sailors—was thought to number about 1200. Arnold had no artillery to breach the walls; the scaling ladders, once made, could not be got across the river; a hundred muskets were unserviceable; and ammunition for those with small arms was only five rounds per man. Only empty bravado was possible. As soon as he was posted, Arnold sent a summons to surrender, but the flag was fired on and a second got the same reception. Arnold paraded his little band within easy cannon shot, which could only have revealed his weakness.

On learning that the garrison was being reinforced and would attack, the Americans beat a painful retreat, some shoeless over the frozen ground, twenty miles up the river to Pointe aux Trembles, where they lay disconsolate for a fortnight. They were not cheered when they learned that the competent General Carleton had taken command of Quebec.

The Americans' prospect brightened with the arrival from Montreal of a schooner bearing General Montgomery, 300 recruits, artillery, and an abundance of captured ammunition, food, and warm clothing.

December 5 found the Americans back before the walls of Quebec. Montgomery knew that a siege was impossible. His New England troops would leave when their term of enlistment was up, on January 1. Trenches could not be dug in the frozen ground. His summons to Carleton to surrender, accompanied by the usual threats, lost force by being several times repeated and as regularly rejected. To give his artillery some play, Montgomery protected a battery of a half-dozen 6- and 12-pound cannon with blocks of ice, reinforced with sticks and straw—"our heap of nonsense," one of his soldiers called it. Carleton's 32-pound balls quickly demolished these improvised works. Carleton now had 1800 men, Montgomery only 800.

The American attack was to be directed against the lower town, on the narrow shelf at the water's edge. Troops under Arnold were to fight their way in at the northern end, those of Montgomery at the southern end then they would join forces to enter the upper town. Several companies objected to the assault as too dangerous, and they needed all of the General's persuasion to make the attempt.

The attack was launched the last night of the year, in a driving snowstorm that piled drifts waist high. Two feints to distract attention from the real objective had no effect; one was disregarded by the defenders, the other never happened because the French Canadians assigned to burn the St. John's gate ran off in a body.

General Montgomery himself, with his aide and another Captain, led the advance of his party of 300. They broke through a palisade and passed unharmed the blockhouse behind it. They cut a second barrier and rushed forward; still they found no resistance. Then a burst of grapeshot from a fortified dwelling on the wayside instantly killed Montgomery and his closest companions. A Captain took command and ordered a retreat.

This had been a one-sided encounter in which the Americans had met swift disaster. The case was different at the other end of the lower town. Arnold led his corps of 600 under musket fire from the main ramparts to a wooden barricade. The plan had been to batter it with a 6-pounder lashed to a sled, but the cannon had been abandoned in the deep snow. Arnold was knocked down by a bullet in his leg and was carried to the rear. Daniel Morgan, now in command, was first to mount a ladder and leap inside the palisade, quickly followed by others. The defenders tried to flee, but they were surrounded and surrendered.

A second barrier spanned the narrow street. Its gate was open, revealing cannon behind. The gunners abandoned their pieces. If the attackers had rushed in, as Morgan cried to them to do, they might have possessed themselves of the waterside quarter. But they were too few; they were actually outnumbered by their prisoners. By the time other companies came up, Carleton had sent reinforcements. Though the scaling ladders were repeatedly mounted, it was sure death to drop inside. The defenders' muskets blazed from nearby houses. The attackers entered one that flanked the barricade, but were expelled by British bayonets. Of course Montgomery had not come up as hoped. The officers determined on a retreat, but it was too late. They were hemmed in front and rear and cannon had been added to the musket fire from the windows. Morgan was defiant to the last, but surrender was inevitable. About 425 Americans were captured, and their sixty killed and wounded were four times those of the defenders.

Arnold lay in pain, with other American wounded, in the general hospital outside of the town, which the Americans had earlier occupied. Five days after the defeat, he wrote: "I believe the enemy dare not venture out, though they threaten it. I pray God they may not, for we are in a miserable condition to receive them." He demanded his loaded pistols and ordered each of his prone companions to have his weapon beside him. If the hospital were invaded the inmates would resist to the death. This was temper, surely, not military sense.

Too late, as a result of disastrous experience, Arnold had more sober ideas. He hoped the Continental Congress would dispatch a general at the head of "not less than eight or ten thousand men to secure . . . a lasting connection with this country." It was essential to take Quebec city, "the key [which] governs the whole country." Otherwise, "the Canadians . . . having been so long habituated to slavery, and having, as yet, but a faint sense of the value of liberty," would not "take an active part."

"Our loss and repulse," Arnold reported to Washington, "struck an amazing panic into both officers and men, and had the enemy improved their advantage, our affairs here must have been entirely ruined. . . . Upwards of one hundred officers and soldiers instantly set off for Montreal, and it was with the greatest difficulty I could persuade the rest to make a stand. . . . I arranged the men in such order as effectually to blockade the city, and enable them to assist each other if attacked." Truly he "put the best face on matters, and betray[ed] no marks of fear." With the remnant of his force— not more than 400, exclusive of unreliable Canadians—he was down to his last hard money, had a precarious supply of provisions, and was out of lead. He had to command from his bed, for he would not be fit for active duty for eight weeks. Still he declared ("Camp before Quebec, Jnuary 6, 1776"), "I have no thoughts of leaving this proud town, until I first enter it in triumph." Actually, Arnold was not so much blockading Carleton as Carleton was ignoring Arnold.

Carleton permitted the baggage of his prisoners to be sent in to them, such as it was. Private Simon Fobes, then nineteen (though his narrative was dictated to his son sixty years later), recorded that the sergeants were required to make out muster rolls of the prisoners, "noting particularly where each man was born." The Provost Marshal "then called out all the prisoners born in England or Ireland, and told them that, according to the letter of the law, they deserved nothing but death; for they had taken up arms against their own country; but, if they would take the oath of allegiance, and enlist in the British service until the first of the following June, they should be reprieved." Joseph Ware, the only diarist who furnished what appears to be a complete casualty roster, put down the names of ninety-three as "Listed in the King's service." However, some of these managed to desert to the Americans.

The worst suffering of the prisoners was from smallpox. Fobes related, "When the pock was coming out on seventy or eighty of our number, our fever very high, with no water to drink, some of the men drank their own urine, which made the fever rage too violently to be endured." After fearful crowding, some were removed to other rooms, and given bunks and blankets and medicine. ". . . [O]ur flesh seemed a mass of corruption; at the same time we were almost covered with vermin. These were a sore affliction. When we were a little recovered we were removed back to our former prison without any cleansing or change of apparel. Our clothes were stiff with corrupted matter." He believed that a twelfth of the prisoners died that winter of smallpox, "some after a partial recovery."

Arnold was made a Brigadier General, but he commanded a ghost "brigade" of which 400, more than half, were down with smallpox, either caught "in the natural way," or induced in a milder form by inoculation. A couple of hundred recruits dribbled in from Montreal; early in April General Wooster came from there with troops that built up the force outside Quebec to 2000. A month later the aged Wooster was superseded by General John Thomas. By now his effectives, because of discharges, desertions, and deaths, were down to 500.

Thomas was awaiting reinforcements voted by Congress when hope was blasted by arrival of a fleet bringing General John Burgoyne with his army of 8000, one-fourth of whom were German mercenaries under Baron Riedesel. Carleton issued from his fortress with a force that instantly put to flight the few hundred Thomas could muster. This wrote *finis* to the attempt to capture Quebec and enlist the Canadians in the cause of the Revolution. The Americans, smallpox or not, abandoned everything, even the headquarters records, in a mad scramble westward. Parties separated, the better to seize food from the inhabitants, until they collected in a demoralized mass at Sorel, at the mouth of the Richelieu. General Thomas died of smallpox as the retreat continued to Chambly.

Congress and Washington sent reinforcements, more than 5000 under Brigadiers John Sullivan and William Thompson, the former in command. They brought food, clothing, ammunition, and artillery. Under unfortunate orders to renew the invasion of Canada, Sullivan assigned Thompson 2000 troops to capture Trois Rivières, which was thought to be weakly held. The night marchers got lost in mosquito-infested bogs and finally emerged for a daylight attack, only to be confronted with 6000 of Burgoyne's army, strongly entrenched.

The result was a two-day rush of the Americans through the woods for safety at Sorel. But there, Sullivan reported to Schuyler, his men were "filled with horrour at the thought of seeing their enemy . . . a great panic among both officers and soldiers . . . no less than 40 officers begged leave to resign." Arnold, now fully chastened, urged Schuyler, "Let us quit [Canada] and secure our own country before it is too late."

Schuyler sent boats to St. John's to take off the sadly reduced Americans. They were barely ahead of Burgoyne's pursuers. It is said that Arnold, the last to embark, actually saw the British van approaching. He shot his horse and pushed off. The Americans' stopping place, the small, swampy Ile aux Noix in the Richelieu River, completed their miseries of smallpox, dysentery, semistarvation, and death. Those who could row took the others up Lake

Champlain to Crown Point. This was another death camp. The fort was in ruined condition; it could not have been held by healthy troops, much less by a corps every day diminished by burials. The Canadian adventure had cost 5000 American lives. Schuyler and Gates, the latter now second in command, chose the only course. They removed the sick to Fort George, at the south end of Lake George, and sent the soldiers who were still on their feet to Ticonderoga, a dozen miles up Lake Champlain.

The tables were now turned, and Carleton was to be the invader. With his army of 13,000, he intended to push through the lakes, down the Hudson, join General Howe at Albany, and sever New England from the other colonies. At St. John's, on the Richelieu, he assembled a fleet of 29 fighting vessels, besides 400 bateaux and 24 longboats for troops and supplies. In the process he took apart a ship and two schooners in the St. Lawrence—they could not be got through the Richelieu rapids—and rebuilt them. He had ample materials, tools, and workmen for his construction, and sailors to man his armada.

The force of the Americans at Ticonderoga had been built up, continentals and militia, to some 9000 rank and file, but only 5000 were fit for duty. Knox had taken the heavier guns to the siege of Boston. Of the 120 remaining at the fort, only 43 could be mounted, and supplies for them were largely lacking. Arnold, from his experience as a shipowner, was knowledgeable about vessels. At Ticonderoga he had four, schooners and sloops, left from the previous summer's operations. These were totally insufficient. How, in that wilderness, could he build a fleet in any way matching what Carleton was preparing?

Arnold had not even axes to fell the timber—not to speak of shipwrights in that army of farmers—nor the many and varied tools and naval materials required. Still, artisans were attracted from the coast by high wages, broken down sawmills were repaired, Schuyler exerted himself at Albany, and somehow the necessary cordage, sailcloth, ironwork, and all else were collected at the boatyards set up at Skenesboro. Four row galleys and twice as many smaller gondolas were constructed and well armed, with 18-pounders down to swivel guns. These slow-sailing, cumbersome craft could best be described as floating batteries.

It was an achievement that Arnold, as early as August 24, 1776, could start his fleet from Crown Point down Lake Champlain, to block the enemy's passage. His crews were made up of 800 landsmen—"very indifferent in general," he called them. After a month of storms and shifting of position, he anchored between Valcour Island and the New York shore.

Carleton began his offensive two weeks later. His squadron sailed past Valcour Island before the American vessels were discovered, tucked in behind. The battle was joined at noon of October 11. It is not necessary to rehearse particulars of the unequal encounter. The British had nearly twice the firepower of the Americans, who nonetheless kept up the fight for five hours, until their vessels were badly disabled and their guns silenced. Though Carleton attempted to cordon off his enemy's exit, night and a dense fog permitted Arnold to slip past. Overtaken by the British fleet the next day, the American vessels were further battered. Arnold beached and burned them, their flags still flying. He marched what was left of his men the ten miles to Crown Point. They stopped only long enough to burn the buildings before continuing to Ticonderoga, completely defeated.

Carleton, in a conciliatory gesture, sent his prisoners to Ticonderoga under parole. He did not attack that fort; he considered it too strong to be taken without a siege, and that would throw his further campaign into the winter months. He withdrew to St. John's.

It has been said that Arnold's defeat on Lake Champlain in the autumn of 1776 was in fact a signal American victory because it postponed for a year Burgoyne's invasion, by which time the patriots could muster their forces to compel his surrender. The argument is that the capture of Burgoyne's army at Saratoga determined the French alliance, and the French army and fleets made possible the final triumph at Yorktown.

More accurately, because Carleton knew that Arnold was preparing to resist on the lake, he delayed the construction of his own fleet, and he delayed overlong. True, Ticonderoga was better garrisoned in October 1776 than it was in July 1777, but then the British captured the fort almost without firing a shot.

It must be concluded that the American campaign against Canada—Arnold's agonized approach, the ruinous defeat at Quebec, the miseries of retreat, the failure at Valcour Island—was an ill-judged venture from start to finish.

The War Within

"THE ANIMOSITY BETWEEN THE WHIGS AND TORIES, REN-
DERS THEIR SITUATION TRULY DEPLORABLE. THE WHIGS
SEEM DETERMINED TO EXTIRPATE THE TORIES, AND THE
Tories the Whigs. Some thousands have fallen in this way, in this
quarter, and the evil rages with more violence than ever. If a stop
cannot be soon put to these massacres, the country will be depopu-
lated in a few months more, as neither Whig nor Tory can live."
Thus witnessed General Nathanael Greene in South Carolina.

The Tory-Whig, or loyalist-patriot, conflict was civil war, Americans against Americans. On both sides the hostility shaded from
regular military action, under army control, down to neighborhood, even personal clashes. Between these extremes were partisan
bands that were more or less organized; generally they had commissioned officers, often rank and file were enlisted, but also frequently the followers were volunteers who came and went. The
fights and raids of these guerrilla parties were usually against enemies, though they were guilty of pillage, burnings, and executions
which carelessly victimized friends as well as foes. The local spo-

radic forays, under no military government—the kind of lawless violence of which General Greene spoke—was more cruel, indiscriminate, and widespread.

In the fury of factions against each other there was not much to choose, except that alleged legal authority permitted the patriots to impose all sorts of penalties (among them, imprisonment, confiscation, banishment) on the Tories. Such punishments were not in the power of the loyalists except in the limited areas that were under British military occupation or domination. Had the loyalists controlled the governmental machinery, they probably would not have been any more tender toward their opponents. As it was, they could not act under color of law.

It is correct to speak of the patriots as composing the popular party. Not that they were clearly more numerous in the colonies as a whole, but that they included more of those of lower income and less recognized social position. The term "Tory," borrowed from England, was accurate in America in implying economic and political conservatism associated with privilege, superior status, and wealth. Of course, individuals and entire communities crossed these lines. Still, on the whole, those who felt they had nothing to gain by a change of regime adhered to the Crown. The allegiance of royal officials, from Governors down to minor functionaries, was to be taken for granted. The clergy of the Church of England were disposed against the Revolution, as were the members of the other learned professions. Men with extensive landholdings or invested funds, and merchants of the port cities, were apt to be on the King's side. Roughly, there was a cleavage between patriot Presbyterians and loyalist Episcopalians, though this difference was as much economic and social as religious; the dissenters were democratic, the Anglicans aristocratic.

Between the definable groups, patriots and loyalists, fell perhaps a third of the population. They were neutral or indifferent to the issue of the struggle. The weight of this large passive party favored the loyalists, since the champions of the Revolution needed to rouse the people to positive action. "Those who are not for me are against me" was the applicable saying in the midst of rebellion. The Quakers, who were especially strong in Pennsylvania, were on the fence because of their moral commitment against warfare.

The Americans' internal struggle was as distressing as the formal war. Actually the two conflicts were intimately connected, for the contest between colonies and Crown was itself a civil war. The strife between patriots and loyalists was the more bitter because the antagonists were neighbors, kindred, former friends. The patriots hated the "Hessians," but those mercenaries fought on command of their princes in Europe and were not concerned with the justice or injustice of the cause they defended. On the other hand, the contending parties of Americans each blamed the other for faithlessness to the best interest of their country; each looked on the other as traitorous. Furthermore, the attacks that most excited rage were not inflicted upon soldiers, but upon helpless civilians, and they often took the form of robbery, arson, and worse.

The grave differences between rebels and loyalists were in the main expressed in the realm of reasoned argument until the minute men were killed on Lexington common; then more, on both sides, fell at Concord; and finally, Bunker Hill earned the name of real battle. If a few months more had gone by without a resort to arms, the colonies might have been willing to remain within the British Empire. But the mother country offered terms a little too late. Revolution, on the part of all but the most fervent, was a reluctant recourse. The patriots and their followers, until the moment of the Declaration of Independence, wanted redress of grievances, not separation with all of its hazards and costs. This was the testimony of leaders whose knowledge and integrity it is impossible to question. Most Americans today are unaware that New York did not endorse the Declaration until several days after it was promulgated by the other twelve states. True, American nationhood would have developed sooner or later, from several causes, and, one would have hoped, peaceably. The menace of the French on this continent had been removed a dozen years earlier; the resources of the country invited exploitation, which could have occurred only under native initiative; the British colonial system, as practiced on a people of similar language and culture, was nearing the end of its era. In any case, time and circumstance were working to produce American self-determination, and if they had been allowed to operate, the results might have been preferable to those achieved by rebellion.

The loyalists were content with the present rather than anticipating the future for America, just as patriots resented current restraints more than they envisioned the national maturity that lay ahead. But abstract rights were cried up, and they obscured both British responsibilities and American opportunities. The Revolution was more than an economic struggle, but the appeal to political principles, as with other excitants, contained poison as well as tonic.

The language of both Whigs and Tories became exaggerated as the conflict intensified. This was inevitable. Americans under British sovereignty did not suffer "chains and slavery," nor did loyalists oppose Congress even at the expense of being "quartered or cut into inch pieces." Orators and essayists in both camps exhausted the vocabulary of vilification. Apostrophes to liberty on the one hand and to allegiance on the other had their counterpart, among the less educated, in acts of extreme abuse and revenge. Sam Adams used his talents as a propagandist to bring on a hysteria. However, even allowing for the disturbed state of the public mind, and mutual fears, the conduct of extreme Tories and Whigs betrayed a moral depravity. Dr. Benjamin Rush wrote Richard Henry Lee, in December 1776, that "every particle of my blood is electrified with revenge." When Cornwallis was overrunning the Carolinas, civil government there almost ceased to exist, which gave rein to outrages. But everywhere the restraints of law were relaxed. Legislative acts permitted arrest, detention, and punishment on the basis of suspicion. In the inflamed state of mind that prevailed, vague terms in statutes were turned to the injury of persons accused. Before the end, all of the states, in one form or another, passed acts for the seizure and trial of anyone who by word or deed brought discredit on Congress, the state legislature, the Commander in Chief, or the paper money. If the accused were found guilty, half of the fine imposed went to the informer.

The legislatures of the states decreed test oaths to determine who supported the Revolutionary government and who retained his allegiance to Britain. The signer testified before God and the world that the war of the colonies was just, promised not to aid the forces of Great Britain, and renounced all obedience to King George III, his heirs, and his abettors. One who refused was held to be outside the law. One purpose of the test oath was to persuade the wavering to declare for the break with the mother country. If unwillingly taken, to protect property or avoid persecution, compliance often covered a secret enemy. Persons appearing before a justice of the peace were given time to consider whether to sign or not, but patriot committees and their agents frequently used force. It was worse than useless. Isaac Sears, helping General Charles Lee to separate goats from sheep on Long Island, reported that he had "ben able to ketch but five Torries, and they of the first rank, which swallowed the oath." Not all administration of the oath was so summary; extensions of the deadline for signing were granted, and many avoided the test by fleeing their homes.

Without a certificate stating that he had pledged obedience to the new government, a man was fair game for patriot restrictions and penalties. Few means of injuring him were left untried. If he did not support the government that protected him, what else could he expect? He was denied the vote, service on juries, the holding of any public office of trust or profit, and access to the courts for any purpose. He could neither buy nor sell land, nor could he leave it to his heirs. Several states forbade lawyers who had not taken the test oath from practicing their profession. The same prohibition was extended to teachers and druggists, on the ground that one poisoned the mind, the other the body. Physicians were not included, but the known loyalist doctor saw his practice dwindle and disappear. To prevent spies from gathering and transmitting information, travelers had to show certificates. Freedom of speech and press were interdicted to prevent "honest and well-meaning but misinformed people" from being "deceived and drawn into erroneous opinion." For example, a humble man might abandon the colonies' cause if he believed, when told by wicked Tories, that the King, next campaign, would send to America 50,-000 Russian Cossacks, led by "masterpieces of inhumanity," along with 90,000 Hessians, Negroes, Laplanders, Fiji Islanders, Japanese, Moors, "Esquimaux," and Persian archers. (The loyalist intimidators forgot cannibals.) Preachers, who were warned against injecting dangerous political doctrine into their sermons, sometimes transgressed in their public prayers. They were sternly told not to seduce the Almighty to Toryism.

It would seem unnecessary to disabuse even the most ignorant of the truth of tales told in Rivington's *Gazette*. This was the main Tory newspaper, published in British-occupied New York, and it was beyond patriot censorship. Before the British came, Rivington's shop was assaulted and his types were scattered in the street. The fanciful rumors that writers in his columns attempted to spread were pathetic evidence of the impotence of the loyalists, shut up in their haven of refuge. News of the French alliance shocked the Tories. The best they could do was to start reports that Louis XVI was preparing to impose Catholicism on America. For this purpose, the French fleets were bringing casks of holy water and consecrated oil, chests of rosaries, crucifixes, and relics to be venerated. For any Americans who proved stubborn against embracing the foreign faith, Louis was providing thumbscrews and racks. Priests were on the way to officiate in confessional or torture chamber. If the Puritan conscience did not revolt at these terrors, the plain patriot countryman would be offended by the promised import of French dancing masters, *friseurs,* and dehydrated frogs and garlic soup.

Where it was not possible to prevent the Tory from mischievous influence, he was confined to his own house or farm or was removed to a distant place in the state or to another state. Some exiles were put on farms; others were held in jail. If the banished returned to their homes on secret visits, their families were compelled to share their exile. Families deprived of the breadwinner were thrown on meager local charity. The formalities of condemning a man to exile were loose compared to the severity of the punishment. Political exile was bad enough, but imprisonment of Tories for alleged criminal acts was worse, especially if the accused was immured in the Simsbury copper mine in Connecticut, a seventy-foot-deep dungeon.

Some loyalists were sent within the British lines; more fled there, especially to New York. In the beginning they told themselves that the British would soon put down the rebellion, but as time wore on their spirits fell, the money they brought with them was exhausted, and they lived poorly on public allowances. They finally formed the Associated Loyalists, which petitioned the military government of the city on behalf of sufferers, and also directed refugee raids into near-by patriot territory. As months passed into years, those who were loyalists from the beginning showed their jealousy of latecomers, whom they believed were acting from policy rather than principle. This rift in refugee ranks was the result of protracted anxieties in close quarters.

Loyalists who could afford the voyage, or whose official positions in America promised them support in England, went there. Reception and reactions of these exiles in the mother country varied widely. Not a few were disgusted by the undemocratic discriminations in English society and resented the low esteem in which American colonials appeared to be held. They were pained when their hosts rejoiced at American defeats. As their money gave out, the government sustained them with small pensions, though a few dignitaries were well provided for.

One Hessian officer, Captain Johann Ewald of the *Jaegers,* was astonished at the thousands of Negroes following Cornwallis' army in the South. They had responded to promises of freedom and protection. Those who performed some camp duties were "followed by about 4,000 more Negroes of every age and sex. The regions through which this train passed were eaten barren, like a field that has been attacked by a swarm of locusts. I don't know what these people lived on. It was fortunate that the army seldom stopped longer than one day or one night."

Captain Ewald's pity was aroused by the sudden expulsion of the Negroes when Cornwallis found himself besieged at Yorktown. "On the same day that we were attacked by the enemy, all our black friends, who had been freed and dragged away to prevent them from working in the fields, and who had served very well in making entrenchments, were chased towards the enemy. They trembled at having to go back to their former owners. I had to make a secret patrol last night and met many of these unhappy ones, who were desperate because of hunger and who sought help because they were between the two firing lines. This act of cruelty became necessary because of lack of food, but one should have thought earlier to save them."

An American sergeant, Joseph Plumb Martin of the Light Corps at Yorktown, confirmed this picture. "During the siege," he wrote, "we saw in the woods herds of Negroes which Lord Cornwallis (after he had inveigled them from their proprietors), in love and pity to them, had turned adrift, with no other recompense for their confidence in his humanity than the smallpox for their bounty and starvation and death for their wages. They might be seen scattered about in every direction, dead and dying, with pieces of ears of burnt Indian corn in their hands and mouths, even of those that were dead."

For a time the substance of loyalists was nibbled away by discriminatory taxes, double or triple what patriots paid. Then Congress, in 1777, recommended that the states confiscate loyalist property. Abandoned estates first invited seizure, but soon the homes and lands of all who would not take the test oath fell under the auctioneer's hammer or were disposed of at private sale. The proceeds were invested in continental loan certificates, except that the dependents of loyalist owners were supposed to be supported from the purchase price. The large acreages were split into smaller holdings in response to democratic demand.

Not all of the confiscating of estates was done by patriots. Where the British military controlled an area, offending patriots were similarly expropriated. At Charleston, South Carolina, on September 6, 1780, a proclamation by the Right Honorable Charles Earl Cornwallis, Lieutenant General of His Majesty's forces, etc., sequestered "the estates, both real and personal, in this province, belonging to the wicked and dangerous traitors," who were then named. The list of thirty-three men who had abandoned their plantations to join the enemies of Great Britain was headed by Christopher Gadsden, Lieutenant Governor, and included Thomas Farr, formerly Speaker, and others who represented the resistance of South Carolina. John Cruden was appointed Commissioner to manage or sell the estates in question and turn over the proceeds to the British Paymaster General.

Loyalists who joined the King's forces or were otherwise conspicuous in giving aid to the British were convicted of treason and sentenced to death, but few suffered the extreme penalty; they remained absent, or proved themselves innocent of the charges, or were pardoned. Washington wisely urged leniency, lest the British retaliate on captured British-born soldiers in American service.

The Tories, content to have things stay as they were, relied too much on the British armies and fleets to keep them so. Still, theirs was not a negative role. It is estimated that, from first to last, 50,-000 loyalists served in the royal army and navy; of the soldiers, about a third were in the militia, as they preferred to choose their own officers. An English historian of the war estimated that New York alone furnished 15,000 men to the army and navy, and 8000 militiamen. Loyalist troops figured importantly in Burgoyne's invasion force in 1777, in the defense of Savannah against French and patriots in 1779, and in the capture of Charleston and the defeat of Gates at Camden the next year. Tarleton raised his Legion in New York, Lord Rawdon recruited his Volunteers of Ireland in Pennsylvania, and other ranger outfits were Tory manned. Benedict Arnold ravaged Connecticut towns and the James River valley in Virginia with Tory troops.

As told elsewhere in these pages, Tories joined forces with Indians, under Colonel John Butler, his son Captain Walter, Sir Guy Johnson, and the Mohawk chief Joseph Brant in the cruelest raids of the war. They desolated the Wyoming Valley on the Pennsylvania frontier, and Cherry Valley on the New York border; they left behind them settlements in ashes and went off with prisoners to be tortured and the scalps of the murdered. These barbarous attacks on ill-defended outposts could have little if any effect on the issue of the war, but they made the name of Tory horrid in patriot ears.

The fiercest single conflict between Tories and patriots, and the largest in scale, was the battle of King's Mountain, fought in October 1780. Some 2000 men were engaged on both sides, and all were Americans save the British Commander, Major Patrick Ferguson. Thus King's Mountain, including its preface and sequel, was an event in the civil war.

Sir Henry Clinton, the Commander in Chief of British land forces in America, was more cautious than Lord Cornwallis, whom he had left in charge in the South after the capture of Charleston, South Carolina. Clinton's operations were all on the seaboard. His policy was to hold the port cities of New York, Charleston, and Savannah, with a possible later descent on the Chesapeake Bay region. He had no taste for invasion of the interior. For example, when he abandoned Philadelphia he did not march into the backcountry of Pennsylvania, but took his large force straightaway to New York City.

Clinton ordered Cornwallis to dominate South Carolina and Georgia, but he did yield, without enthusiasm, to his aggressive subordinate's ambition to possess himself of North Carolina as well. Cornwallis went further. He argued that the whole tier of Southern states right up to Pennsylvania would have to be conquered if South Carolina and Georgia were to remain secure.

From his interior posts in South Carolina—Ninety-six, Camden, and Cheraw—Cornwallis would thrust northward and westward. Major Patrick Ferguson was to subdue the upcountry of South Carolina and move in an arc northeastward, to join Cornwallis and Tarleton at Charlotte, North Carolina. Ferguson was the boldest of the British partisan leaders, with the possible exception of Tarleton. He attracted to his command a large number of South Carolina Tories. Many of them were Scots, traditionally pledged to the King's standard, while others were emboldened by the fall of Charleston and the total American defeat at Camden. Ferguson's recruiting was as much by threat as by persuasion. A backwoodsman had to be stouthearted to cling to his patriotism while his house was plundered or burned and he and his family were abused. The stories of outrages committed by Ferguson's parties lost nothing in the telling as they flew through the district, though the truth was bad enough. These tales reached over the mountains and fired resistance in those parts.

Ferguson made the mistake of further exciting patriotism by his proclamation to the western mountain men. Citing a recent Whig

[28]

atrocity, he challenged, "if you choose to be degraded forever by a set of mongrels, say so at once and let your women turn their backs on you, and look for real men to protect them." If they refused to be real men—loyal British subjects—he would march his army over the mountains and punish them for their weakness.

These were the wrong things to say to those particular patriots. Frontier hunters and Indian fighters, they were proud and self-reliant. Settled in the district where the states of Virginia, North Carolina, and Tennessee now meet, they were cut off from the seaboard by the Appalachians and had developed their own habits of community defense. With one accord, they resolved to go after Ferguson and his band of 1300 Tories before he could come into their country.

Colonels Shelby, Sevier, Williams, Cleveland, McDowell, Campbell, and others led their neighbors to the place of rendezvous, Sycamore Flats on the Watauga (now Elizabethton, Tennessee). The various companies numbered from fewer than 200 to twice as many, and made a total of 1400, all mounted. In frontier hunting shirts, leggings, and moccasins, they traveled light, each man carrying no more equipment than a blanket, a pouch of parched corn, and a long-barreled rifle, the use of which he understood perfectly. John Sevier and others did scare up a war chest of $12,000, and for forage and beef in their campaign they camped on Tories in their path.

Before they set out, on September 26, 1780, they were exhorted by their volunteer chaplain, Reverend Samuel Doak, who knew how to align God on their side of the enterprise. The mountain passes through which they rode in chilling rains and clinging mists are today identified by historic markers, for theirs was the eruption of the West into the American Revolution.

At the Cowpens, in northwest South Carolina, they took a brief rest and food, and decided that 900 of the fittest would press ahead to find Ferguson. The leaders invited any who flinched from the danger to back out. None did so, though many were youngsters in their teens. The battle orders were simple: each man was to be his own officer, and each was to fight Indian style, without waiting for commands.

The advance horsemen rode all night and half the next day to come up to Ferguson's force, which was perched on a mountain spur that rose sixty feet above the plain. The flat summit was a third of a mile long. At the outer end, where Ferguson had his camp, it widened out to 120 yards. The steep sides were covered with rocks and trees. Of the 1100 Tories on this eminence (200 of Ferguson's corps were off on a foraging expedition), 100 were rangers, regulars, from New York and New Jersey; the others were well-disciplined militia, mostly from South Carolina. Their muskets were fitted with bayonets or, serving the same purpose, long knives thrust into the barrels.

Ferguson's position was strong, except that his tongue-like hill could be assailed on three sides at once. The patriot frontiersmen tied their horses in the woods and clambered upward with menacing yells. As they approached the top they were forced backward by solid ranks of stabbing bayonets. In hand-to-hand fighting the mountaineers, who had no bayonets, were at a disadvantage. But their rifles, aimed from cover at the red-coated defenders, were more deadly than the musket fire from above. After each repulse the patriots returned to the attack. Themselves half-concealed, they thinned the lines of the exposed Tories. The riflemen worked up closer on all sides. Then Sevier's men were at the top. Ferguson concentrated on them, but so weakened his defense elsewhere that in minutes three more companies of attackers reached the summit.

Soon the redcoats, massed in the open plateau, were easy targets for the rifles in the forest. Ferguson dashed about, now here, now there, furiously facing his men to their assailants. But the end was near. A white flag was raised in the turmoil of sound and smoke, and Ferguson, with a slash of his sword, cut it down. Then he fell in a fusillade of bullets. His troops, now demoralized, huddled behind the camp wagons.

Captain Abraham dePeyster took command, promptly surrendered, and begged for quarter. He got none, for the blood of the mountain men was up. They fired away at their helpless enemies. Finally Colonel Campbell and Colonel Shelby stopped the murder.

Every Tory on that hilltop was killed, left to die of wounds, or captured. What could be done with 700 prisoners? The victors, an impromptu corps, had no continuing organization and were eager to return to their homes. On the march back, Colonel Campbell had to issue orders to stop "the disorderly manner of slaughtering and disturbing the prisoners." On the following day the "manner of slaughtering" took the semblance of form. Patriot officers who were magistrates summoned a (not impartial) jury; after "trial," thirty-six of the captured were found guilty of robbery, arson, and murder. Nine were hanged forthwith, chiefly in retaliation for alleged crimes of the British and Tories against patriots. Soon thereafter, practically all of the remaining prisoners were allowed to escape.

After King's Mountain, the passions of the divided Americans, loyalists and rebels, did not cool. However, British commanders put less dependence than ever on inhabitants who opposed the colonies' cause. Major Ferguson had been their best recruiter and leader, and he, wrapped in a bull's hide, lay in a shallow grave on his battlefield.

The loyalists, besides going into standup fights, marauded up the Hudson, on Long Island, along the Jersey coast, and, incessantly, in the Carolinas. These forays against open villages and individual farms hardly had the dignity of foraging expeditions, for the horses, cattle, sheep, and hogs driven off were frequently the booty of private bands. Naturally, the patriots replied in kind. Even the recognized patriot partisans—Sumter, for example—supported themselves on plunder.

One would not expect pillage of a loyalist by troops selected for General Washington's bodyguard. In October 1778, Alijah Fisher returned to camp after a short furlough to find some of his comrades had new clothes, though they had received no money from home. It transpired that John Herrin had been out with a horse and a pass "to bye things for the Generals Famely . . . he Come to an old Tory's house and they would not Let him have any thing and he see several things that he wanted so when he Come home he go to his messmates and tales them and they gos and robed him." The thieves "ware all blacked." Howlen, the Tory, complained; John Herrick, one of the messmates, turned state's evidence; and Herrin, Moses Walton, and Elias Brown were sentenced to be hanged. Herrick got off with a hundred lashes.

The Tories distributed counterfeit continental and state currency, quantities of which were supplied by the British in New York. The intent was to damage the economy; however, the patriots were already doing so by spewing paper money from their own presses.

In March 1782 loyalists compelled the surrender of a blockhouse at Tom's River, New Jersey. The events that followed caused formidable resentment in America and extreme anxiety in Europe. Captain Joshua Huddy was first imprisoned in New York, then returned to New Jersey by the loyalists and, without trial, summarily hanged. With the approval of his chief officers and of Congress, Washington ordered the selection, by lot, of an English Captain in American hands. He was to be executed in retaliation for the murder of Huddy. The choice fell on Captain Charles Asgill, nineteen years old, the only son of a titled family. Before proceeding further, General Washington demanded of Sir Henry Clinton the punishment of Captain Lippincott, whom Americans held responsible for the outrage.

General Clinton expressed his abhorrence of the execution of Huddy, and he appointed a court-martial for Lippincott. Then followed a delay of months, in which Washington held to his resolve that Huddy's death should not go without reprisal. He resisted appeals from several quarters to spare the innocent young hostage. The outlook for Asgill darkened when Sir Guy Carleton, who had succeeded Clinton in command, informed Washington that the court-martial had acquitted Lippincott on the ground that he acted on order of the semi-official Associated Loyalists.

However, General Carleton disowned Lippincott's act and said he would make further investigation to bring the guilty to justice; the directing board of the loyalist irregulars was dissolved. Washington was himself disposed to accept apology and promise of prevention in future, and he was pained by the procrastination of Congress in coming to his view.

Lady Asgill implored the King and Queen of France to intercede to save her son. Washington submitted their entreaty to Congress, but the insensitive legislators took ten days to get around to their order for young Asgill's release. This was after he had been held in jeopardy for more than six months. Washington expressed his own profound relief to Captain Asgill, to Lady Asgill, and to Their Majesties of France.

During the war thousands of loyalists—the banished, the proscribed, the voluntary exiles—made their way to Canada. They chose the parts they could reach from the port of New York or through the northern counties: either Nova Scotia (which then included New Brunswick) or the Ontario frontier. These wartime expatriates were mostly poor people who were colonized ("staked") by the British government. When the last hope of military success vanished with the coming of peace, there was a mass exodus of loyalists, who feared their fate at the hands of the victorious Whigs. Sir Henry Clinton, in the King's name, promised that when the troops left the refugees would not be abandoned. Ten thousand went from Savannah and Charleston when those towns were evacuated; many of them were planters, bound for Florida or the Caribbean, but others joined the throngs in New York. Loyalist families fleeing the country were supplied by the British government with clothing, tools, and food sufficient for a year; the King's ships transported them and their belongings, chiefly to Nova Scotia. As a result, Canada received about 60,000 *émigrés*.

Making a start in a northern wilderness was a severe trial. Abundant land was granted, but clearing the forests was a heartbreaking task and not all of the pioneers were fit for the toilsome life. Whole regiments of Tories who had enlisted in the British army went together, which ensured community cooperation. Able individuals, trained in public life, were available to set up simple governmental machinery. However, years were needed, and much suffering was endured, before these Canadian provinces were well established, much less prosperous.

In the peace negotiations, the British Commissioners tried in vain to secure the return of confiscated estates to their loyalist owners. The Americans conceded only that Congress would recommend this to the states. The recommendation had no effect, nor was the promise against future confiscation kept, for seizures of loyalist property continued for years. Parliament accepted the responsibility of compensating those who had suffered losses because they had supported the King's cause. Diligent commissioners, sitting in London, Canada, and the United States, in six years examined some 5000 claims totaling about $40,000,000. Some claims were fraudulent; others were thrown out or reduced for good reasons. In the end $19 million was ordered paid. Including the sums for settlement in Canada, the British government spent $30 million in restitution to the loyalists.

However much the Revolution was an irreparable stroke to the expatriates, their expulsion was a greater deprivation to the United States. Had the peace been followed by generous reconciliation instead of continued bitter hostility, the valuable talents, experience, and industry of the loyalists would have been preserved to the young Republic. The years of faltering government under the Confederation might have been ameliorated, and prosperity under the Constitution would have been aided by the cooperation of the thousands expelled. This was foreseen by wise patriot leaders, but they could not prevail against the public rancor. Not the least cost of the Revolution was the civil strife, the war within the war, and its aftermath.

Disabilities of Congress

THE REVOLT OF THE AMERICAN COLONIES AGAINST IMPE-
RIAL RULE WAS BOUND TO THRUST THEM INTO PECULIAR
DIFFICULTIES—MILITARY, ECONOMIC, AND POLITICAL.
In the midst of war they had to summon physical and social resources for which they were unprepared. The British government
was corrupt and unenlightened in policy, but it was a going concern, with all the machinery of internal and external control. The
colonies, by contrast, had to lift themselves by their bootstraps, had
to learn the hard way, by doing.

The principal factor in protracting the colonies' struggle and increasing the suffering of the war was inexperience in united action.
The errors of omission of the Continental Congress were not cured
after the Confederation came formally into being, near the end of
the contest. This is not to assess blame, but merely to observe a
condition. To focus effort, Congress needed to be a lens, which col-
lects and concentrates rays; instead, it too far resembled a prism,
which breaks up white light into rainbow colors. The history of
America from 1774 to 1789—from the First Continental Con-

gress to the formation of the national government under the Constitution—is a history of the growing awareness of the merits of organization.

This progress was clouded by the persistent controversy between rights and duties, liberty and responsibility. Heated, costly, and inevitable as this conflict was, the partisans of freedom on the one hand and of feasibility on the other were in fact speaking each other's language. Forces that appeared to be hostile were in truth supplementary. Voluntary and individual qualities were fostered by collective decision and action. The trend of a strenuous period endorsed the oneness of liberty and law. However, passions disputed the prospect of any harmony. A beneficial blend of views could not have been reached without fierce debate.

The pity is that some who have told the story deny the sincerity of one side or the other. It is natural and desirable for the propositions of political parties to clash. Antagonistic advocacies intended for the public good are praiseworthy. If partisans were portrayed as honest advocates, much confusion about the Revolution and its aftermath would be avoided. But no, one side or the other is presented as disingenuous. Unquestionably, the Revolutionary worthies, being mortal, were not devoid of selfish impulses. Personal interest and individual environment flavored or prompted their public principles. However, that is not to say that the forefathers were willing, even anxious, to subordinate the common good to their private advantage. It is generally agreed that an abler and more high-minded lot of legislators has never been witnessed in American experience, nor, for that matter, in any country at any time.

The accusing finger has been pointed at the men of property and position along the Atlantic coast, merchants in the North and planters in the South. These privileged ones wanted a conservative government with ample protection against control by the majority, who were small farmers, frontiersmen, and town workers. Those of lesser means, on the other hand, favored a broad suffrage and the maximum of state and local autonomy. Having no riches to conserve, they were attached to the ideal of individual freedom. The contrast between the designs of the wealthy and the desires of the poor has led to the contention that the Revolution was as much a rebellion of the common people against the aristocrats as it was a revolt against British dominion. This class struggle, it is alleged, showed itself before, during, and after the war. It was evident in the refusal of many loyalists, and the reluctance of patriots who were basically content with things as they were, to break with the mother country. It appeared in the disbelief of Southern slaveholders in the egalitarian doctrine of the Declaration of Independence. Finally, it is said that the replacement of the Confederation by the Constitution was the ill-concealed conspiracy of the propertied to seize power and perpetuate it in their own hands. In the face of this machination, the nameless majority suffered invasion of democracy and the aggrandizement of central government.

Leaving aside the question of whether the few were guilty and the many wronged, the Continental Congress lacked the structure and powers required to conduct the war. This is abundantly evident in law and in fact. The prime weakness was its inability to command the resources of the country. Since the states held themselves to be severally sovereign, Congress had not the authority to tax them, much less to tax their individual citizens. Congress could only ask the states to contribute to the common treasury in accordance with quotas determined by the value of improved lands. The states laid taxes as they chose, and they forwarded funds for the use of Congress in various proportions to their quotas. Most were tardy and delinquent in their remittances. Other lacks were material, but the confining of Congress to the role of beggar was the crucial crippling.

It is plain in every provision of the Articles of Confederation that they were written by men who were rejecting authority. The more remote the governing power from the local community, the more it was attenuated. The authors saw tyranny lurking in every quarter. They went to the other extreme from King George's divine right, making all power temporary, at the will of the grudging member states. The Articles, proposed in 1776, were not formulated until 1778, and they were not completely ratified until 1781, when the fighting war was within eight months of being over. Meantime, the states were as well satisfied to conduct the war with no constitution, under a Congress which sat at sufferance as a *de facto* extension of previous trade conferences. Such powers as the Articles allowed were not fit for peace and less fit for war.

Congress was a single chamber, composed of delegates chosen, recallable, and paid by the states, no fewer than two nor more than seven from each. No delegate could serve in Congress more than three years in six. Each state, large or small, had one vote; that is, all were sovereign and therefore all were equal. The President of Congress was elected by that body annually; he was a presiding officer, not the chief executive of the Confederation. Legislation and administration were confused, the latter being conducted by committees of Congress. Except for courts that passed on crimes on the high seas, there was no federal judiciary. Thus the scrupulous "checks and balances" installed in the later Constitution of the United States were not needed in the Confederation, because there were no branches of government to be insulated from each other.

The votes of nine states were required for any important action, and those of a majority of states (seven) were needed for determining all lesser matters except for adjournment from day to day. This was a severe restriction, the more so because the proportions applied to states which were members, not those which were then represented in Congress. Furthermore, as the vote of a state depended on a majority of its delegates, if its delegates were evenly divided on a question, that state had no vote. A committee composed of one member from each state could be appointed to sit during the recess of Congress, but its authority was limited to minor matters.

Congress had the exclusive power to make treaties, except that no treaty of commerce could restrain any state from regulating its own foreign trade by duties and prohibitions. This nullified the power of Congress over foreign trade. Congress was given no authority over commerce between the states; each state could impose duties on imports from other states.

Congress had the exclusive right to declare war, make peace, and maintain a navy, but for a land force it had to depend upon quotas of soldiers furnished by the states in proportion to their white inhabitants. The states raised and equipped their men at the expense of the United States. If a state was called on to march more than its quota of troops, it could refuse the order on the plea that its own safety would be endangered. The states appointed all regimental officers, that is, from Colonel down. Thus Congress had the responsibility for waging war, but could not recruit troops directly, nor support and pay them except with money supplied at the will of the states, or with paper money issued on the authority of Congress.

Not only did Congress, during most of the war years, have no constitutional existence, for much of the time it threatened to have no physical existence. This was because of slim attendance, representation frequently falling below the nine states needed for transacting important business or even the seven required for passing on lesser concerns. Once, when Congress was supposed to be in session, and had a pressing agenda, delegates of only three states were present. This takes no account of the intervals when the members were assembling; then the lonesome few who appeared had no choice but to adjourn from day to day while waiting for their tardy colleagues. The winter months, when travel was hardest, were favorites for delegates to hug their own firesides, but this was just when Congress was busiest, preparing for the next military campaign.

For example, on December 9, 1777, the President, Henry Laurens, was directed to write to Connecticut, New York, Pennsylvania, Maryland, and South Carolina, "representing to them the great and important matters to be transacted in Congress during the winter, and the few members now attending, and that he request them to send forward, without delay, an additional number of members." He was also ordered to press New Jersey and Delaware, which were unrepresented, to send delegates immediately.

A few days later President Laurens proposed raising a South Carolinian to the rank of Brigadier. But, he lamented, "there was nobody on the floor to take up and improve the suggestion from the Chair, or to reply to the Specious reasonings for postponing. . . . We deserve the Evil of this delay. . . . for our shameful unpardonable delay in filling up our Delegacy with sensible vigilant faithful Citizens."

When Congress moved from Philadelphia—to Baltimore, York, Princeton, Annapolis—there was delay in gathering at the new place of sitting. Once the members collected in the small town of exile, they complained of cramped lodgings, poor but high priced "diet," and lack of congenial society. True, this last amenity was abundantly offered in Annapolis, where the pleasure-loving inhabitants invited them to "plays, Balls, Concerts, routs, hops, Fandangoes, and fox hunting," with gaming to fill the gaps of formal entertainments. But these diversions were not to the taste of New Englanders, whose "education in youth" was sterner, even if their expense allowance of four dollars a day had admitted of "mixing with the *bon-ton.*" Elsewhere the deprivations of village sojourn brought on nostalgia for the lost comforts and company of Philadelphia. From the members' yearnings to return to the capital city, one would suppose that they had been more eager in attending there than was their wont.

The Congress was particularly thin at York in the winter of 1777–78, when fifteen to seventeen delegates "made a very full House," and at times representation was "reduced to nine States

. . . in Units," a single faithful from each. President Laurens complained in February that "we have sometimes been stagnant for want of Members—and oftener running whole days into weeks of unmatured conversations" because the knot of conferees was too small to take action. John Banister of Virginia protested that, amidst the vacuity, "affairs of the greatest magnitude . . . lie dormant and give place to local Trifles." And Charles Carroll of Carrollton wrote, "The Congress do worse than ever: We murder time, and chat it away in idle impertinent talk."

Delegates absented themselves from public councils for "the improvement of their private Estates," departed the national body to attend on the state legislatures, or deserted in order to be "Governors, etc., at home." "It is a practice with many," William Grayson remarked sourly, "to come forward and be very assiduous till they have carried some State jobb and then decamp with precipitation." Those who remained, being few, were overburdened with demands of committee work. Their health suffered from their fatigues, leave aside "the Lime water [of York] which tears your Bowels out" and "has driven several Delegates home to their native springs." Members who had reached the limit of endurance, they declared, summoned colleagues to report for duty and release them. Nathaniel Folsom of New Hampshire begged the slacker Josiah Bartlett, "in twenty four hours after Receiving this mount your horse and Come and Relieve me, . . . as I have worne allmost all the flesh off my Bones being Exercised in my mind night and Day, and no time to Relax." John Mathews of South Carolina, after a short tour in Congress, implored Governor Rutledge, "For God's sake procure [home leave] for me, and I'll be dam'd if you ever catch me here again." Cornelius Harnett, a self-sacrificing patriot, besought a fellow North Carolinian, "For God's sake . . . get some Gentlemen appointed in my stead," as he had exhausted his toleration. He complained that, after he had sat all day in Congress, the treasury board often kept him until eleven o'clock at night. He called York "the most inhospitable scandalous place I ever was in. If I once more can return to my family all the Devils in Hell shall not separate us."

The few in Congress made an official appeal to the states to send at least three delegates each, in order that they would be able to dispatch important business and save the health of the corporal's guard that had been constant. The response was disappointing.

When Baron von Steuben visited York, Pennsylvania, then capital, in February 1778, his aide, Pierre Duponceau, described the debility into which the legislature had fallen. "The Congress of the United States," he wrote, "were not at that time the illustrious body whose eloquence and wisdom, whose stern virtues and unflinching patriotism, had astonished the world. Their number was reduced to about one half of what it was when independence was declared. All but a few of the men of superior minds had disappeared from it. Their measures were feeble and vacillating, and their party feuds seemed to forebode some impending calamity."

The pace of decision was also slowed by dawdling and wrangling that shed little light on the issues under consideration. Bare as the Journals are, they reveal tactics that served to delay action. Henry Laurens stigmatized members who had "a knack of starting questions of order, raising debates upon . . . captious, and trifling amendments, protracting them by long speeches, by postponing, calling for the previous question, and other arts." Of the ebullient oratory nothing was recorded in the minutes. The verbal vapors that habitually arose, fragrant or toxic, persuasive or repellent, found no place in the concise jottings of the secretary, Charles Thomson. In the modern day of media of mass communication, when the inducement to displays of gifts of speech would seem to be greater, the old-time flourishes are omitted. Two centuries ago the virtuosos of the cunningly contrived sentence emoted, undiscouraged by the tiny company of listeners. Then "a way with words" was admired in, and downright expected of, a legislator.

From time to time—not often enough for dispatch of business —the members of the small Congress recognized that they indulged their talents to excess, and resolved to limit the length of their speeches and to rise only once, or perhaps twice, on a given question.

Since vexing matters were commonly long under discussion in Congress, the shifts in delegates attending often brought to the floor members who were ignorant of what had taken place. Those who had remained in their places through the tedium of debates tended to discount the merit of fresh voices. Still more time was needed to inform the newcomers of the stage to which deliberation had reached. This was preferable, however, to a state's neglecting to elect any delegates, which sometimes happened.

On the head of a Congress crippled by absentees, the closing scene of the war years was melancholy. The discredit was piercing because the body was unfitted for two prime acts. One was the affecting acceptance of General Washington's resignation of his commission as Commander in Chief. The other was ratification of the definitive treaty of peace.

Congress adjourned at Princeton on November 4, 1783, to meet at Annapolis on November 26. In the interval, John Thaxter, secretary to John Adams, arrived bearing the treaty from the peace commissioners at Paris. He delivered the document to President Thomas Mifflin in Philadelphia. It disclosed that ratifications were to be exchanged within six months of signing, no later than March 3, 1784. About half that time had elapsed, so Mifflin sped letters to the states, urging them to send forward their delegates for a full Congress. If ever these dignitaries could be expected to put spurs to their horses, now was the occasion. But they lagged or occupied themselves elsewhere, and it was not until December 13 that seven states, two states short of the needed nine, were represented, though single delegates had appeared from New Hampshire and South Carolina. Then followed a month and a day in which attendance did not improve, and sometimes worsened.

Meantime, on December 23, General Washington presented himself to tender his commission and bid "an affectionate farewell to this august body, under whose orders I have so long acted. . . ." Delegates of six states in that august body did not share in the tears and thanks, for those of New Hampshire, Connecticut, New York, New Jersey, South Carolina, and Georgia were elsewhere. Just the same, the snug chamber in the State House was crowded with Maryland officialdom and the society of Annapolis.

That very day fresh entreaties were sent to the delinquent states to build the number on the floor to at least nine to assure "the safety, honor and good faith of the United States" by ratifying the treaty. The better prospects seemed to be the states that already had single delegates in Annapolis, though it would be six weeks before a second could arrive from New Hampshire, and the Carolinian's colleague, Richard Beresford, was sick abed in Philadelphia. New York had not so much as elected delegates, and none could be expected from distant Georgia in that winter season. One of the Delaware delegates, Eleazer McComb, chose that moment to say that he had to quit Congress to go about his private affairs. Renewed appeals then went to Connecticut, ravaged in the war but reputed for its contributions, and to New Jersey, the scene of American triumphs at Trenton and Princeton and smart resistance at Monmouth.

Anxiety lest formal approval of the treaty get off too late produced the proposal to act by seven states and conceal the illegality from the British. Others objected to the violation. Rather, Congress could take horse for Philadelphia, convene in Beresford's sickchamber, and just maybe the Jerseymen would report to make nine states. The trouble was, despite prevailing winds from the west, no ship was likely to reach Europe by the deadline. Congress, making the best of a bad case, wrote the ministers in Paris on January 5, 1784, to beg an extension of time, or, that failing, to exchange the treaty as ratified by seven states with the promise of the assent of two more to follow.

There were eight more agonizing days of waiting. Then two Connecticut Yankees were welcomed, and John Beatty—solo, alas!—came from New Jersey. By now the date was January 13, and only fifty-six days were left to comply with the stipulation for clinching the peace. Would nefarious Britain take advantage of the forfeit to renege on her terms?

Happily, the next morning the invalid Beresford arrived in Congress, barely in time to prevent his frenzied colleagues being carried out in straitjackets. Instanter the treaty was ratified by the votes of nine states, twenty-three delegates, for once unanimous!

Not a moment was lost in committing the original ratification, a duplicate, and a triplicate to three messengers who were to sail by different ships. The first Mercury, Colonel Josiah Harmar, found no departing vessel at Philadelphia, but he caught a French packet at New York on January 21, with forty-two days left for the crossing. Robert Morris, who knew most about shipping, and who was to dispatch the duplicate, after twelve days was informed that his own agent was still rooted to the American shore. Nevertheless, Congress took heart in the belief that Harmar was on his way to France. This balm was lost when it was learned in mid-February that the precious packet had run aground and had been obliged to limp back to New York. Nor had Colonel David Franks discovered a passage from any port.

It was now too late to win the race for ratification by the appointed date. The sloth of Congress had combined with the sloth of ships to put the messengers to Paris a month behind time. If the legislators blamed themselves, they should have. But in fact they need not have fretted over the outcome. The British were villains, but they were also gentlemen. They made no fuss about the delay, the exchange of ratifications took place just the same, and so all ended happily. Happily for the nonce, though vexations arose in the sequel. But those trials are no part of this story.

What has been the chief political development in the United

States during the last two hundred years? A likely answer is the growth of the power and variety of actions of the central government. This trend has encountered a succession of organized protests, most violent and protracted in secession and civil war. Today the objection to conformity to national standards takes the guise, among others, of reluctance to overcome race prejudice. But the process of amalgamation has gone on even in the realm of defiance, for the cry of states' rights has broadened to sectional dissent. It goes without saying that the autonomy of counties and towns within a state has long since faded, and that the great urban concentrations now look to the federal treasury for help.

It is difficult, therefore, to understand the strength of local attachments at the time of the Revolution. Nowadays, the whole continent gets the same news in the same moment, and simultaneously views the same picture; not long ago, two hundred million people focused on three fellow citizens exploring the moon. We know the doings of national figures in White House, in Congress, on campaign platforms, or in sports arenas better than we know our next door neighbors. Two centuries ago, sparse population and primitive means of transport, travel, and communication accented differences of occupation, interest, and loyalty. "My country" to a member of the Continental Congress was apt to mean not America, but South Carolina, Virginia, or Connecticut; if one probed deeper, the identification was with a particular part of the colony or state.

Public men—most, not all—were circumscribed. Horizons were close to home. The average man, if he was not a seafarer or soldier, probably lived out his life within a radius of some twenty miles; lawyers rode limited circuits, clergymen remained for years in the same pulpits, physicians sat at familiar bedsides. As a seeming contradiction to this localism, newspapers contained little of affairs in their own communities, but took their material from distant, often European, columns. Why? Circulation was so small that

[47]

everyone knew what was happening at hand; besides, editors (printers) did not stray from their typecases.

The challenges confronting the Continental Congress, suddenly guiding a rebellious war against powerful Britain, were staggering, even leaving aside the disability of local priorities. How could the Congress face the common foe with full force when unity was impaired by internal conflicts, jealousies, and defections?

In the beginning, the colonies acted together, both in protests against invasion of their rights and in desire for reconciliation with the mother country. The First Continental Congress, in 1774, unanimously adopted the trade boycott of Britain, and, at the same time, presented loyal petitions to King and Parliament. Though this appeal to the King was ignored, another was forwarded the next year, and with like result. Several delegates forswore primary attachment to their states; Patrick Henry exclaimed, "I am not a Virginian but an American."

Cooperation of the colonies in coercive measures, and, at the same time, professions of submission to royal authority if grievances were redressed, were soon surpassed by cooperation in collective defense. Washington was elected Commander in Chief of the armies of America, forts on Lake Champlain were captured in the name of the Continental Congress, the British forces were expelled from Boston, privateering against British shipping was authorized, and millions of paper dollars were issued for the support of warlike resistance.

The Declaration of Independence would seem to be the consummation of the common cause. It was adopted only after most of the colonies had reluctantly relinquished hopes of remaining within the British realm, and after individual colonies had yielded their fears of each other. But independence did not mean unity. Five years, often marked by discord, elapsed before the Articles of Confederation were approved, by which time the fighting war was almost over. Nor did the instrument of government, when it came into force, serve to bind the states closer to each other. It had not been necessary to consent to a constitution in order to form the all-important military alliance with France. The war exhibited, throughout, an imperfect cohesion of the states, and the peace was the signal for positive internal dissension.

It was professed in Congress that independence, confederation, and the obtaining of foreign allies (France, first and foremost) were parts of a whole. How could Congress negotiate treaties if it did not have constitutional power to bind the country? Independence and treaties dealt with externals. The components of the Declaration were juridical philosophy, verbal eloquence, and specific grievances; the treaties called for mutual trust and assistance. Once it was decided that the colonies would either separate from England or make a military and commercial association with France, no sooner said than done. But a frame of government, especially if it was expected to be "perpetual," involved long pondering, bargaining, and adjustment. A constitution could not be a done thing, but contemplated working relationships of the states with each other and with the central authority. It embraced, in one way or another, the most important public interests and the dearest private rights, civil and material. The instrument was to be fashioned, moreover, by a body which had originally been deputed for defiance and which came to be absorbed in defense. As was several times suggested in the course of the wrangles, a specially empowered constitutional convention, had that been possible, would have been better fitted to arrive at rules for American self-government. Yet neither would that have succeeded at the time. Peace and several years of experience were necessary for the construction of an enduring plan.

In July 1775, Benjamin Franklin laid before Congress tentative "Articles of Confederation and Perpetual Union," but they were forthwith dismissed and denied a record in the Journal. Still, Franklin's scheme, then shunned, was superior in many respects to that of John Dickinson, drawn by order of Congress almost a year later (June 12, 1776). Both outlines were tender to the authority of the states, but Dickinson was more inhibited than his fellow Pennsylvanian. Far from envisioning a competent national government, he strongly opposed—and voted against—American independence. Then, having deposited his unwanted child on the doorstep of Congress, he departed, not to reappear until the infant, differently clothed, had been adopted by the Continental body. It is illustrative of the difference of the two projects of union that what Franklin called the "General Congress," Dickinson described as "Meeting of the States."

From the first, the delegates in Congress were sharply at odds over the terms of confederation; they quarreled, day after day promised to return to the debates but failed to do so, and once dropped the problem for six months together. The Articles were not whipped into shape and agreed to in Congress until after a year and four months of discussion; then three years and more went by before they were ratified by the states. Meantime, Congress functioned by acquiescence of the states and people; it was, in fact, an *ad hoc* body. However, approval of the Articles made little or no difference in the powers exercised by the representatives.

The principal bones of contention in framing the Confederation were three. First, should all of the states, small as well as large, have an equal vote in Congress? Or should the voice of each be proportioned to population, property, contribution to the common treasury, or some combination of these criteria? Second, since the states were of different capacities, what was to be the basis of financial contribution? Third, to meet the demands of those states that had no claims to Western lands, would the states that presumed to reach to the "South Sea" (the Pacific Ocean) accept more easterly boundaries and surrender their more distant regions to the Union for the common benefit? Manifestly, the western pretensions of New York, Connecticut, and Virginia were intimately bound up with provisions for representation and revenue. If these states held to their claims to lands north of the Ohio, they might some day dwarf not only Rhode Island, Delaware, and New Jersey, but more considerable states, such as Massachusetts, Pennsylvania, and South Carolina.

On the question of voting in Congress, the small states insisted on keeping the existing rule of equality. Their argument was that, though they were smaller than others in area, population, and wealth, they were, as sovereignties, risking their all in the bid for American independence. Furthermore—and a crucial point, since Congress was to act on states, not on individuals—superior population or property should not be reflected in greater weight in councils of the Confederation. The large states, on the other hand, wanted representation proportioned to their size and contribution. A compromise proposal was that the states should vote proportionately on money matters. The Lilliputs would have none of this, for their treasure was in their very existence as political entities.

What would be the criterion of contributions? Both the Franklin and Dickinson drafts used population. The Southern colonies contended that if people were to be the basis, their slaves should be excluded from the calculation. Chase of Maryland, Hooper of North Carolina, and Edward Rutledge and Lynch of South Carolina in similar phrases defined slaves as "goods and chattels, property," no more suitable for levies by the central government than "sheep, cattle, horses, etc." John Adams properly rejoined that it was persons as workers who produced wealth, and it made no difference whether they were called freemen or slaves. Then followed some North-South discussion which resulted in the sloppy statistic that a slave was half as productive as a free laborer. James Wilson of Pennsylvania thereupon objected that if only half of the slaves were counted as people in fixing quotas of contribution, this would discriminate in favor of the South; moreover, to omit half of the slave population would encourage slaveholding. Nobody seems to have considered the idea that perhaps slaves as a group were more productive than freemen as a group, because the slaves' whole lives were devoted to labor, while many whites were relatively idle. In any case, these ruminations had no issue at the time; they came up again in the Constitutional Convention of 1787, where a slave was finally denominated three-fifths of a freeman.

Dr. John Witherspoon shifted debate from population to land and improvements, which he considered to be a truer measure of wealth of a community. (In a later Congress, another delegate with Scottish economic insight went further and explained, convincingly, that no one feature of a society is a sufficient gauge of its productive capacity). Disputants heatedly asserted "jarring Claims and interests." Many members of Congress despaired of progress in forming a confederation, and they went home. Those who remained persisted, and they worked out a provisional plan by mid-August 1776. Then came peace overtures from the Howe brothers, who had arrived just too late to check adoption of the Declaration of Independence, but in time, they hoped, to avoid a military attack on New York. Few expected peace, but Congress thought it best to send a committee to discover what Admiral Howe had to offer. He had nothing, really; if the colonies returned to British allegiance, he personally assured them, their grievances would be redressed, but he could not particularize. Though this conference took place on September 11, a fortnight after the disastrous American defeat in the battle of Long Island, Congress did not soften its refusal of blandishments.

However, furthering the resolve to stand together in the test of arms, Congress adjourned the bitter debate on confederation. It did not return to that project for a full six months. Then it did so spasmodically, with one firm insertion in the fluctuating plan. This was introduced by the vehement Thomas Burke of North Carolina and was, appropriately, seconded by South Carolina. Reservation by the states of control over their internal affairs, it was insisted, was not enough. It must be declared that they kept for themselves every authority not expressly delegated to Congress. Burke inveighed against giving unlimited power to any body of men whatever. He must have had a peeled eye to glimpse, as he said he did, evidence that Congress was already poaching on the sovereignty of the states.

Burke's view of the anemic Confederation was neither unusual nor extreme. When the Articles were completed in Congress he characterized them in a memorandum to the Assembly of his state: "I consider the Congress at present as a General Council of America instituted for the purpose of opposing the usurpations of Britain, conducting the war against her, and forming foreign alliances as necessary thereto. Incident to this must be the General direction of the Army and Navy, because they are the instruments of the war. Also for the providing the necessary funds for the disbursements, because without them neither Army or Navy could subsist." He allowed no more latitude to the central government. "This idea of the Powers, use and authority of Congress, excludes all coercive Interpositions within the States respectively, except with respect to the Army and Navy because the States are competent to every exertion of power within themselves."

Congress could summon ways and means only "by recommendation, which always implies a power in the State to reject." Nor would Burke subscribe to any "pretence for continuance of a Congress after the war is concluded, or of assuming a power to any other purpose."

Congress fled Philadelphia barely ahead of the British army, which marched in on October 19, 1777. Capture of the American capital, though it appeared significant to Europeans, was of little military advantage. Capture of Congress, inchoate though that body was, would have been a military and political blow to the states. Resettled in York, Pennsylvania, Congress addressed itself in earnest to completing confederation, for its own sake and because constitutional union was considered a necessary preliminary to drawing France into open military alliance.

It was decided, almost unanimously, that each state should have one vote in Congress, since each was sovereign. After days of tussle, the delegates determined to assess contributions to expenses on the value of land and improvements, but the vote was close, five to four, and two states divided. This was a victory for the South. A victory for nobody was the provision for representation in Congress. A state could send no more than seven delegates, no fewer than two, and no delegate could serve more than three years in the space of six years. This meant that the delegates from a state changed places with each other at uncertain intervals, and a dutiful delegate might be best acquainted with problems and most useful as a legislator when he had come to the end of his term.

The third chief question was whether Congress could set bounds to those states that claimed to stretch across the continent. The Dickinson draft had conferred this power and, with foresight, had allowed the division of the public domain into new states as occasion required. Several efforts to approve this proposition were rejected. Only Maryland was constant for it. As might have been guessed from the obstinacy of Maryland, the decision to leave the claimant states untrimmed was to delay approval of the Articles of Confederation for several years.

Weary of their good (or bad) works, the members, one by one, took their departure, and soon Congress became only a skeleton body. Those who stuck made minor alterations in, and additions to, the proposed Articles. They completed the task on November 15, 1777, and referred the document to the states. Said the letter of transmittal, the plan was "the best that could be adapted to the circumstances of all," differing as the states did "in habits, produce, commerce, and internal police." The legislatures were asked to view the offering seriously, with their patriotism offsetting their local preferences.

When Congress returned to Philadelphia in July 1778, following the British evacuation, the engrossed Articles of Confederation were signed by the representatives of ten states. The delegates of New Jersey, Delaware, and Maryland were not empowered by their legislatures to do so. Though some talked of a confederation embracing fewer than the thirteen states, Congress appealed earnestly to the holdouts to come in. New Jersey proved amenable (November 1778), then Delaware (January 1779). But Maryland, as a Massachusetts delegate foretold, continued to "take airs and plague us."

Failure to complete the Union was awkward on two occasions. The treaties of alliance and commerce with France (concluded in February 1778, ratified in America in May) were negotiated and accepted by Congress, even though that body could not speak for an American nation. However, the statesmen of this country need not have been embarrassed, because, as was later recognized, France had her own reasons for coming to the rescue of the rebels against Britain. A month later the second group of British peace commissioners (with the Earl of Carlisle as chairman) arrived. Even if they had come before the French alliance was consummated, Congress would still have clung to independence as the condition of treating. As it was, the envoys resorted to offensive means of persuasion. They did not further their cause by pointing out that Congress, in fact, had no authority to bind the colonies, since the Confederation was still hanging fire. This was a gratuitous taunt to which Congress paid no attention.

It was not until February of 1780 that New York, at the instance of Philip Schuyler and others, ceded part of her western lands to the United States with the special purpose of inducing Maryland to approve the Confederation. Connecticut followed, then Virginia. Luzerne, Minister from France, stepped out of his diplomatic role to nudge Maryland to be satisfied with these overtures. Maryland consented, and on March 1, 1781, Congress proclaimed "the final ratification of the Confederation of the United States of America."

Inglorious General

WASHINGTON'S SECOND IN COMMAND, MAJOR GENERAL CHARLES LEE, WAS MORE OF A LIABILITY THAN A HELP TO THE COMMANDER IN CHIEF. FORTUNATELY, FOR HALF the time that Lee held his commission he was a prisoner of the British. In captivity, his obstructionism progressed to a positive design to defeat the American cause, though the Howes did not respond to his treacherous overtures. Charles Lee illustrated the familiar observation that if an officer, no matter what his skill and experience, is not committed to his assignment, his performance will be discreditable. The German officers on the British side were not politically involved, but with them professional pride was a sufficient substitute. Lee's reluctance to further the colonies' cause, or worse, stood in contrast to the devotion of other commanders, such as Lafayette, Steuben, and de Kalb, who, like him, were not native born.

Charles Lee was born in Chester, England, in 1731. He was the son of an army officer. After a good preparatory school education, he purchased a lieutenancy in a grenadier regiment. He came to

America with Braddock's expedition in 1754, but saw no fighting in that General's campaign. He was slightly wounded in Abercrombie's futile attack on Ticonderoga. Under Amherst at the siege of Niagara, he saw much of the northwest frontier; there a Mohawk squaw bore him twins, boy and girl. In 1762, as a Major in Portugal under Burgoyne, he won distinction in a charge against the Spanish. Two years later he visited Frederick of Prussia, who recommended him to the King of Poland, for whom, as aide with the rank of Major General, he went on a mission to Turkey. In 1769 he had a shadowy part in the Russian army fighting the Turks. He toured the Mediterranean, then returned to England, the vitriolic critic of the government in its dealings with America. Lee may have written some of the *Junius* letters.

In 1773 he came to America again, this time for the rest of his life. He went up and down the country, a super-advocate of American rebellion, though he was living on his Major's half pay from the British army. He bought a plantation in western Virginia, next to that of his friend Horatio Gates. As fighting approached, he vastly impressed the patriots with his professional military knowledge and experience. In June 1775, Congress named Lee Major General and third in the line of command—Washington, Artemas Ward, then Lee. His vigorous sponsors, the Adamses and Mifflin, continued to be his partisans at the expense of Washington. When General Ward retired after the evacuation of Boston in 1776, Lee became second to Washington. Before that, Lee gave good service at Cambridge and Boston and in the fortification of New York. He was credited with the victory over Clinton, Cornwallis, and Parker at Charleston, which Colonel William Moultrie did more to win.

Of middle height, Charles Lee was excessively thin; the fierceness of his hooked nose was not relieved by his drawn-down, sour expression of mouth. His dress was unsoldierly, untidy.

Always vain, he was spoiled by admiration. If he had been less self-centered, his natural penetration of mind would have allowed him to see the excellent qualities in those less egotistical than himself. His genuine gift of language made his rudeness not only offensive, but destructive. He had enduring affection for his one sister, in England, and for the large collection of dogs who were his constant companions. The wonder is that he was so long esteemed and trusted by Washington and others who, in good will, tolerated his failings.

Washington's retreat across New Jersey in November–December 1776 marked for the Americans the most dismal, desperate period of the war. British successes on Long Island and at Kip's Bay, Harlem, and White Plains had left to the Americans on the lower Hudson only Fort Washington, on the northern tip of Manhattan, and Fort Lee, on the palisades in New Jersey. Hardly had Washington crossed the Hudson to Hackensack than his misplaced confidence in the river strongholds was crushed. The Fort Washington garrison of 2800 surrendered, and Fort Lee was evacuated barely ahead of the entrance of a large enemy detachment under Lord Cornwallis. These disasters stripped the Americans of cannon, tents, food, entrenching tools, 2800 muskets, and 400,000 cartridges.

Washington's force of 5000 was drastically reduced by the expiration of enlistment of militia and by wholesale desertions. The conduct of New Jersey people was "most Infamous"; instead of turning out to defend the country, they made their submissions (took the oath of loyalty) to the British. New Jersey now lay open to General Howe, and he was close on the Americans' heels in the race to the Delaware. Washington's "wretched remains of a broken army," as Joseph Reed described it, lacked tents, blankets, in many cases shoes, and even shirts. This was when the Commander in Chief confided to a kinsman, "I think the game is pretty near up."

His little army shrinking by the day, and due to expire by the first of January, when enlistments ran out, Washington called on

General Charles Lee to reinforce him. Lee was at North Castle, New York (now North White Plains), with 5500 effective men. "His Excellency thinks it would be advisable in you to remove the troops under your command on this side of the North River," was Washington's message through an aide. And next day Washington himself wrote that he was "of opinion . . . that the public interest requires your coming over to this side."

Lee presumed to the full on the fact that Washington's wishes were at first expressed in the form of requests, rather than being direct orders. He made a succession of excuses for failure to comply with Washington's repeated calls upon him. He contended that, as commander of a separate army, he enjoyed independence of decision; besides, Washington, by the wording of his messages, expected Lee to exercise his own discretion. Lee said he had to stay where he was to prevent the enemy from moving into New England. His men, he complained, were poorly clothed and shod, in no condition to cross the Hudson and march to Hackensack. If troops from the east of the river were to join Washington in New Jersey, let them come from the force of General William Heath at Peekskill. Heath had more than 3000 fit for duty, said Lee, and could spare 2000 to go to Washington's assistance. Lee promised he would replace those sent from Heath's command. Heath flatly refused. He had his orders from Washington, from no one else, and would obey them to the letter. Heath—"stubborn ox," Lee called him—rejected Lee's assumption of authority over him.

Lee wrote to Washington's Adjutant, "His Excellency recommends me to move . . . to the other side of the river . . . but we could not be there in time to answer any purpose." As Lee continued to hang back, the Commander in Chief's dispatches could no longer be called recommendations. "My former letters," he wrote, "were so full and explicit as to the necessity of your marching as early as possible, that it is unnecessary to add more on that head. I confess I expected you would be sooner in motion."

This finally fetched from Lee the promise to bring 4000 troops to New Jersey on December 2. However, he could not yield to Washington's demands without expressing the "wish you would bind me as little as possible . . . detached generals cannot have too great latitude unless they are very incompetent indeed."

When Lee got to Haverstraw, he answered a "pressing letter" from Washington. In his reply, he gave further reason for not hastening to his superior's aid. His intelligence was that Washington had "quitted Brunswick, so that it is impossible to know where I can join you." He believed Washington had already been reinforced, therefore he would hang on the enemy's rear instead of catching up to the Commander in Chief. Washington, writing from Trenton on December 10, was of different mind. The enemy were on the Delaware, and they doubtless intended "to pass the river above us, and to prevent your joining me. . . . Do come on." If Lee arrived promptly, he could be the means of preserving Philadelphia, "a city whose loss must prove of . . . fatal consequence to the cause of America. . . . I entreat you to push on with every possible succour you can bring."

Lee's lethargy in face of Washington's beseeching messages did not prevent him from boasting that he would be the savior of New Jersey. That state, he declared, "was really in the hands of the enemy before my arrival." He basked in the flattery of himself and the disparagement of Washington that came from Colonel Joseph Reed, at headquarters, who should not have written as he did: "I . . . think it is entirely owing to you that this army—the Liberties of America . . . are not entirely cut off. You have Decision, a quality often wanting in Minds otherwise valuable." Lee should come to Hackensack, where his superior talents "are like to be necessary." The Commander in Chief's hesitant judgment had lost Fort Washington. "Oh, General," Reed exclaimed, "an indecisive mind is one of the greatest Misfortunes that can befall an Army —how often have I lamented it this Campaign." Lee, in reply, agreed.

Lee crept along at three miles a day, then rested two days at Morristown. From there he wrote to General Gates, who was marching to Washington's assistance, that "a certain great man is most damnably deficient. He has thrown me into a situation where . . . if I stay in the Province I risk myself and Army and if I do not stay the Province is lost forever. . . . Our Counsels have been weak to the last degree."

This was pride before his fall. He made Vealtown (Bernardsville) after a spurt of eight miles, but instead of taking quarters near his troops, he went on four miles, to an inn at Basking Ridge. This "eccentric movement," as Lord Stirling called it, with just his personal staff and a small guard, Washington thought was "folly . . . for the sake of a little better lodging." It turned out to be anything but better. After slumbers interrupted by calls of messengers and visitors, Lee had a late breakfast. He had just sat down, coatless and in slippers, to his correspondence when outside there arose a clatter of shouts and shots.

Major William Harcourt and Cornet Banastre Tarleton, with a patrol of thirty red-coated troopers, surrounded the house. They put Lee's guard out of action and demanded the General's surrender. After spluttering and blaming others for what was his own fault, Lee handed over his sword and was tied on a horse for the ride to New Brunswick. The date was December 13, 1776.

Lee's capture did not prevent patriot successes in New Jersey. General John Sullivan, who had remained with Lee's army, promptly took command and led the troops to Washington's camp across the Delaware. Philadelphia volunteers, Pennsylvania and Maryland Germans, and Gates with 500 men brought the force to 6000. General Howe did not cross the river, but Washington recrossed it twice, to rout and make prisoners of the Hessians at Trenton on Christmas night, then to defeat the British at Princeton and spend the winter at Morristown.

Lee was soon taken to New York, where he was treated more like a guest than a captive, though there was some question of whether he should be tried for treason instead of being subject to exchange as a prisoner of war. Refugee Tories, who were living poorly in crowded quarters, naturally complained when the rebel General was given the best room in the City Hall. He talked familiarly with General James Robertson, who was in command of the city.

Lee's absence from the army made the hearts of his partisans grow fonder, to the point of preferring him to Washington for the chief command, a bias which he shared. Since he was not available, prejudice in his favor shifted to sponsorship of Horatio Gates, a candidate who was no more worthy. This cabal to undermine confidence in General Washington is described elsewhere in these pages.

What was not known of Lee's captivity until long after the Revolution was his plan, dated March 29, 1777, explaining to the British how they could quickly win the war. Military operations should be against Pennsylvania, Maryland, and Virginia. In response to an offer of general amnesty, these states would yield the demand for independence, the others would follow, and the colonies would be reunited to the mother country with the least further cost in lives and money.

A few historians have interpreted this as an ingenious attempt to deceive Sir William Howe for the benefit of the American cause. If most of the British army went south, Burgoyne's invasion from Canada would fail, since he would not be joined up the Hudson by a force from New York. Lee well knew that America would not make peace until independence was won. It is argued, moreover, that Lee did in fact influence Howe to make Philadelphia the object of his next campaign.

The majority view is that Lee's strategy offered to the British was flagrant treason to America. If not dictated by the desire to save his own neck, it at least showed that he designed to subvert the Revolution. Admittedly, Lee was a quixotic character, but his plan for British victory was not American patriotism in disguise. If the advice he gave to the British had become known to Congress and Washington, he would have been treated as a traitor. If the British had followed Lee's recommendations, to their sorrow, that might mean that Lee was acting on behalf of America, but there is no evidence that Howe was fooled by Lee. Howe's descent on Philadelphia was his own idea. As for Howe's failure to join Burgoyne, it was Lord Germain, managing the war from England, who forgot to notify Howe of his part in the campaign. Lastly, Lee's tardy obedience to Washington's orders prior to his capture, and his disobedience of orders after his release, point to sabotage of America's efforts.

On April 21, 1778, General Charles Lee was exchanged for Major General Richard Prescott, commanding at Newport, Rhode Island, who had been captured in his quarters by a bold band of Americans. Two days later Lee was welcomed at Valley Forge with honors accorded to no one else. The army was drawn up in lines reaching from headquarters two miles toward Philadelphia. Washington, with his general officers and their staffs, rode farther "and waited till Gen'l Lee appeared. Gen. Washington dismounted & rec'd Gen. Lee as if he had been his brother. He passed thro' the Lines of Officers & the Army, who all paid him the highest military Honours to Head Quarters, where Mrs. Washington was and here he was entertained with an elegant Dinner and the Music Playing the whole Time. A Room was assigned him back of Mrs. Washington's Sitting Room. . . ." This was Elias Boudinot's description.

Washington gave Lee the command of the right wing, but before he assumed it, he was given permission to visit Congress at York. From there he immediately renewed his relations with British officers. He wrote General James Robertson, who turned the letter over to Sir Henry Clinton, the new Commander in Chief, that if his advice had been followed the war would have been ended before this. Now that he was no longer in danger of being tried as a deserter, the sincerity of his motives could not be doubted. He anticipated by a month the peace proposals of Lord Carlisle's commission. Lee advised that Britain should offer universal amnesty and renounce any right to tax the colonies. On these terms the Americans would gladly abandon any idea of separation from the mother country. In early June, back in the American camp, Lee congratulated Clinton on his appointment to succeed General Howe: "General Lee presents his most sincere and humble respects to Sir Henry Clinton. He wishes him all possible happiness and health and begs, whatever may be the event of the present unfortunate contest, that he will believe General Lee to be his most respectful and obedient humble servant."

If this was not treasonable, it was forbidden correspondence and in flat contradiction to the oath he took five days later, that he would, to the utmost of his power, support the independence of the United States and defend it against King George, his abetters and adherents.

Lee returned to Valley Forge a fortnight after a council of war had determined on a basically defensive policy in the coming campaign. There would be no attack on Philadelphia or elsewhere unless good opportunity offered. Lee signed the decision.

It was evident that the British were preparing to evacuate Philadelphia. Most believed they would go to New York. Washington was informed by his secret agents that Lord Howe could not furnish enough shipping for the water route, and hence Sir Henry Clinton would have to march across New Jersey. The British began to move on June 18, and, within hours, advance brigades of the American army, under General Lee, made for Coryell's Ferry (New Hope, Pa., to Lambertville, N.J.). Washington left Valley Forge early the next morning with the main army. The situation now was the reverse of what it had been nearly two years earlier. Instead of the British pursuing the Americans' feeble force westward, Washington with superior numbers (about 14,000) was tracking his enemy eastward. Actually, Washington's problems sprang from the fact that Clinton was in retreat. If the enemy were indeed fleeing, should they be assailed? If so, what was their route, and when should they be struck?

Not that Clinton moved rapidly. New Jersey troops under Maxwell and Dickinson had gone ahead to break down bridges over the many streams, fill up wells, and otherwise impede the British march. Clinton was encumbered by a wagon train nearly twelve miles long; he admitted it was excessive, except that, since he was passing through a hostile country, he had to carry food and forage with him. A large drove of cattle slowed his pace, as did the carriages of loyalists and the contingent of unruly camp women. To make all worse, the days were blistering hot, and they were not cooled by the frequent downpours of rain. Troops, particularly the heavily equipped Hessians, fell out of column from exhaustion.

For several days the armies marched more or less parallel to each other, thirty or forty miles apart, the British to the south of the Americans. At Hopewell, a dozen miles northwest of Princeton, Washington's army rested for two days, cleaned arms, and cooked rations. The British were some twenty-five miles away, in the vicinity of Allen Town, southeast of Trenton. Washington was uncertain whether the enemy crawled at the snail's pace of five or six miles a day because of obstructions and impediments, or whether Clinton was trying to tempt him to the lower country for battle.

On the morning of June 24, Washington called his chief officers into council. Should he seek a general action? If not, how could they best annoy the enemy's march? Charles Lee's inhibitions swayed all but Wayne, who stood out for a full-scale fight. Lee argued, as always, that American troops could not match the better trained and better equipped British and Hessian soldiers in pitched battle. To commit them to the test would be criminal. Better build a bridge of gold for the enemy to cross than risk an attack. The

Americans should march directly to the Hudson and let Clinton pass to New York as he chose. French military aid, with D'Estaing's fleet already present, was America's hope for winning the war. Impatience now would court disaster.

Lafayette—Greene and Wayne agreeing—declared that it "would be disgraceful and humiliating to allow the enemy to cross the Jerseys in tranquility." At least Washington should send 1500 men to reinforce the detachments hovering on the British flanks and rear. Lee grudgingly assented to this compromise. This was the decision of the council, but afterward Lafayette, Greene, von Steuben, and Duportail wrote Washington their second thoughts. They urged that a stronger force should plague the enemy's progress, while the main army should be kept in easy supporting distance. If partial attacks brought on a general engagement, so be it. Lieutenant Colonel Alexander Hamilton, Washington's aide, had no voice in the council, but he vigorously dissented as he took the minutes. The conclusion, he said afterward, "would have done honor to the most honorable society of midwives, and to them only." He deplored the opinion "that we should keep at a comfortable distance from the enemy" and be content with "a vain parade of annoying them by detachment." It was degrading to permit "an undisturbed passage to an enemy . . . dispirited by desertion, broken by fatigue, retiring through woods, defiles, and morasses . . . in the face of an army superior in numbers, elated by pursuit. . . ."

Washington made the most of the cautious advice. He ordered General Charles Scott, with 1500 excellent troops, "to gall the enemys left flank and rear." Morgan's 600 riflemen would hang on the right flank, and smaller parties of foot and horse would advance. These new units would cooperate with Maxwell's corps and General Philemon Dickinson's Jersey militia, which from the first had harassed the British march.

At Kingston, four miles northeast of Princeton, on June 25, Washington no longer heeded timid counsel. As Clinton was tak-

[66]

ing the shortest route to the sea, at Sandy Hook, he had to be attacked in force or would escape. Wayne, eager for action, was ordered to advance with 1000 troops, and the command of the entire forward contingent, upwards of 5000 men, more than a third of the American army, was offered to Charles Lee as the ranking Major General. Lee shilly-shallied. The assignment, he objected, was fitter for "a young volunteering general" (Lafayette). Stirling promptly asserted his own claim, which induced Lee to change his mind and demand the position nearest the enemy. Then he again resigned it to the Marquis, and again recanted. In the end, Lee was given over-all command of the advance brigades, with instructions to aid any design formed by Lafayette.

When the British halted at and about Monmouth Court House, Washington collected the American force at English Town, seven miles to the west and north. Around midnight of June 27, Hamilton put in writing Washington's orders, previously given orally, which Lee was to follow next morning. In the hurry of last-minute preparations, no copy of the letter was retained at headquarters, which opened the way to later dispute, since Lee did not produce the original. As Washington's aide remembered it, the Commander in Chief intended Lee to attack, with his whole forward body if necessary; then the main army would come up for a fight to the finish. Washington, unable to foresee all contingencies, properly allowed Lee an amount of discretion. It was known that Lee would encounter the best British troops, those under Lord Cornwallis, for Clinton had shifted them to protect the rear of his march.

The character of the terrain was important to what followed. The flat farm fields immediately to the west of the village of Monmouth were cut by three "ravines," really marshes, trending roughly north and south and more or less equally spaced. The westernmost was passable for artillery only over a narrow causeway; the others were spanned by boggy roads. Enclosing the western end of the plain were hills, the highest, that in the middle, crowned by the Tennent church, which is still standing. General Lee made no effort to learn these features of what had to be the battleground, nor did he outline any plan of action to his subordinate generals.

He marched his force from English Town a couple of hours after sunrise next morning, September 28, the day already hot and destined to reach 96 degrees. He came up with the enemy about eight o'clock, near the village.

Four hours later, Washington, leading the main army from English Town, was astonished, on approaching the Tennent church, to meet soldiers hurrying toward him from the direction of Monmouth. They reported that Lee's force was in retreat. Washington sent two aides galloping ahead to discover what was happening. Soon he knew, for battalions were pressing past him, their commanders unable to say by whose orders they were flying the field. Riding forward, Washington met Lee and angrily demanded of him the cause of the backward rush. The Commander in Chief did not tarry to hear Lee's stammered answer. He gave rapid orders to Lee and others to check the advancing enemy, then posted fresh infantry and artillery on the high ground above the west ravine. With Stirling on the left, Greene on the right, and himself in the center, the Americans repelled and drove back the enemy.

"I never saw the General to so much advantage," Hamilton declared. "A general rout, dismay, and disgrace, would have attended the whole army in any other hands but his. . . . Other officers have great merit in performing their parts well, but he directed the whole with the skill of a master workman." Said Lafayette, "I thought . . . that never had I beheld so superb a man."

After the longest battle of the war, in punishing heat, the British withdrew to the village of Monmouth and the American army occupied the field. It was Washington's intention to renew the fight next morning, but he did not pursue when he found that at midnight the enemy had stolen away toward Sandy Hook. One private gave a summary of the battle: "On Sunday our army had the Engagement with the British at Monmouth . . . where Gen. Lee went Contrary to his orders but our army Drove them and if that he had managed according to his orders it was likely in all probability we should have taken the howl or the bigar Part of there army. It was a very hot Day and a grate many died a drinking water."

Smarting under the disapproval of the army, Lee wrote to Washington insulting letters in which he demanded a court-martial to permit him to defend his conduct on the field of Monmouth. Washington immediately appointed a court to consider charges against Lee: first, of "disobedience of orders, in not attacking the enemy . . . agreeable to repeated instructions," second, of "misbehavior before the enemy . . . by making an unnecessary, disorderly and shameful retreat," and, third, "disrespect to the Commander-in-Chief in two letters. . . ."

The court sat many times at different places as the army moved northward to the Hudson. Lee's main defense was that by retreating he had saved his large forward force from destruction. The enemy was too strong, particularly in cavalry, to be withstood; if the Americans had not fallen back in time, they would have been caught between the marshes and slaughtered. Washington's orders to attack had allowed Lee a degree of discretion. If this were not enough, Lee pleaded that he had received contradictory information and that certain of his directions were not obeyed.

The court-martial held Lee guilty as charged, except that the word "shameful" describing his retreat was expunged. He was suspended from any command for twelve months, then, following an altercation with Congress, was dismissed altogether. During the remaining years of his life (he died in October 1782), which he spent as a solitary on his farm in Berkeley County, Virginia (now West Virginia), he disparaged Washington and the army with tongue and pen.

In his overtures to the enemy, including the proffer of his plan for subjugation of the colonies, Lee was a traitor to America. Since his advances were secret and not accepted, he was saved from being charged with treason. His demonstrated crime was half-hearted, faltering execution of his military responsibilities. At Monmouth, by acts of omission or commission, he imperiled the American cause.

Washington's dramatic reversal of Lee's retreat gave the American army the victory, in the sense that it occupied the field of battle. More than that, Monmouth proved that American soldiers, disciplined and responding to inspired leadership, could stand in open combat against the best troops of Europe.

Anti-Washington Clique

IT WAS IRONICAL THAT THE ONE BRIGHT SPOT IN THE FALL
AND WINTER OF 1777–78 CAST THE REST OF THE SCENE IN
DEEPER DARKNESS. THE VICTORY OVER BURGOYNE CONTRASTED
with the failure to prevent Howe from taking Philadelphia. Following Washington's defeats at Brandywine and Germantown
came the fall of the forts on the Delaware. As though these misfortunes were not enough, Washington's dispirited army was forced
into what may be called stationary retreat, first at Whitemarsh and
then in dreary quarters at Valley Forge. The purpose of haunting
the purlieus of Philadelphia was to prevent the British from ravaging the neighboring regions of Pennsylvania, New Jersey, and Delaware. Actually, not only was it impossible to shut off supplies to
the enemy, but the American camp was threatened with starvation.

Washington's plight the winter before, when he had been
driven from New York across the Delaware, had been acute, but
then he reversed his peril by the descent on the Hessians at Tren-

ton and followed that stroke by a second at Princeton. Valley Forge, on the other hand, was prolonged misery, made worse because the prospect of again taking the field was clouded.

Improved organization of the army was called for, but progress could not be made while the mere day-to-day existence of the camp was endangered for want of food and clothing. The committee sent from Congress to Whitemarsh—Robert Morris was the chairman—wrote to General Washington, on December 10, 1777: "Among the many reasons against a Winters Campaign we were sorry to observe one of the most prevalent was a general discontent in the Army and especially among the Officers. These discontents were ascribed to various causes and we doubt not many of them are well founded." Congress wished to see "a reform . . . take place in the Army, and proper discipline be introduced." James Lovell, delegate from Massachusetts, was so infected with distrust of Washington that he proposed to Samuel Adams, a fellow doubter of the Commander in Chief, not a reform of, but a revolution in the military force. Washington, Lovell said, would cooperate with Congress in measures to make the army vigorous, "but verily my own Share of Hope is not great enough on this Promise as to make me relinquish the Idea of an annual Choice of *all* officers." Probably no one joined the suspecting Lovell in this quixotic remedy. In any event, the near starvation that staved off such a proposal was a blessing in disguise.

In the patriot ranks, dejection produced dissension. In Congress, in many parts of the country, and in the army itself dissatisfaction arose over Washington's leadership. The complainants put forward Horatio Gates, "the conqueror of Burgoyne," as the champion who could rescue the cause from disaster. If not Gates, then General Charles Lee or General Thomas Conway inspired hopes. These proposals to displace Washington were fumbling, for not one of the three erected as substitute was eligible for supreme command. Gates' success at Saratoga was in fact not of his own doing. Lee was a prisoner of the British as a result of his own carelessness. Conway was a fault-finding braggart under whom his fellow officers would not have served. In spite of these disabilities, the three stood recommended to their supporters as professional soldiers of experience, while Washington for the moment was made to appear as a Virginia planter in uniform. Jonathan Sergeant, formerly a delegate in Congress from New Jersey but in November 1777 the Attorney General of Pennsylvania, gave James Lovell his opinion that Washington had been guilty of "such blunders as might have disgraced a soldier of three months' standing."

The protest episode is known accidentally, and too narrowly, as the "Conway cabal." There has always been a question whether it was an organized movement, or simply consisted of angry, envious voices simultaneously raised in different quarters. The term "cabal" is mistaken if it is considered to mean "conspiracy," for the opposition to Washington was not secret; if it was a plot, it was open enough. Washington was sure of his enemies, and he was reluctantly goaded into identifying them to the President of Congress and to others of his friends. Many of his close associates had no doubt that a concerted effort was being made to dismiss him.

One day, an anonymous paper charging Washington with incompetence on many counts was picked up on the stairs of Congress. President Henry Laurens thought it fit only for the fire, but in friendship he sent it to Washington, who replied at the end of January 1778: "I was not unapprized that a malignant faction had been for sometime forming to my prejudice; which . . . could not but give me . . . pain on a personal account; but my chief concern arises from an apprehension of the dangerous cosequences, which intestine dissensions may produce to the common cause. . . . My enemies take an ungenerous advantage of me; they know the delicacy of my situation, and that motives of policy deprive me of the defence I might otherwise make against their insidious attacks. They know I cannot combat their insinuations, however injurious, without disclosing secrets, it is of the utmost moment to conceal." It had been his "unremitting aim to do the best circumstances would permit; yet," he continued, "I may have been very often mistaken in my judgment of the means, and may, in many instances deserve the imputation of error." He wanted Laurens to lay the accusations before Congress. It was later believed that the attack, unworthy in any case because it was unsigned, was the work of Dr. Benjamin Rush of Philadelphia, who had recently resigned as physician general following a quarrel with Dr. William Shippen, Jr., head of the army medical service.

Washington comforted himself with the reflection, which he sent to Henry Laurens: "Why should I expect to be exempt from centure; the unfailing lot of an elevated station? Merit and talents, with which I can have no pretensions of rivalship, have ever been subjected to it." "Fifty thousand pounds," Washington had said earlier, "would not induce me to undergo what I have done." It was true that no amount of money could buy what he gave freely. During the siege of Boston he had confided to Joseph Reed: "I know the unhappy predicament I stand in! I know that much is expected of me; I know, that without men, without arms, without ammunition, without anything fit for the accommodation of a soldier, little is to be done; and, what is mortifying . . . I cannot stand justified to the world without exposing my own weakness, and injuring the cause by declaring my wants, which I am determined not to do. . . ."

The first tangible sign of antagonism to Washington was in the tipsy babbling of Colonel James Wilkinson, Acting Adjutant of General Gates. Gates chose Wilkinson, his favorite aide, to take to Congress—not directly to Washington—official news of Burgoyne's surrender. Washington's remonstrance to Gates, dated October 30, 1777, was, "I cannot but regret that a matter of such magnitude and so interesting to our general operations shoud have reached me by report only . . . not bearing that authenticity which the importance of it required, and which it would have received by a line under your signature, stating the simple fact."

Dawdling in his journey, young Wilkinson spent a convivial evening at the headquarters of Lord Stirling * at Reading. Stirling, out of loyalty to Washington, informed the Commander in Chief of a statement made by Wilkinson to Stirling's aide, Major William McWilliams. This provoked a crisp note from Washington (November 9, 1777) to Brigadier General Thomas Conway: "Sir: A letter which I received last night contained the following paragraph. In a Letter from Genl. Conway to Genl. Gates he says: 'Heaven has been determined to save your Country; or a weak General and bad Councellors would have ruind it.' "

Brigadier General Thomas Conway, of Irish birth and long service in the French army, was brave on the battlefield, but obnoxiously boastful. Some others of the European professional soldiers, early in the war, disparaged the fitness of American military leaders who had come from civil life. They found fault with Washington and his close associates, such as Henry Knox, the former Boston bookseller, and Nathanael Greene, the Rhode Island iron forger. Even Baron de Kalb, in the beginning, while praising Washington's character and motives, thought he lacked necessary aggressiveness; in fact, while in France the Baron had been instructed to promote the substitution of an accredited French General to head the patriots' revolt. Before long de Kalb revised his initial impressions and gave the Commander in Chief his full support.

Not so Conway. Though free with his shafts, he loftily threatened to resign whenever he himself was the object of criticism. Congress favored him with appointment as Inspector General and advancement to Major General. The board of war meant him to be second in command, under Lafayette, in the projected Canadian campaign in the winter of 1778. By more than accident, his

* William Alexander, of New Jersey, whose claim to the Scottish title was honored in America.

name has been given to the enclave of prejudice against Washington (the Conway cabal), though he was a figure secondary to Generals Horatio Gates, Charles Lee, and Thomas Mifflin, and several prominent politicians.

Washington's first tilt with him, because of Conway's reported snide comments to Gates, ill prepared the Commander in Chief to receive the Irish Frenchman as Inspector General, and at advanced rank. Washington had earlier discussed at headquarters the need for an officer who would promote uniformity of drill and efficiency of administrative departments throughout the army. Manifold other duties, in field and camp, had prevented the maturing of his plans.

When Conway, fresh from the smiles of Congress at York, presented himself at Valley Forge to assume his new function, Washington was correctly respectful of his assignment, but made no pretense of personal welcome. At the same time, for the good of the service, Washington earnestly tried to calm the dissatisfaction of many officers with Conway's promotion. Conway resented his chilly treatment. He protested that he accepted the inspectorship from loyal motives, and that the rank of Major General was essential to performance of his duties. If his appointment was disagreeable to the army, he was "very ready to return to France where I have pressing Business. . . ." Washington answered that complaint of officers was not on the score of the inspectorship. However, "By consulting your own feelings upon the appointment of the baron deKalb you may judge what must be the Sensations of those Brigadiers, who by your Promotion are Superceded." Washington would always be obedient to the actions of Congress, but he trusted that "no Extraordinary promotion [would] take place, but when the Merit of the Officer is so generally acknowledged as to Obviate every reasonable cause of Dissatisfaction thereat."

This remark, which was for Congress as well as for Conway, provoked the latter to offensive flattery. ". . . the General and universal merit," he wrote, "Wh you Wish every promoted officer might be endowed with is [known only in] the great frederick of europe, and the great Washington in this continent. I . . . never was so rash as to pretend to such a prodigious height." Conway regretted that he was not acceptable to Washington and could "expect no support in fulfilling the Laborious Duty of our inspector general." He was prepared to return to France.

Washington sent this correspondence to Congress with a covering statement: "If General Conway means, by cool receptions . . . that I did not receive him in the language of a warm and cordial Friend, I readily confess the charge. I did not, nor shall I ever, till I am capable of the arts of dissimulation." He deemed Conway his enemy, but treated him with proper respect to his official character.

In spite of being poised for France, where he hoped he would "Meet with no frowns," General Conway did not immediately quit the army. He clung to his inspectorship, though he accomplished nothing in the main camp at Valley Forge. Three of the five members of the board of war—Gates, Mifflin, and Francis Lightfoot Lee—were his partisans. (The others, William Duer and Richard Peters, were Washington's supporters.) The war board, with compliance of Congress, projected a new "irruption" into Canada, to be led by Lafayette with Conway as his second in command. This harebrained scheme, thought up in mid-winter (January 1778), was testimony to the giddiness of its sponsors. It took no account of the disastrous history of the attempt of Arnold and Montgomery in 1775, even to the extent of ordering John Stark, who had been of Arnold's party, to submit himself to a second adventure in suffering and frustration. Washington, who was not consulted in the decision, confided his opinion of it to his friend Thomas Nelson, Jr.: "An expedition is . . . on foot against (rather into) Canada, wh I am well persuaded is the child of folly, circumstanced as our affairs are at present, but as it is the first fruit of our new board of War, I did not incline to say any thing against it."

Washington was asked to release Hazen's regiment for the expedition (Hazen was a Canadian) and to hand Lafayette his instructions. The Commander in Chief declined to give any advice on the undertaking, as he knew neither what was intended nor the means to be used. Though he could ill spare Hazen's corps, it was ordered northward. Lafayette set out, not for Albany, but for York, where Congress was in session. He was anxious for a command; his high rank was until then in effect honorary. But he would not be party to an affront to Washington, and he would serve only under Washington's orders. Nor would he accept Conway as his next in command. Lafayette knew all about Conway's aspersions on his chief. He demanded a Major General on whom he could rely— McDougall or de Kalb. Congress and the war board, on the other hand, were willing to insult Washington. However, since France was about to become America's ally in the war, they gave in to Lafayette's stipulations rather than see him depart for France and take other officers of his nation with him.

The Marquis, his old friend de Kalb, and six of their companions in the voyage to America rode through bitter weather to Albany. There they found that the promised 2500 troops, warmly clothed and fully supplied for a winter campaign, were in fact only half as many, lightly clad even for summer operations, and disgusted at the prospect before them. Gates had promised that Stark would already have burned British shipping on Champlain, but the means of doing it had not been furnished him. All knowledgeable advisers, including Schuyler, Arnold, and the empty-handed commissaries, condemned the enterprise as reckless.

Lafayette resented thus being made a fool of. Congress in March "suspended," then called off the crazy junket. Lafayette and Baron de Kalb returned to Valley Forge. In fact, the laugh was not on them, but on the board of war and Congress. If part of the plan had been to seduce Lafayette from his loyalty to the Commander in Chief, it was defeated by the Marquis' firmness and by the shabby treatment he had received from the politicos at York. By that time (spring of 1778) Washington's enemies had been discredited. He himself told Governor Patrick Henry, "I have good reason to believe that their machinations have recoiled most sensibly upon themselves."

As for Conway, he resigned, but for his sniping at Washington he was challenged to a duel by Colonel John Cadwalader. Cadwalader's ball struck Conway in the mouth, as Dr. Thacher said, with some restraint, "greatly to the derangement of his tongue and teeth." Conway believed his wound was mortal. He propped himself in bed to pen to Washington a complete apology "for having done, written, or said any thing disagreeable to your excellency." He declared as his "last sentiments . . . You are in my eyes the great and good man. May you long enjoy the love . . . and veneration of these states, whose liberties you have asserted, by your virtues!" That was the *amende honorable.* Conway lived for a score of years longer, rejoined the French army, served in India with distinction, chose the royal cause in the French Revolution, and died in exile.

So much for Lafayette's discard of Conway in the abortive Canadian project. The story returns to the mischief of Wilkinson. He discharged his errand to Congress at York, then, belatedly, reported to Valley Forge. There Conway pounced on him for loose talk that had drawn Washington's censure on himself, Conway. Gates, at Albany, was alerted to be ready for Washington's ire at Conway's reflections. General Thomas Mifflin, at Reading, where Wilkinson had been more winey than wise, reported to Gates, "An extract from General Conway's letter to You has been procured and sent to headquarters." Washington had taxed Conway with the slur which, Mifflin admonished, was "such as should not have been entrusted to any of your Family. My dear General," he continued, with an eye to his own comfort, "take Care of your Generosity &

Frank Disposition; they . . . may injure some of your best friends."

Gates, flustered, did not catch Mifflin's tip that it was Gates' aide, Wilkinson, who had spoken out of turn. He promptly addressed Conway: "I entreat you . . . to let me know which of the letters was copied off. It is of the greatest importance, that I should detect the person who has been guilty of that act of infidelity; I cannot trace him out, unless I have your assistance." Then he quickly decided that he did not need Conway's help to identify the culprit. It was not his own aide, but Washington's who was guilty. To Wilkinson, on his return to Albany, Gates exploded: "I have had a spy in my camp since you left me!" He explained (in Wilkinson's account) that "Hamilton had been sent up to him by General Washington; 'and would you believe it, he purloined the copy of a letter out of that closet,' pointing to one in the room . . . Colonel Hamilton was left alone an hour in this room, and during that time, he took Conway's letter out of that closet and copied it, and the copy has been furnished to Washington.' "

Wilkinson saw trouble for himself in the offing, but he knew that his peril was not lessened by casting Hamilton in the role of sneak thief, not to say espionage agent for the Commander in Chief. Was it not likely, Wilkinson offered, that Hamilton had learned of the embarrassing business from his bosom friend Robert Troup, Gates' aide, and had passed on Conway's criticism to Washington? While in Albany, Hamilton and Troup had been much in each other's company.

Gates pursued his conviction that Hamilton was the original miscreant, and insinuated as much to Washington. "I conjure your excellency, to give me all the assistance you can, in tracing out the author of the infidelity which put extracts from General Conway's letters to me in your hands. Those letters have been *stealingly copied*. . . . It is . . . *in your* . . . *power* to do me and the United States a very important service, by detecting a wretch who may betray me, and capitally injure the *very operations under your imme-diate direction.*" He added that he was sending a copy of this letter to the President of Congress.

Washington expressed puzzlement that Gates wished to share his perturbation with Congress, but since he had done so, Washington was answering through the same channel. He lifted the blinders from Gates' eyes by reciting that Wilkinson, at Reading, had disclosed Conway's reproaches, and not in confidence. Lord Stirling had so informed Washington, along with the remark, "such wicked duplicity of conduct I shall always think it my duty to detect." Washington had let Conway know that he "was not un-apprized of his intriguing disposition." The Commander in Chief had kept Conway's censure to himself, "so desirous was I, of con-cealing every matter that could, in its consequences, give the small-est Interruption to the tranquility of the Army, or afford a gleam of hope to the enemy of dissensions therein."

Washington closed by including Gates in his resentment. He had not suspected that he, Washington, was the subject of a confi-dential correspondence of Conway with Gates. He first supposed that Conway's ill disposition had been revealed by Gates "with a friendly view to forewarn me, against a secret enemy . . . a dan-gerous incendiary; in which character, sooner or later, this Country will know Genl. Conway. But, in this, as in other matters of late, I have found myself mistaken."

Henry Laurens, President of Congress, writing to a close friend, deplored the "unhappy dispute . . . between our Commander in Chief and Genl. Gates . . . a letter written by Genl. Conway to Genl Gates fanned up this alarming flame." Conway, who had re-cently spent an hour with Laurens, "assured me that Genl Wash-ington had been deceived and imposed on, that his Letter con-tained no such expressions as had been reported to the General." But Laurens added, "I have seen the Letter this day . . . it is true

Genl. Washington was misinformed, the letter does not contain the words which had been reported to him, but ten times worse in every view."

Gates answered Washington's strictures from York, where he was now president of the board of war. He sought release from the cleft stick by a flat denial of what both he and Conway had earlier tacitly admitted: "I declare, that the paragraph conveyed to your Excellency as . . . genuine . . . was in words as well as in substance a wicked forgery."

Washington did not allow Gates to squirm out of his predicament so easily. More than the tart exchanges concerning Conway's recriminations and Gates' reception of them had, for once, got on the Commander in Chief's nerves. A succession of untoward developments in the preceding three months had made him anxious for the army and for the country. He had refrained, so far as the public knew, from resenting slights upon himself. Gates had not announced to him Burgoyne's surrender, and then had been grudging in sending him reinforcements. The last hope of shutting off supplies to the British in Philadelphia had vanished with the fall of the forts on the Delaware. He had been criticized for going into winter quarters at Valley Forge instead of keeping his troops on the offensive. Congress had made Gates head of the new board of war, thus elevating him, in more than a technical sense, to be Washington's superior. Conway, whom he would not have chosen, had been appointed Inspector General, and his promotion to Major General had caused outcries from other officers besides the Brigadiers. Beyond all this, Washington was obliged to see his soldiers at Valley Forge endure wintry sufferings which he could not remedy.

Galled by this turn of affairs, he sat himself down to vent his feelings on the equivocating General Gates. With his own hand he wrote Gates a lecture-letter, some 1500 words. The mere inscribing of it was more than he should have burdened himself with. He observed that he was unable to reconcile the import of Gates' various letters, and sometimes could not match parts of the same letter. Gates had first appeared to recognize the genuineness of Conway's detraction and had seemed to be anxious only to discover who had reported the discreditable remarks to Washington. Then he had proclaimed that no such passage in Conway's correspondence with him had ever existed. Why, Washington asked, if Conway's letter was faultless, had not Gates produced it as proof?

Gates kept on protesting that Conway had shared with him no reproaches. For the sake of official relations, Washington was ready to forget the controversy into which he had been forced. "Your repeatedly and solemnly disclaiming any offensive views . . . makes me willing to close with the desire, you express, of burying [those matters] hereafter in silence, and so far as future events will permit, oblivion."

Having wriggled free of Washington's censure, Gates relieved his guilt by upbraiding Wilkinson. That cherished subordinate, learning at York that Gates had denounced him "in the grossest language," challenged the General to meet him behind the English church. Gates arrived, armed with tearful apologies only. Wilkinson had promised to make Lord Stirling "bleed for his conduct," but concluded to accept disdain in place of a duel. He backed down in another way also. Congress, when he had brought the news of Saratoga, had promoted him—he was twenty—to be Brigadier General, but protests of other officers persuaded him to resign the new rank.

The carping at Washington, aside from that of discontented or scheming army officers, was localized in New England and Pennsylvania. New Englanders such as Sam and John Adams and James Lovell had trembled for the safety of their section from Burgoyne's invasion while General Schuyler was the commander of the Northern army. This was as much hostility toward New York as distrust of Schuyler, the upper Hudson personage. Schuyler was a leader much like the Commander in Chief, of aristocratic background, large landed possessions, and not a professional soldier; his steady patriotism, unlike Washington's, was unworthily questioned by certain of his enemies. Not until General Gates, the New England favorite, supplanted Schuyler at Saratoga, and New England Generals Lincoln and Arnold were added to his command to resist Burgoyne, did the northeast corner of the country gather confidence.

Pennsylvanians were resentful of Washington because he had not prevented the enemy from occupying Philadelphia. Not all Pennsylvanians did, for Benjamin Franklin rejoined that Sir William Howe had not taken Philadelphia, Philadelphia had taken Howe. This proved to be true; the British lay idle in the captured city for eight months, Howe was displaced by Sir Henry Clinton, and Clinton evacuated the city, rejoining the forces at New York. Capture of the national capital was not the political stroke that it appeared to European eyes to be, for the American Congress, such as it was, functioned as well as ever in York. Nor were the plaints of some that their dear Philadelphia had fallen to the enemy as genuine as was pretended. Dr. Benjamin Rush and General Thomas Mifflin, among the principal attackers of Washington at this juncture, were soured on him, and, indeed, on the army, for other reasons. Rush had been uncooperative within the medical department, and Mifflin had been derelict as Quartermaster General.

Long years afterward, Duponceau, who had come to America as von Steuben's youthful secretary, and thus was of the headquarters circle at Valley Forge and later, wrote that there had been a clear design "to raise the Conqueror of Burgoyne to the Supreme command." But "Washington stood firm, and undaunted in the midst of his enemies; and . . . 'looked them into silence.' " That was true, so far as public utterance went, for he would not endanger united effort. But in private his strictures on his foes were unsparing. The picture often drawn of Washington as a man above the battle, impervious to personal hurt, is contradicted by his expressed resentment of unfair thrusts. His emotions were as strong as his self-discipline, which usually held them under wraps.

Though beset by disaffection in Congress and mischievous jealousies in the army, the Commander in Chief refused to be discouraged. After reviewing these annoyances for the faithful Lafayette, he ended on his habitual note of confidence: ". . . we must not, in so great a contest, expect to meet with nothing but Sun shine. I have no doubt but that every thing happens so for the best; that we shall triumph over all our misfortunes, and shall, in the end, be ultimately happy; when, My Dear Marquis, if you will give me your Company in Virginia, we will laugh at our past difficulties and the folly of others."

Money Troubles

ONE SERIOUS CAUSE OF HARDSHIP, CONFUSION, AND IN-JUSTICE WAS THE RESORT TO FINANCING THE REVOLU-TION MAINLY BY THE ISSUE OF IRREDEEMABLE PAPER money. Grants and borrowing, which were less relied upon, were perfectly allowable, indeed, inescapable. And taxation, which was most desirable, was least practiced. Complicated by political and administrative disabilities, the war exhibited every fiscal error. To unwisdom was added governmental dishonor.

On February 25, 1780, Congress abandoned its futile attempts to purchase military supplies with worthless money and called on the states to deposit grain, meat, rum, clothing, and forage at designated depots. In addition, quartermasters and commissaries impressed what they needed, simply seizing food, wagons, horses, and arms, and gave receipts for what they took. This method of procuring the means of making war was awkward, unpopular, and unequal as it bore upon the people, but government had no other resort; public finance had broken down. Critics of the devices used to obtain revenue were not silent: ardent patriots such as John

Witherspoon, Pelatiah Webster, Thomas Paine, Robert Morris, and Alexander Hamilton remonstrated and urged reforms. However, the errors committed were not basically Congress'.

Material support of the rebellion brought an unexampled emergency, sudden and protracted. The colonies were innocent of political, much less constitutional, organization for united action. This was the root cause of the financial floundering. Combined effort was hortatory, without legal underpinning. The colonies, by habit, geography, and climate, were separate societies; they had had little cooperation in fact and less by sanction of public machinery. It is remarkable that they envisioned joint, even national independence, and that, to achieve that goal, they were able to pool their resources as well as they did.

The war was proclaimed a revolt against foreign taxation, but the colonists had been accustomed to only the few and small taxes levied by their own local representatives. Since the economy was an agricultural one, wealth was fairly evenly divided, and poll taxes and property taxes were not discriminatory; besides, the colonies relied on indirect income from customs dues and excise taxes on luxuries. As gold and silver were scarce, having been drained away to correct an unfavorable balance of foreign trade, the colonists used barter and, more largely, paper money. All of the colonies, plus numerous public and private "banks," issued circulating notes, for ordinary conduct of government as well as to meet occasional exceptional expenses. These notes were of many sorts, subject to several limitations on their use, but their common characteristic was a lapse into depreciation; if eventually redeemed, it was at a fraction of their nominal value. Redemption was often merely in other notes of "new tenor"; these in turn lost value and were replaced, or were supplemented by still more paper money. So dependent were the colonists on fiat money that when Parliament, in 1764, forbade further issues it was bitterly resented. That ban figured among the causes of the break with the mother country.

As soon as the Americans were free of British restraint, they answered the demand for prompt and large funds by employing the printing press, for state as well as continental currency. For a time, due to the genuine need for additional media of exchange incident to war activity, and bolstered by patriotic acceptance, the paper maintained its face value. However, the day was not long deferred when, with mounting issues, its volume became superabundant and its value progressively declined in spite of coercive governmental and other efforts to support the purchasing power. The paper was given legal tender quality; there were attempts to limit the prices of common commodities by compulsion; punishments were imposed for refusal to take the disparaged money at par. Congress reiterated promises and righteously exhorted and scolded, but all to no purpose. The fatal degeneration could not be denied. Finally, the last reproach of those who refused to take the paper money at face value had not died on the legislative lip when Congress itself decreed a mass repudiation. The traditional practice of the separate colonies was now followed by the central government. Congress foisted off on the holders of bad paper money another issue, bearing interest, which was expected to retain its purchasing power. The new tenor notes were damned from the outset, and they soon joined in the accelerated decline of the old currency. Though some of both were eventually received at trifling valuation in public dues, they had lost all acceptance in trade.

Fiscal inexperience has been offered as excuse for the wholesale recourse to paper money. One member of Congress exclaimed, "Why should I burden my constituents with taxes when I can send to the printer for a cartload of money, one quire of which will pay for the whole?" But the majority of the population not only knew the bad tendencies of uncontrolled paper currency, they also knew the good. They preferred to have the bitter, if necessary, to enjoy the sweets. Depreciation was expected; indeed, by some it was advocated. Rising prices stimulated trade. Debtors, who were more numerous than creditors, coveted the legal license to discharge their obligations at a pleasing discount. In that democratic society the popular demand could not be gainsaid.

Nor is it surprising that public spokesmen rationalized ills into merits and benefits. The paper money, unlike specie, it was observed, did not fly the country to enrich others, but remained to enliven business and promote wealth at home. Further, as the paper passed rapidly from hand to hand, the depreciation was fairly distributed; it did not penalize one group more than any other. Others took a different tack in exculpating the paper issues. The rising prices of goods, gold, and silver, they claimed, were not due to superfluity of the money, but to positive scarcity of commodities relative to legitimate demand. The dearth was intensified by wicked speculators who withheld products from the market and at the same time cried down the currency. The fall of the foreign exchanges was similarly explained away. It should be remembered, however, that the same delusions were vocal in sophisticated Britain a generation later, during the Napoleonic war.

Pelatiah Webster pronounced: "Paper money polluted the equity of our laws, turned them into engines of oppression, corrupted the justice of our public administration, destroyed the fortunes of thousands who had confidence in it, enervated the trade, husbandry, and manufactures of our country, and went far to destroy the morality of our people." And Witherspoon wrote, "For two or three years we constantly saw and were informed of creditors running away from their debtors, and the debtors pursuing them in triumph, and paying them without mercy." Thomas McKean, a President of the Continental Congress, lost £6000 by inflation, Governor William Livingston of New Jersey was similarly defrauded of much of his fortune of £8000, Richard Henry Lee in 1779 received for the rent of 4000 acres paper money that would buy only four barrels of corn. Jefferson was not above offering a creditor paper worth a fourth of the value he had borrowed, but later he thought better of it and paid in full. The further the paper currency depreciated—though still legal tender—the more desirable it was to dishonest debtors in discharging their obligations; it was forced on creditors when the ratio was as low as seventy to one of specie. Trustees and guardians, who were thought to be especially trustworthy, defrauded their wards ("widows and orphans") with paper money worth a fraction of their original funds. Ties of family and friendship were ruthlessly severed in these barefaced cheats.

The opportunities for quick war profits were multiplied by the availability of debased paper money, which the law said had to be accepted at its face value. Unscrupulous operators would have been busy without this assist, which increased their glee. General Washington, like many others, was slow to understand that bad morals were promoted by bad money. He applauded "bringing those murderers of our cause, the monopolizers, forestallers, and engrossers, to condign punishment." They were "pests of society, and the greatest enemies we have to the happiness of America. . . . I would to God that . . . the more atrocious [were] hung . . . upon a gallows five times as high as the one prepared for Haman." He lamented that "idleness, dissipation, and extravagance seem to have laid fast hold of most [men]; . . . speculation, peculation, and an insatiable thirst for riches seem to have got the better of every consideration. . . ." Later he realized that fraudulent legal tender was the fillip to these vices. The laws and prosecutions to prevent commercial malpractice proved mischievous while the guilty paper money was sanctioned. Pelatiah Webster likened them to sprinkling water on a blacksmith's forge, "which deadens the flame for a moment, but never fails to increase the heat and force of the internal fire."

The provincial congress of New York suggested to the Continental body, as if the latter needed any prompting, the convenience of financing the war by paper issues. Beginning with authorization, on the heels of the battle of Bunker Hill, for printing $300,000, a total of $6 million was provided for in that year of 1775. The amounts approved increased annually, except in 1777, a year of moderate reduction; then there was a violent increase in 1778 (when there were fourteen acts for issues passed, to a total of more than $63 million). In 1779, the last year of issues, the amount was in excess of $140 million, more than twice that of the year before. The whole sum of continental emissions was $241,550,780. Not all of the notes printed were in circulation at a given time, for small quantities were redeemed. On the other hand, it is believed that treasury officials took it on themselves to exceed the issues authorized.

Besides all this, the states thrust into circulation $209,524,776, Virginia and the Carolinas being most prodigal. Also, in spite of curlicues and other fancy devices in the engraving, changes of plates, and two official signatures on each bill, the paper money was counterfeited, and to an unknown amount. Both unscrupulous Americans, and the British (as a means of economic warfare), injected large amounts of spurious currency into the economy. Congress attempted to call out of circulation the heavily counterfeited emissions of May 20, 1777, and April 11, 1778, giving new notes in exchange, but the correction was difficult and imperfect. The great variety of bills put out, especially by the states, made detection of counterfeits vexing even for officials. A Pennsylvania act of 1776 prescribed the death penalty for anyone who counterfeited the paper currency of Congress or of any state. That penalty was never enforced. Even those who were proved to have uttered counterfeits (put them into circulation) seem to have been imprisoned, but not given the full punishment. The letter of the law required that the offender be placed in the pillory, which was decorated by his severed ears; then he or she was to receive thirty-one lashes on the bare back, and was required to compensate the person to whom the bad money was passed. Lastly, if the criminal had no estate to indemnify his dupe, he was to be sold into service for not more than seven years.

Of course, the smaller the denominations of bills, the more general and rapid was their circulation and the greater their effect in raising prices. The continental notes ranged from top nominal value down to one-sixth of a dollar. The legal tender property, which was intended, of course, to promote their acceptance, was conferred by the states at the urging of Congress. As Congress had no power to tax, the states were pledged to redeem the paper money in a rough apportionment according to population.

Depreciation, which was not acknowledged by Congress, commenced in the late months of 1776; by January 1779 one specie dollar exchanged for eight in paper, and by November of that year the ratio was 38½ to 1. Two months prior to this, when the amount of continental notes in circulation had been estimated to be $160 million, Congress had resolved that no more should be issued after the total outstanding reached $200 million, which occurred before the end of the year. It was evident that increasing the issues was of no advantage; the whole volume of currency promptly lost more value than the increments supplied in purchasing power.

Long after depreciation had become too plain to be denied, Congress kept on spitting into the wind, solemnly assuring the public that the paper money would be redeemed at face value. These declarations were hollow and childish, and they deceived nobody. In September 1779, when the money was practically worthless, Congress proclaimed: "A bankrupt faithless republic would be a novelty in the political world, and appear among respectable nations like a common prostitute among chaste and respectable matrons." In six short months Congress entered the ranks of the prostitutes. On March 18, 1780, when the paper dollar was worth one or two cents, Congress resolved on substantial repudiation. Thereafter it would accept the old bills at 40 for 1 of new issues of supposedly unquestionable integrity. The mechanism was to requisition the states for $15 million a month for thirteen months, the amount to be paid in the old money, which, when received, was to be destroyed. The new tenor bills would not be issued in excess of one-twentieth of the face value of the old emissions; the new bills were to be redeemable in specie in five years, were to bear interest at 5 per cent, and were to be receivable for taxes.

Congress adopted a scale of depreciation intended to protect creditors against fraud under color of law. It was assumed that the stages of depreciation were from $1.75 paper for 1 Spanish milled dollar (silver) on March 1, 1778; six months later the rate was 4 for 1, after another six months it was 18 for 1, and a year later, at the date of the act of practical repudiation, it was 40 for 1. The scale greatly underrated the true depreciation.

Of the old bills, slightly less than $120 million were paid into the treasury and destroyed; of the new tenor, $4,400,000 were issued. Naturally, after the 40-for-1 act, which the Scotsman Witherspoon branded "The first and great deliberate breach of public faith," the old notes lost value faster than ever. They stood at 100 to 1 at the opening of the year 1781, and six months later they no longer circulated. Thereafter, the only demand was from speculators at prices from 500 down to 1000 for 1. David Ramsay's kind obituary—the money "gently fell asleep in the hands of its last possessor"—was corrected by Horace White: "it passed out of the world like a victim of delirium tremens."

The new tenor notes, issued by a government that had confessed bankruptcy, depreciated from the start and soon stood at 6 to 1. Small amounts were subscribed for stock in the funding of 1790. Of an estimated $78 million of the old notes outstanding, some $6 million were accepted for stock at 100 to 1; the remainder had gone "where the woodbine twineth."

In no case could inflation have been avoided, though it would have been less if the central government had been able to tax the people directly and forbid the issue of paper money by the states. If the circulating media are to be swelled, the appropriate—though partial—corrective is to draw purchasing power into the public treasury. Domestic loans aid this purpose, but taxes, being coercive, are superior. The radical defect was that Congress had no immediate power over the national resources. Requests of the states to lay taxes for the common cause were scandalously disregarded. The states, like Congress, found it simpler to manufacture money than to extract it from the people.

Most members of Congress knew the evil tendency of reliance on paper money, but they were helpless because the states refused to compel sacrifices. "Our finances are in such a situation," Cornelius Harnett, at York, wrote to Thomas Burke in November 1777, "that unless the States agree immediately, to tax as high as the people can possibly bear, the credit of our money must be ruined. Another very large emission must take place, there is no preventing it. The Treasury Boards see the fatal consequence of this measure, but they also perceive that when we have no money, we shall have no Army. The prospect before us is truly distressing, we must however continue further emissions. I tremble at the consequences." Laurens, the President of Congress, confided to John Rutledge, "Our Treasury was lately exhausted, New Emissions were made instantly . . . the demands upon us which . . . are in daily growth are Mountainous, but happy indeed are we, that any quantity of brown paper will answer the calls of our necessities. alarming as this appears we must for the present submit. further necessities may, must, in a few months perform a work which wisdom ought to have effected many months ago."

So far from taxing for the benefit of the continent, Connecticut, a full five years later, defrauded its own soldiers with spurious currency after paper emissions by Congress had been forsworn. Officers and men of militia companies stationed at Forts Trumbull and Griswold (New London and Groton) complained to the legislature

in October 1782 that they had been shortchanged in 1781, the
year of Arnold's attack, and many of them for a longer period.
Their wages "had been in Pay Table orders & State Connecticut
bills, which fell very short of real money. Though they [the paper
issues] speak good money, they carry not equal credit with the
people of the country;" they would not make payment "unless put
off at much less value than they express." The soldiers begged that
"your Hons would be pleased to Devise and Direct a mode of pay
that may be equal to real money."

"Leonidas," in the *Pennsylvania Packet* (July 3, 1779), scolded
the lawmakers for allowing the inflation to reach its desperate
stage. "It is vain," he admonished, "to blame the arts of your enemies, or the infamous practices of monopolizers and forestallers.
The present depreciated state of your money must be traced only to
the mistakes of Congress. Your money . . . your money . . . demands every thought and every hour." It is surprising to find that
Elbridge Gerry would hale the printer before the house to answer
for his infamous publication.

The strictures of "Leonidas" did not prevent Congress, a fortnight later, from issuing 5 million more paper dollars. By September 1, however, the resolve to stop the pernicious practice was
hardening. Congress "on no account whatever" would exceed the
amount of $200 million. John Jay, then President of Congress, no-
tified the states that the paper flood was being dammed. In a long
address, he went on to combat distrust of the continental bills. He
declared that the Confederation was a fact (even though the Articles had not won full assent), that the paper money had been legally issued, and that it would be faithfully redeemed. Any act of
Congress "to annihilate your money . . . would be null and void."

Jay had worked himself into a patriotic fervor which blinded
him to the lack of revenue for Congress. At about this time a
young officer at Washington's headquarters was setting down a
more realistic fiscal prescription. Alexander Hamilton, in a letter

intended to reach Congress, insisted that a foreign loan was imperative. The proceeds should not be used to purchase war materials abroad or to buy up the superfluous paper; rather, the loan should form part of the capital of a Bank of the United States, the major portion of the shares of which should be privately subscribed. The notes of the bank should be exchanged for the depreciated paper at the rate of 1 to 60. That would reduce the volume of currency to the point where it could be supported. Moneyed men, stockholders in the bank, would have an immediate interest in preserving the value of the currency. The resources of the bank would be available for loans to government.

Under the delusion that high prices were due primarily to avarice of sellers, a series of conventions in different parts of the country recommended that the states pass laws fixing prices and wages and compelling all persons to accept the paper money as of equal value with specie. A violator of such regulations was branded an enemy of his country and fined, and he could be set in the pillory or jailed. Creditors were required to accept the paper money at face value or the debt was legally canceled. One convention stated that no person should buy the necessities of life except in small quantities, to prevent forestalling and monopoly. Rhode Island decreed that if some persons were suffering for goods while others were over-supplied, justices of the peace might order constables to break open the premises of the latter and seize the commodities, at lawful prices, for the benefit of those in need. Since foreign goods were scarce and dear, it was urged that importers be limited in the advance of price over prime cost.

These compulsions were rigorously enforced in some states and towns, were less obeyed in others, or were not adopted at all. This brought complaints from complying communities. The strictest controls were then amended and particular licenses and exceptions were permitted. All the while, the wisest observers, though they did not deny that self-seeking was at work, insisted that depreciation of the paper money was due to its excessive issue. Many leaders contended that the restrictions promoted the very scarcity and high prices which they were designed to obstruct. A Bostonian wrote, in June 1777: "We are all starving here, since the plaguey addition to the regulating bill. People will not bring in provision, and we cannot procure the common necessaries of life." However, the temptation to damn the wicked rather than pay taxes to reduce the superfluity of paper died hard.

One device, related to the states' various conventions, that was used to make goods plentiful at reasonable prices, especially provisions and salt, was the laying of embargoes on export by water or land. (This was also done to prevent capture of supplies by the enemy.) The embargoes were imposed by the states, for the most part, and there was protest that their rights were invaded when Congress, in 1778, enacted a general prohibition on export of provisions in order to be sure of food for the army. The embargoes were usually for limited periods of weeks or months, though they were sometimes extended. Since enlistment on privateers hindered recruitment of troops, Rhode Island and Connecticut at times forbade the fitting out of privateers, and Pennsylvania at one point stopped the sailing of all private vessels, to be sure of men for the state's ships. An embargo might be partial, permitting flour to be exported if a third of the stock were first offered to the army commissary. Penalties for violation included forfeit of double the value of the goods. Leather, cloth, wool, and unshorn sheep appeared in the lists of articles covered. To reserve enough oxen for plowing, only one pair could be yoked to any wagon or cart transporting private or public goods.

Each state acted selfishly to protect its own people, even though neighboring states were deprived of scarce commodities. In revenge, a disadvantaged state would lift all prohibitions in order to invite imports. This produced internal jealousies and wranglings. Attempts at joint action by the states were ineffectual.

Gradually it was seen that the embargoes, like other commercial restrictions, had results that were the opposite of what had been intended. Farmers and merchants refused to make their goods available, and prices rose. When Robert Morris was about to become Superintendent of Finance (June 1781), he secured repeal of the Pennsylvania embargo by pledging that he would furnish that state's quota of supplies to the government. He wrote General Washington that since the ships had been allowed to take flour to the French and Spanish islands there had not been a day when he could not obtain five or ten thousand barrels for the army, and the price was halved from what it had been. When North Carolina proposed to lay an embargo on army provisions, Morris urged that "all such restrictions be taken off. They sour people's minds, destroy the spirit of industry . . . producing a dearth of the things embargoed; eventually enhance the prices far more than they could have been increased by any other mode." Freedom of commerce ensured plenty and enabled the people to pay taxes.

When Congress, on September 1, 1779, limited the paper money outstanding, it in effect admitted that too much of it was the cause of rising prices. In the months following, prices continued to soar. A committee confronting this further inflation contended that "the real causes of the great and alarming depreciation are wholly owing to the acts of some disaffected to our government, and others whose extortion and avarice scandalize all goods, and not to scarcity of Commodity or over quantity of a circulating medium, nor want of faith in Government, the causes heretofore assigned with so much plausibility."

To substantiate this, the committee observed that the paper dollars in circulation were not over seven times the quantity necessary for a common medium of exchange. Though the buying power of these dollars might fall, "yet no calculation can carry [the depreciation] to fifteen prices." However, "it is notorious that the article of flour of this market [Philadelphia] is not only now at fifty prices but that it has raised 150 p.ct. since the limitation of future emissions and other articles have advanced nearly in the same proportion." Having exculpated Congress, the committee urged wage and price controls by the states, no price to exceed twenty times that prevailing in the base year; salt and military stores should be exempted.

The argument that increase in the circulating medium to seven times the normal did not justify a greater than proportional advance in prices was shallow reasoning. Beyond a certain point, the extra quantity of money gave warning of inferior quality. The fact was, the community had lost faith in both the currency and the Congress. The promises to restrict issues in the future, and the declaration that the mass of paper money would be redeemed, were not accepted at face value. The doubts of the credibility of Congress were soon proved to be well founded.

In this situation of damaged faith, the tendency of sellers of goods and labor to hedge against expected further price increases was inevitable. This was recognized by General Washington at about that time. He inquired of a coachmaker his charge for "a genteel plain Chariot with neat Harness for four horses." He added, "That the workman may be at no loss to fix a just price on these things on Acct. of the fluctuating, and uncertain state of our Curr [enc] y he may make his estimates in Specie which shall either be paid him immediately upon delivery of the Work, or in paper money at the difference of exchange then prevailing, be it little or much; this will put the matter upon so . . . unequivocal a footing that he can be at no loss in fixing prices, nor be under the smallest inducement to ask an enormous price in order to g [uar] d the evil consequences of depreciation." The fluctuating state of the currency of which Washington spoke was illustrated in Congress' need to double the paper pay of its own secretary in a single month (from $2000 to $4000 per annum), and thereafter to increase it to $14,000.

Depreciation of the continental and state paper money had an especially unfavorable impact on the army. Quartermasters and commissaries found suppliers reluctant to accept the sinking currency, but the purchasing agents did have several means of coercion. Not so the soldiers, whose pay, long in arrears anyhow, when finally received was speeding toward the vanishing point in value. True, the troops did have maintenance, such as it was, but worry for the plight of their families contributed to chronic discontent and outright desertion. A memorial of Virginia officers recited that continental pay, in 1776, was $90 for a colonel, $45 for a captain, and $7 for a private. These wages, in May 1778, were worth $18, $9, and $1.54. Congress raised the pay, but prices increased faster, so that by August 1779 the buying power for the different ranks had fallen to $6.50, $3.25, and 33⅓¢. In spite of two more raises, the real values in November 1781 were $3.33, $1.66, and 20¢. Paper money retained a vestige of value in the South longer than it did in the North, but in September 1781 it finally ceased to circulate at Williamsburg, just as the army was moving to the siege of Yorktown.

The people's bitterness at the galloping inflation was sometimes expressed in humorous disparagement. All sorts of mocking stories were afloat. A merchant deposed that in June 1779 he bought a hogshead of sugar and sold it at a profit, but the sum he received would buy only a tierce. He sold the smaller cask, also at a profit, but with the proceeds he could buy only a barrel. It was said that a man could lose his wages while he was earning them. Decorating the walls of barber shops with worthless paper was good for a laugh, but a dog in Philadelphia could not have appreciated the joke when sailors tarred and plastered him with the despised stuff. No sooner had Rhode Islanders gathered for a mock burial of continentals than the state issued a new sort of paper money. The funeral orator held up a fistful of this, exclaiming, "Be thou also ready, for thou shalt surely die." It was recorded that in Virginia in 1778 the state paper money was at 40 for 1 of continental paper, and the continental at 60 for 1 of silver, so that a single Spanish dollar would discharge $2400 of debt in Virginia money.

Among the very incidental sources of revenue of Congress was a lottery, which limped along for four or five years after 1777. The enemy occupation of Philadelphia interfered with the sale of 100,000 tickets. The best prizes were continental five-year bonds, which were not attractive, judging from the necessity of raising the interest on those of the second class from 4 to 6 per cent. Drawings were several times postponed. The receipts were disappointing, though their exact amount is not known.

The monetary cost of the Revolutionary War may be stated only loosely. The figures have little meaning anyhow because they do not, cannot, include sacrifices that were by their nature inestimable. Such were the physical suffering and death of soldiers, the deprivation of their families, the expropriation and expulsion of loyalists, the diversion of labor and capital from constructive uses, the destruction of homes, industries, and stocks of goods in warehouses, the burning of whole towns. The economic depression in America that followed the war also ought to be counted in the cost. The economic drain on France was one of the direct causes of the French Revolution, which is another story.

A calculation of the income of the Continental treasury, 1775–83, specie value, is:

Paper money	$37,800,000
Domestic loans	11,585,506
Foreign loans	7,830,517
Taxes	5,795,000
Miscellaneous	2,852,802
Total	$65,863,825

To this sum must be added outstanding certificates of indebtedness, $16,708,000, and expenditures of the states, $21 million, making a grand total of $103,571,825. Other statements ran higher; Jefferson put the cost at $140 million.

England spent more, some £91 million, and France, on America's account, perhaps 300 million livres, or $60 million.

One of the embarrassments of Congress, and, more particularly, of General Washington, was the failure of the United States to perform its part in the alliance with France. Since the United States was the original (and considered itself the chief) belligerent, prodding by France, though timely, was unwelcome. On January 25, 1780, Luzerne, the French Minister in Philadelphia, informed Congress of orders he had received from his master: ". . . the present situation of the affairs of the alliance in Europe announces the necessity of another campaign which is indispensable to bring England to an acknowledgment of the independence of the United States, which is the essential purpose of the . . . war." France was making necessary preparations in conjunction with the King of Spain; "it is absolutely necessary that the United States, on their part, should make efforts proportionable to the greatness of the object for which they are contending." Luzerne spelled out his lecture. "The only means of putting an end to the calamities of the war is to push it with new vigour; to take effectual measures immediately for completing the army, and putting it in condition to begin an early campaign."

The Congress, which responded six days later, so far from apologizing for backwardness, blithely promised more than could be performed. ". . . the United States," Congress declared, "have expectations on which they can rely with confidence of bringing into the field an army of 25,000 effective men, exclusive of commissioned officers . . . this army can be reinforced by militia so as to be in force sufficient for any enterprises against the posts occupied by the enemy within the United States." Congress could pledge supplies for cooperating French armies. Congress would rely "on the contributions of the states by taxes, and on moneys to be raised by internal loans for the pay of the army." However, clothing, tents, arms, and other warlike stores must come principally from France, and the United States must have the assistance of French naval forces.

At this juncture Washington's army was on the edge of disintegration at Morristown winter quarters, Congress was being driven to desperate expedients, and calamities were impending in the South. How could Congress pretend to ample resources from taxes and domestic loans, when experience gave the lie to such boasts? And a moment's thought must have persuaded the representatives of America that Luzerne knew the true situation too well to give credence to false optimism. This was one of numerous times when Congress seems to have lost touch with reality, in spite of having among its members at this period such able figures as Schuyler, R. R. Livingston, Oliver Ellsworth, and Roger Sherman.

It was by stages that Congress approached devaluation of the continental currency. Fixing of prices by the states might or might not work, but meantime Congress, for support of the army, abandoned the money mechanism (on February 25, 1780). The states were to contribute two-thirds of their quotas in physical supplies which were to be deposited within their borders at those points the Commander in Chief should designate. Money and prices did not enter into this except for accounting purposes. The kinds and quantities of goods required of each state were specified, and they were to be credited at values stated in Spanish milled dollars. Transport of goods to the places of deposit was at the expense and risk of the states, but, once delivered, Congress would stand any loss from seizure or destruction by the enemy, or by spoilage.

Some specimen allotments illustrate this system of revenue in kind. Massachusetts was to furnish 56,000 hundredweight of beef, 12,126 bushels of salt, and 195,628 gallons of rum. New York was to supply 11,200 hundredweight of beef, 13,069 barrels of flour, 500 tons of hay, and 30,000 bushels of Indian corn or other "short forage" equivalent. Of course the supplies asked of a state varied with the character of its production. South Carolina, which was to figure so prominently in the coming campaign, was to furnish 52,000 hundredweight of rice, along with 16,000 hundredweight of beef, 5000 bushels of salt, 120,000 gallons of rum, 800 tons of hay or corn blade, and 80,000 bushels of corn. Virginia's list included 47,000 hundredweight of beef; Pennsylvania was to contribute no beef, but was to provide 40,000 barrels of flour. Tobacco (7000 hogsheads from Virginia and Maryland) was not to go to the points of deposit for food and forage, but to be under the direction of the commercial committee of Congress, for export. Any state could deliver pork in lieu of beef "in quantities proportioned to the prices assigned to each."

The resolution stated the prices at which supplies were to be credited to the states: flour, per hundredweight, $4.40; beef, best grass fed, delivered between July 1 and December 1, $5.50 per net hundredweight, and best stall fed, delivered in December, $6.50 for the same amount. Fresh pork, well fattened with corn or rice, was valued at $7 per net hundredweight, while salt pork was $22 per barrel of 220 pounds. Corn and rice were credited at 75¢ a bushel, good inspected tobacco at $6 per hundred pounds, West India rum at $1.66 and domestic rum at $1 a gallon, and salt at $3 per bushel.

This scheme of taking the greater part of state quotas not in money, but in supplies, required a system of inspection, custody, issue, record-keeping, and over-all supervision. Effort was made to avoid a burdensome bureaucracy by strictly limiting the number of officials representing Congress. The law provided for three superintendents of magazines and transportation, one for each of the geographic divisions. Each of these top supervisors was to have a deputy in every state of his division, and each magazine was to have a bonded storekeeper. These officials would have one clerk apiece and no more. The staff was skeleton, but the work to be done let Congress in for the formulation of elaborate rules covering rejection of substandard supplies, proper authority for issuing goods, and record-keeping and reporting. It was recommended that warehouses be hired, but if none were available, they were to be erected. Transportation involved constructing boats and bridges, repairing roads, and clearing rivers.

The delivery of supplies from the storehouses to different military units, from an independent army down to detachments of troops passing in the vicinity, called for detailed specifications. The ration for a saddle horse was fourteen pounds of hay and six quarts of oats per day; for a draft horse, sixteen pounds of hay and twelve quarts of oats. Sixty men, including officers, were to have a quarter-cord of wood per day; six men, including officers, were entitled to twenty pounds of straw for three days, but no straw in summer, except in rainy weather and for the sick. If a state's quota of supplies were insufficient for an army quartered there, its legislature was asked to furnish additional quantities, to be paid for by the continent in specie.

Receiving the bulk of continental revenue in specific supplies, if it worked well, would relieve Congress of the need to purchase food and forage for the army in the depreciating currency. But how could it cope with the continental paper money, whose downward plunges were distracting the whole economy? Congress promptly adopted the plan of accepting the old paper at the rate of $40 for $1 in the new issue. It took time for the expedients of securing physical supplies from the states and jacking up the value of the currency to produce results. Meantime, if the troops were naked, one solution would be to have fewer troops. Robert R. Livingston at once moved that the Commander in Chief be directed to dismiss all soldiers whose enlistments would expire by April 1 and to reduce the number of regiments from eighty-eight to sixty.

Though Congress lacked the power to tax, the continental paper money, as it lost value in the hands of the holders, was in fact a heavy tax. Those who had furnished the government with supplies or services—farmers, merchants, soldiers—paid, in the depreciation, a public tax. Dealings within the population as a whole, with paper money that was losing purchasing power, caused a redistribution of wealth. Those who paid off old debts in currency of less worth were gainers exactly in the degree that their creditors were cheated. This was true even after the scale of depreciation was officially announced, for the values at successive dates were less than those declared. For example, in March 1780, when the government accepted the outstanding paper at 40 to 1 of new notes, the true ratio was about 60 to 1. The poor were hardest hit by the depreciation. Prices rose earlier and faster than wages, and limitations on wages were better enforced than restrictions on prices of articles of common consumption. Those who could hold their government securities for years were fairly compensated, but the poor, including veterans and their dependents, had to part with their certificates at a third, fourth, or fifth of their later worth.

The people had little specie with which to pay taxes. At the outset, prior to certain proceeds of foreign loans and the specie expenditures of British and French forces, the country contained only some $12 million in hard money. Those areas that were occupied by the enemy could furnish nothing to Congress. At various times this was the case in all or parts of Massachusetts, New York, Pennsylvania, Virginia, the Carolinas, and Georgia. Obviously, every war is paid for, in treasure as in blood, at the time it is fought. Except for actual goods and services received from abroad, the Americans of the Revolutionary years bore the whole cost of the war. But this expense could not have been recruited in the form of taxes alone; paper money, loans, and such means as the capture of enemy property on land and sea were necessary. In war, this has always been true, even of the richest nations.

Americans during the Revolution and for years afterward were chary of giving authority to their public officers. They had chafed under submission to the King's agents, and were not about to endanger their new freedom by creating another set of executive masters. This fear of conferring power palsied the conduct of the war, particularly in the sensitive field of finance. Until late in the war (1781), such funds as were furnished to the central government were thought to be more safely administered by committees and boards than by a single responsible superintendent.

The result was confusion, inattention, and waste. Day-to-day management of foreign affairs and of the war department by members of Congress who had to divide their efforts between legislative and executive functions was likewise inefficient. But fiscal control required the technical skill and exactitude of record-keeping best entrusted to a qualified individual officer. (That too many cooks spoil the broth was the point of an anecdote told a century and a half later. One morning in 1927, a junior executive burst into his boss's office, excitedly exclaiming, "Did you hear the news? Lindbergh has flown the Atlantic alone!" His employer, impassive, did not raise his eyes from his desk. The youngster repeated, *"Alone! alone!"* "I heard you," came the tired response. "Now let him try it with a committee.")

As soon as bills of credit were issued, two treasurers were appointed to receive and disburse the funds. Tangles occurred, and within months a committee of accounts or claims, composed of no fewer than thirteen members of Congress, was appointed to examine and report on all matters in its jurisdiction. Early in 1776, this large body was supplemented by a standing committee of five delegates, who were to supervise the treasury operations. While this top committee added to the cumbersome machinery, it was empowered to engage a clerk, or several clerks, and provide books and an office for them, which was progress. Further advance was made by naming an auditor general to head the office of accounts and oversee the bookkeepers. The auditor and his subordinates were under the standing committee of five, which was thereafter known as the treasury board. Overlapping was reduced by dropping the committee of claims, but responsibility was already being diffused by the continuous addition of special committees and commissions charged with particularly knotty problems.

When the first domestic loan was opened, in October 1776, loan offices were established in the states. They were manned by receivers, who also paid out the interest. These offices, necessarily distant from the capital, were often negligently, even fraudulently, managed. Abuses increased when the government no longer paid interest in specie, and the loan officers issued certificates of indebtedness ("indents") for the payments due to lenders. This practice piled paper on paper. The indents later were given some standing when they were made receivable for taxes. Besides the loan officers who were to oversee domestic borrowing, continental receivers of taxes were appointed for each state (in 1781), but there was little for them to collect, even if they had been zealous, which most were not.

Commissioners were named to certify approved claims to the Auditor General, a treasurer of loans was added, and, more important, a standing committee on finance was appointed to investigate treasury operations. It was as chairman of this committee that Robert Morris, the capable Philadelphia merchant, demonstrated his fitness for his later distinguished service to the public finances. Morris urged reforms in the uncoordinated treasury structure.

In 1778 an attempt was made to unify the treasury administration. All officers at the capital were to be in one building; it did not have to be large, since the principal functionaries (an auditor, a treasurer, and a comptroller) were to have only one or two clerks each. The small number of clerks spoke of the meagerness of the treasury, but it was significant that Congress now allowed their superiors to appoint them. Six commissioners of accounts were cautiously divided into two chambers, and their clerks, two for each chamber, were chosen by Congress. Congress kept further control by retaining the treasury board. The need for a supervisory expert was acknowledged when Congress invited to this post Dr. Richard Price, the celebrated English writer on public finance. Price cordially favored the Revolution, but he declined the assignment. Congress was not yet ready to repose supreme trust in an American. The legislators contented themselves with abolishing the treasury board and setting up a board of treasury—they were running out of names for agencies—but they did provide that only two of the five members should be of the congressional body.

After two years, the loose management of the board of treasury led to the appointment of investigating committees, which uncovered the incompetence and offensive manners of members rather than fraud. Large payments had been allowed without proper vouchers, certain agents had refused to render any accounts, and all business dragged interminably. Some $4 million expended in France, mainly for army supplies, was never fully accounted for. The honesty of Silas Deane, one of the American commissioners in France, was attacked in Congress by his fellow commissioner, Arthur Lee. A committee of investigation reported that the suspicions and animosities among the commissioners were prejudicial to the honor and interests of the United States, and that the existing commissioners should be dismissed in favor of new appointees. Only Franklin retained his post. From 1779 to 1782 the expenditures in France were in Franklin's hands. In vain he begged Congress to have his accounts examined. Wartime procurement, habitually wasteful and corrupt, left more mistrust than reliable financial records. The absence of documentation in this period of fiscal confusion is evident in the fact that Hamilton, a decade later, was obliged to state the federal expenditure in 1780 at the guesswork figure of $3 million.

Several knowledgeable observers had urged that the executive departmens of finance, war, and marine, which had been mismanaged by legislative committees and boards, be placed in the hands of single responsible individuals. Robert Morris was considered the best man for the office of Superintendent of Finance, the most crucial for continuance of the struggle. Experienced, wealthy, and patriotic, in both the Pennsylvania Assembly and in Congress he had demonstrated his capacity to reform the treasury operations.

Morris was elected February 20, 1781, but he did not accept until three months later, on May 14, when his sense of public duty overcame his reluctance to sacrifice his important private interests. In the interval, Congress dithered over the reasonable conditions which Morris set. First, he asked specifically that he be allowed to continue in the business engagements to which he was already committed. This was earlier granted than his second demand, that he be empowered to appoint and dismiss his subordinates. Samuel Adams, who had a voice for independence but was sometimes blind to the means necessary to achieve it, led the opposition to delegating congressional authority. Only when the treasury was on the verge of disaster did the claims of efficiency overcome insistence on legislative interference at every point in the conduct of affairs.

Morris entered vigorously on the manifold tasks of his arduous assignment. The immediate problem was to recruit means for the campaign which was to end in the victory over Cornwallis at Yorktown. Besides straining every American resource, Morris turned to the French for specie and expense of transport. He also advanced $12,000 of his own money in the undertaking. In his tenure of office—he was induced to hold on until November 1784—he reduced expenses, enlarged income, and introduced more system in the finances than anyone else could have done. He was aided by the final collapse of the paper currency, after which he was able to operate on a specie basis, or at least keep his accounts in terms of hard money. By the time American independence was manifestly within sight, silver had become available from expenditures of British and French armies, and from Morris' commercial dealings with the Spanish at Havana. These benefits would not have been sufficient without his wisdom in establishing a public bank, his persistent entreaties to the states to lay and collect taxes, and his willingness to issue his own notes to pay the soldiers when the army was disbanded. The inevitable confusion of his private and his public dealings brought a sequel of undeserved doubt of his honesty in office, and his life of personal success and patriotic service ended in tragedy. A savior of his country, he could not save himself. Because of his extravagant speculations, he was imprisoned for three years for debt, and his last five years he spent in distress as a bankrupt.

A favorite expedient of Congress was to draw bills of exchange on the envoys in Europe and sell these bills in America for continental currency. Congress did not wait to find out whether its ministers had the means of meeting these drafts. By the time the demands reached Europe and it was reported to America whether they were paid or not, five or six months would have passed, and in the interval—or afterward, for that matter—the blithe Congress did not worry about the straits to which its agents abroad might be put. Franklin's remonstrance in the spring of 1779 was typical of many plaints of moneyless servants of Congress in foreign capitals. "The drafts . . . coming very fast upon me," he lamented, "the anxiety I have suffered and the distress of mind lest I should not be able to pay them, has for a long time been very great indeed. To apply again to this court for money for a particular purpose which they had already over and over again provided for . . . was extremely awkward." The French told Franklin that the treasury had been strained by their sending a fleet to America. The best the King could do was offer to guarantee the interest on an American loan if it could be obtained in Holland or elsewhere. But the Dutch lenders were not responsive; Germany and England paid higher interest than America, several American states were competing with Congress for loans in Amsterdam, and reports of squabbles in Congress had damaged American credit. Franklin was devoting his own salary toward meeting drafts on him. He besought Congress to draw no more unless he had notified them that he was in pocket.

As France seemed to be reaching the limit of her loans, Congress assigned Henry Laurens to Holland and John Jay to Spain. Bills were drawn on both of them before they left America! The final absurdity came when Laurens, captured at sea and imprisoned in the Tower of London, still received demands from Congress.

The prospect of loans from Spain was poor from the first. That government did not want to encourage colonies to rebel; she feared that her claims in North America would be threatened by the rise of a strong independent nation and had allied herself with France against England chiefly to regain Gibraltar. Spain advanced to the United States slightly less than $175,000.

Thus the bills drawn by Congress on European envoys recoiled upon Franklin, the most successful and most trusted of American beggars. He protested to John Jay: "I had worried this friendly and generous court [of France] with oft-repeated demands, occasioned by these . . . unexpected drafts, and was ashamed to show my face to the Minister." Yet he did face the Minister, again and again, and extracted additional sums. These and other deposits were placed with Grand, the banker of Congress in Paris. He paid out during the war $2,477,099 on account of bills drawn on the envoys, and in the end was owed by the American government $1,576,591.

The Soldier and
His Arms

THE ORDERLY BOOK OF THE NORTHERN ARMY AT TICON-
DEROGA REPORTS THE EXECUTION OF A MAN WHO HAD
DESERTED SEVEN TIMES AND SEVEN TIMES HAD RE-ENLISTED
for the bounties. This nimbleness in offering himself, however in-
constantly, was in contrast to the backwardness of Carolinians in
joining the small force of General Nathanael Greene, who was
desperately resisting Lord Cornwallis. On the last day of January
1781, the American commander wrote to Colonel Francis Locke,
from Beatty's Ford on the Catawba: "The enemy are laying on the
opposite side of the river, and seem determined to penetrate the
country. General Davidson informs me he has called again and
again for the people to turn out and defend their country." Greene
found this sloth "unaccountable." "If you neglect to take the field
you will deserve the miseries ever inseparable from slavery. Let me
conjure you, my countrymen, to fly to arms, and to repair to headquarters without loss of time, and bring with you ten days provision." The enemy did cross the river, the very next day.

Based on General Knox's estimates, the continentals and militia who served during some part of the eight years of war numbered in excess of 232,000. Probably the largest American force ever commanded by Washington in the field, some 13,000 or more, was that which pursued Sir Henry Clinton across New Jersey in the summer of 1778. At the siege of Yorktown, with the addition of the French, he had between 5000 and 6000 more. The Revolutionary army fluctuated in size, mostly because of expiration of enlistments, but also because of desertions, casualties, discharges on account of disease, and the brief, emergency spells of militia.

In the beginning, at Cambridge, the volunteers who flocked in, mainly from New England, enlisted for nine months, until January 1, 1776. The journal of Simeon Lyman, of Sharon, Connecticut, reveals the unwillingness of these troops to remain even a little while longer. It was often observed that troops from the Southern states, where the organization of society was more authoritarian, accepted discipline and control more than did those from New England, where every man was his own master. On November 30, 1775, Simeon wrote: "In the afternoon we was ordered out to see who would stay 3 weeks longer, and there was but 3 that would stay, and they had listed to stay another year." "December, Friday, 1th [sic]. We was ordered to parade before the general's door, the whole regiment, and General [Charles] Lee and General Solivan came out, and those that would not stay 4 days longer after their enlistments . . . was ordered to turn out, and there was about 3 quarters turned out and we was ordered to form a hollow square and General Lee came in and the first words was 'Men, I do not know what to call you, [you] are the worst of all creatures,' and flung and curst and swore at us, and said if we would not stay he would order us to go to Bunker Hill and if we would not go he would order the riflemen [Morgan's continentals] to fire at us, and they talked they would take our guns and take our names down, and our lieutenants begged us to stay and we joined the rest, and they got about ten of their guns. . . ." Simeon's non-stop sentence is too long not to be broken. The obstinate ones were marched off to be confined, but "they agreed to stay the four days, and they gave them a dram and the colonel told us he would give us another the next morning, and we was dismissed."

Since his pleas were of so little avail, General Lee had a further threat. On the next day "there was a paper set up on the general's door not to let the soldiers have any victual if they would not stay 3 weeks longer . . . and some was mad and said they would not stay the 4 days, and the paper was took down as soon as it was dark, and another put up that General Lee was a fool and if he had not come here we should not know it." Lee's answer to this retort was another paper pinned on his tent, which Private Lyman copied into his journal. Addrsssing the innkeepers on the roads running into Connecticut, Lee begged them to "show a proper contempt . . . towards those disaffected miscreants who are at this crisis deserting [your country's] cause. Those who by a traitorous desertion in the hour of trial would open the possibility to the enemy of enslaving you, have forfeited all title to be treated . . . as men." Do not admit to your houses those "reprobates to virtue, honor, God, and their country." Lee ended, however, by assuring that "this vile dastardly spirit" was far from being general in the army.

Six months later, in June 1776, Congress wanted to enlist 30,-000 militia into continental service, but the bounty of $10 had little appeal, since the men could get more from their local communities for a shorter engagement. So Congress offered the gift of land and provision for those disabled in the line of duty. When voluntary enlistments fell off, drafts were used, of one in four or five of those eligible. It was possible to pay a fine or furnish a substitute, and so "not go a Soldier when Draughted by the Town." This last expedient opened the way to abuses. General von Steuben, recruiting in Virginia, was offered a boy not yet in his teens. The indignant von Steuben immediately ordered the draft of the able-bodied man who had hoped to escape service by having the child enrolled. Washington wrote, in July 1779, "excepting about 400 recruits from the State of Massachusetts (a portion of whom I am told are children, hired at about 1500 each for 9 months' service), I have had no reenforcements to this army since last campaign." When the French joined the American army on the Hudson in the summer of 1781, Claude Blanchard, a French commissary, observed of Washington's troops, "There were some fine looking men, also many who were small and thin, and some children twelve or thirteen years old. They have no uniforms and in general are badly clad."

The British also had youngsters in arms. The day after the battle of Freeman's Farm, Lieutenant Anburey and a squad were sent out to bury the dead and bring in the wounded. "Our army abounded," he said, "with young officers, in the subaltern line, and . . . three of the 20th regt were interred together, the age of the oldest not exceeding seventeen." He told of Lieutenant Hervey, of the 62nd, "a youth of sixteen." Several times wounded, Hervey refused to leave the field. Then a ball in the leg knocked him out, and, as he was carried off, yet another wound proved mortal.

It is known from several sources that some of Washington's soldiers were under the age of sixteen. He said that "our young troops," posted behind shelter, would give a good account of themselves, but "they will not march boldly up to a work nor stand exposed in a plain." Therefore he never spared the spade and pickaxe.

Recruiting for the eighty-eight battalions to serve for the war slowed when men waited to see whether bounties would be increased. Troops who had enlisted for the duration were jealous of those who came in later at higher bounties. Congress therefore gave $100 to every soldier who had enlisted for the war before

January 23, 1779, though of course the payment was in depreciated paper money.

Competing opportunities discouraged enlistment. Perhaps as many as 10,000 went privateering from New England, attracted by the freedom of the life and the prospect of booty. Recruiting of sailors by investors in the privateers was also intense, with music in the streets of coastal villages and liquor in the taverns for those who would go aboard on adventurous cruises. As wages rose, artisans were deterred from enlisting, and as prices increased, married men became reluctant to leave their families in want. Naturally, militiamen in the ranks at harvest time were profoundly restless.

Officers who left camp on recruiting missions often were not industrious in their efforts and stayed away overlong without giving their commanders an account of their whereabouts or doings. In any case, the system of recruiting by officers was incompatible with good discipline to be enforced by the same officers later; first persuasions and promises would be disappointed by later demands of subordination.

Privates lacked respect for lower officers, if they were known in their communities as men of little worth or knowledge who had pushed themselves forward for commissions. This was understandable but soon after the outset of the war, and later also, the authority of even the highest officers was sometimes disregarded. When General Schuyler, at Ticonderoga, ordered Wooster's Connecticut troops to go to St. John's, they did not "choose to move." Schuyler exlaimed to Congress, "Do not choose to move! Strange language for an Army. But the irresistible force of necessity obliges me to put up with it." General Montgomery and other officers at St. John's had to consult the troops before adopting a plan of attack. "They felt it necessary to call a sort of town meeting" and let the privates vote on the question. When the New Englanders had been wet and hungry for days on end they showed a "leveling spirit,

such an equality among them, that the officers have no authority.
. . . The privates are all generals," said Montgomery. "I cannot
help observing to how little purpose I am here. Were I not afraid
the example would be too generally followed, and that the publick
service might suffer, I would not stay an hour at the head of troops
whose operations I cannot direct."

The generality of troops were more dutiful. Sergeant Joseph
Plumb Martin repeatedly described being exhausted—"almost
tired off my legs"—by long marches on little food. "Fighting
the enemy," he said, "is the great scarecrow to people unacquainted
with the duties of an army. To see the fire and smoke, to hear the
din of cannon and musketry and the whistling of shot, they cannot
bear the sight or hearing of this. But believe me . . . I have felt
more anxiety, undergone more fatigue and hardships, suffered more
every way, in performing one of those tedious marches than ever I
did in fighting the hottest battle I was ever in." The rear guard
was especially tried if the army was transporting its food on the
hoof. "To march in the dark behind a thousand animals, along a
narrow, muddy road, already cut to pieces by heavy artillery, was a
test of patriotism."

Lord Germain and King George planned that Burgoyne should
employ Indians in the fighting. Until he knew more of what he
was doing, Burgoyne invited the savages' worst excesses. Their immediate commander was Colonel LaCorne St. Luc, who told the
British the secret of Indian success in warfare: "Il faut lâcher les
sauvages contre les miserables rebels, pour imposer le terreur sur
les frontiers. . . . Il faut brutalizer les affaires." General William
Tryon, who had talents for spreading terror, reported this advice
and added that he was "exactly of opinion with Colonel LaCorne
St. Luc." Captain Frederick Mackenzie of the Royal Welsh Fusi-
leers approved a scorched-earth policy. "The expedition of Colonel
Butler, and his Indian allies . . . advancing thro' the back parts of
Pennsylvania . . . spreading Terror, and dismay promises much

and may prove of singular advantage in favor of Government. . . .
'Tis surprising what an effect the burning & destroying their property, has had upon the Rebels." That was the only way to bring them to a sense of their duty and turn them against Congress.

Tories operating with Indians, as at the battle of Newtown, New York, stripped and painted themselves to look like their ferocious forest allies. However, the Indian warriors with the British made themselves scarce when Daniel Morgan's riflemen were around, for those sharpshooting frontiersmen were deadly foes of the savages. Morgan's corps had been at Saratoga only a few days when Colonel Henry Dearborn noted in his journal, "An Indian Scalp was Brought in to Day by a Party of our men which is a Rareety with us."

Burgoyne's Indians were busy with the scalping knife before one particular outrage produced orders that they should stop collecting their favorite trophies. As Burgoyne was advancing toward the Hudson, young, reportedly lovely Jane McCrea set out for the British lines to visit the provincial officer to whom she was engaged. Near Fort Edward she was seized by a party of Burgoyne's Indians, who murdered and scalped her. For fear of losing all of the Indians, none was punished for the crime. However, the atrocity helped to bring New Englanders to defeat of the British at Saratoga. As Lieutenant Anburey had observed, "The appearance of a dead body is not a pleasing spectacle, but when scalped it is shocking; two in this situation, we met with, in our march from Skenesborough to Fort Edward. After so cruel an operation, you could hardly suppose any one could survive, but when we took possession of Ticonderoga, we found two poor fellows who lay wounded, that had been scalped in the skirmish the day before the Americans abandoned it, and who are in a fair way of recovery. I have seen a person who had been scalped, and who was as hearty as ever, but his hair never grew again."

The American success at Bennington was not long past when

Congress, on October 25, 1777, ordered that $200 be paid to Abraham Nimham, for the use of himself and his companions, "and as an acknowledgement of their zeal in the cause of the United States." That day the Stockbridge Indians applying to be employed in the service of the United States were referred to General Gates, to whose army they were required to repair. These were Chrisian Indians, but, on the other hand, Congress did not scruple to set on the enemy some of the fiercest and most dreaded of the savages.

A month later, Fort Pitt reported incursions and massacres on the frontiers by Indians who were believed to have been urged on by Lieutenant Governor Henry Hamilton at Fort Detroit. Word was also sent that disaffection had been fomented "among some worthless and evil-disposed persons on the Frontiers, who have been induced to aid our merciless enemies." The Shawanese and Delawares remained American allies. Congress oppointed a committee to go to Fort Pitt "empowered to engage as many of the Delaware and Shawanese warriors in the service of the United States as they judge convenient." The committee should plan with Brigadier General Hand to "carry the war into the enemy's country."

Within weeks Congress agreed to a long speech to the Six Nations. It promised forgiveness for past offenses and begged friendship for the future, but threatened that "if we must take up the hatchet, the blood to be shed will lie heavy on your heads." The commissioners for Indian affairs were told that a main object of the speech was to induce the Six Nations "to surprise Niagara, which will be practicable, if the Senecas heartily embrace the measure and it is conducted with prudence and secrecy." The tribes were to be rewarded if they attacked Niagara according to plan.

Joseph Galloway, who may not be a reliable witness, since he was civil administrator of Philadelphia during the British occupation, reported in March 1778 that 1134 deserters from the American army had come into the city and had taken the oath of alle-

giance to the Crown. However, he said that three-fourths of the
deserts were foreign born. At the end of 1779, when Sir Henry
Clinton left New York for the siege of Charleston, Baron Knyphausen succeeded him in command in the North. There is reason
to believe that desertion from the American army, especially of
Jerseymen, prompted Knyphausen to stimulate dissatisfaction by
his raids on Elizabethtown and Springfield, New Jersey, in 1780. It
was reported that a stream of deserters came into New York, 160
in one day, declaring themselves ready to return to British loyalty.
Little dependence can be put in the particular numbers, for both
sides exaggerated the amount of desertion from the other.

A committee of Congress sought to combat the desertion problem (this in February 1777), but, as with so much else, it did so in-
directly and tentatively. It recommended that the state legislatures
provide by law that any constable, freeholder, or keeper of any
public ferry might apprehend any suspected deserter and deliver
him to a justice of the peace. The informer should receive $5.00
for every mile he conveyed his prisoner. If found guilty, the deserter should be turned over to the nearest commissioned officer or
lodged in jail and be advertised in a newspaper. Anyone guilty of
harboring a deserter, purchasing his arms or clothes, or altering the
brand of a horse should be punished by fine, jail, thirty-nine lashes,
or all of these penalties. But no one looking for deserters should
break into a house without a warrant. Pending passage of such
laws, committees of observation should try to detect deserters and
return them to their duty.

The severest punishments in the British service, which were
worse than in the American, really amounted to torture and death.
Such was the sentence of 1000 lashes, administered in installments
after the lacerated back had been washed with salt water but
before any healing had occurred. "Removal to the navy" might
mean "keelhauling," trussing a man and pulling him with ropes
from rail to rail beneath the vessel's bottom, scraping him against

the barnacles. "Riding the wooden horse" (fencerail) might cripple a man for life. Daniel Morgan, when a colonial in the British army, received 500 lashes for asaulting an officer.

Many lashes with the cat-o'-nine-tails, repeated the very next day, were inhumanly cruel. Dr. Lewis Beebe wrote in his journal at Ticonderoga, September 26, 1776, "this ofternoon see a private of Col: Maxwells Regt received 100 stripes 62 more he is [to] receive tomorrow agreeable to the sentence of the Court martial; he was convicted of desertion, thiefing and a number of other crimes."

As late as September 1783, when the war was over, Lieutenant von Krafft entered in his diary, "Was present at the execution of sentence on a drummer of our Company who had been sentenced by Court Martial to 24 times gantlet on 2 days through 2000 men, and then to be driven out." Running the gauntlet was a punishment for offenses less than the most serious, especially among the German troops. Krafft noted, on February 18, 1782, "Attended on Court Martial of a rascal who was sentenced to run the gantlet 12 times in one day through 200 men." "15 Aug. Thur. At a gantlet. 2 thieves, 3 times."

The soldiers between whose lines the condemned had to run were supplied with switches or sticks. If the culprit was too fleet, and escaped the due number of cuts and blows, he might be slowed by the bayonets of two men walking backward before him. One cannot think that he was retarded in this way if he was compelled to make the painful passage a dozen times in one day, or, as happened, that often on several days. If clubs had been rained on his back, Indian fashion, he would have emerged a mere pulp.

Though the Germans deserted in numbers, when caught they were not as apt to be executed as an Englishman was, to judge from Krafft's diary. On September 27, 1781, "Several desertions having occurred among the Hessians, a gallows was built in front of Fort Knyphausen [formerly Fort Washington] in order to excite fear." In April 1783, when the war was manifestly over, a "deserter was sentenced to receive 24 lashes," and, a few days later, "I had a man who had deserted sworn into the Company again." The next month "We [Hessians] were informed in the order of Gen. Carleton that all English deserters, who should come back, were to be received; but not in service again on account of their perjury, but with leave to be taken back to England."

A sergeant in the Connecticut line was ordered by his superior officer, in the midst of an action, to fetch more ammunition. He was stopped by another officer who accused him of deserting his post. The sergeant explained his errand, but in vain. The officer drew his sword. Seeing his life threatened, the sergeant "cocked his musket, and stood in his own defense. He was, however, taken, confined and tried for mutiny, and condemned to be shot." The Commander in Chief approved the sentence. On the day set for execution an embankment was thrown up to prevent the shot fired at the condemned man from hitting others. The Connecticut troops were formed in a square, and they showed their exasperation at the unjust deed they were compelled to witness.

The sergeant was blindfolded and bound in the kneeling position; a corporal and six executioners stood before him. One of the chaplains gave "a long harangue to the soldiers setting forth the enormity of the crime charged . . . repeatedly using this sentence, 'crimes for which men ought to die,' which did much to further the resentment of the troops already raised to a high pitch." Then the chaplain read a reprieve, which was greeted by "lively and repeated cheerings."

Shortage of arms was chronic. It is believed that, in July 1776, one-fourth of the American army had none, though this was only a few weeks before the battle of Long Island. Often recruits came in without muskets. In certain wild retreats militiamen threw away their weapons, along with their knapsacks, to speed their escape. America lacked arms factories, properly speaking; a gunsmith, a craftsman, would make the complete musket or rifle. No two were precisely alike, which increased the difficulty of repair because replacement parts had to be specially fitted. Eli Whitney's epoch-making invention of manufacturing uniform, interchangeable components of muskets was a generation away. Even good gunflints were hard to get, as few workmen knew how to chip them. Cartridge paper was scarce. The American Revolutionary soldier carried only twenty-five to forty cartridges, as against the sixty that an enemy bore.

At the time of the Revolution the most advanced gunshop would contain three or four barrel forges, a water mill for grinding and polishing barrels, a lock shop with seven forges and benches for forty filers, ten benches for gunstock makers, a brass foundry for mountings, a couple of forges for bayonets and ramrods, a mill for grinding and polishing them, a forge for fittings, and an assembly shop. Here there was division of labor, with its advantages of specialized skills and speed of production, though there could not be perfect uniformity in the different parts.

Most American-made weapons were manufactured in a much more modest operation. Thus Thomas Smyth, of Chestertown, Maryland, in December 1776 introduced Robert Read, a blacksmith of the town, to the council of safety. Read waited on the council to sell them seventeen muskets he had made, and he proposed contracting for a good many more. His muskets appeared to be substantial. He was said to be of good character, possessed some property, and "would be pretty punctual." The year previous it was said, perhaps optimistically, that the 192 gunsmiths in Pennsylvania could furnish 10,000 stands of arms annually. That would be, on the average, fifty-two each. A committee of the Maryland legislature reported in September 1776 that the gun factory established at Fredericktown yielded no adequate returns for the expense. Of £1200 appropriated, £1076 9s. 8d. had been expended and only thirty-eight gunlocks had been produced. The committee recommended that the factory be leased to Elisha Winters, who would pay 6 per cent of the value of the plant, give proper wages to the state-owned slaves, and furnish, monthly, at least 125 muskets, fitted with bayonets, at £4 5*s.* each.

It was expected that when a man joined the army he would bring along whatever weapon he had at home. The Massachusetts council, on October 17, 1776, enlisting eighty-six men for the duration of the war, prescribed that they should carry into the service "a good effective fire-arm and bayonet (if to be obtained,) cartridge-box, knapsack, and blanket, and if no bayonet, in lieu thereof a sword, hatchet, or tomahawk."

Since the manufacture of firearms and the securing of ammunition for them was such a problem, Benjamin Franklin suggested the use of bows and arrows; arrows could be shot faster than a musket, or, especially, a rifle, could be loaded. This proposal was turned down, but the Pennsylvania committee of safety favored the use of pikes in one or two rear ranks; any blacksmith could make pikes.

In the absence of powder mills, the Massachusetts provincial congress, two months before the encounter at Lexington, resolved on a committee to draw up easy directions for the making of saltpeter (potassium nitrate), which composed 75 per cent of the black powder then in use. The instructions were to be printed and sent broadcast in the colony. The Philadelphia committee of safety went a step further, calling on each county to send two men to be trained in extracting saltpeter; then, at the committee's expense, they went from town to town teaching others. The source of saltpeter was earth from under old buildings where wood had rotted; from beneath privies, where the organic content was high; and, more abundantly, from caves. Caves in Virginia yielded eight to ten pounds of saltpeter from a bushel of earth; other soils contained considerably less. From two pounds of rough stems of certain types of Virginia and Maryland tobacco an ounce of saltpeter could be obtained by leaching.

The New York convention, in October 1776, offered 8*s.* 6*d.* per pound for saltpeter of materials collected within the state, and a bounty of 1*s.* a pound for all powder made of saltpeter brought in from neighboring states or abroad. Such encouragement by the states produced saltpeter in considerable quantities. In the same month the Massachusetts council voted £2200 to enable Thomas Crane to pay for the saltpeter he had received at the powder mill at Stoughton. The New York committee of safety gave Henry Wisner, Jr., £100 as a premium for building a powder mill in Ulster County, and Wisner and Moses Philips were entitled to receive a loan of £1000 for two years without interest, provided they complied with resolves for that purpose.

In the first years of the war many gave themselves to gathering the materials of gunpowder, but this ardor cooled after French fleets gave protection for imports. However, the wages of those willing to go to the mountains for "mine work" were high, and the government never possessed as much powder as was needed. Powder of American manufacture did not command the home market until about 1790.

Dueling was an evil not peculiarly chargeable to the Revolutionary war, except that military officers were especially prone to defend their honor in prearranged personal combat with deadly weapons. Someone has observed that the epaulet readily became a chip. "The code" was the possession of those who considered themselves gentlemen, to which class officers as a whole, though by no means all of them, belonged. Common soldiers settled their quarrels with words, fists, and kicks, or perhaps with weapons, in hot anger on the spot. Their friends might join to make a melee, but there was no punctilio of designated seconds, or preparatory negotiations. Officers, on the other hand, were accustomed to the use of pistols and swords, they could afford the wine which frequently led to offensive words, and their resentments were not supposed to cool while the particulars of time and place of armed encounter were arranged. Dueling was respected, but also frowned upon, hence the secrecy of the "meetings" or "interviews." High officers of the American army countenanced the practice and engaged in it themselves.

Instances of officer duels are mentioned in the war diary of the disapproving Dr. James Thacher. In August 1780, he happened to dine at a tavern in the vicinity of Dobbs Ferry, New York, with General Philip Schuyler and others. "Here I learned that a duel had just been fought between Lieutenant O. and Mr. P., both of Colonel Mayland's [Moylan's] regiment of dragoons, and both of whom yesterday were on the most intimate terms of friendship. Mr. O. killed his antagonist on the spot, and received a dangerous wound in the thigh. When I visited him his wound had been dressed, and I was astonished at the calmness . . . with which he related all the particulars of this murderous catastrophe, and the agonized state of mind of his late friend in his dying moments." Aside from anything else, Thacher lamented that the army had lost a valuable officer.

Hardly had the surgeon diarist put down his pen when he recorded "Another dreadful appeal this day made to combat on a point of honor. The parties were Lieutenant S. and Mr. L a volunteer in the army; the latter gentleman fell, and instantly expired; his murderer escaped uninjured." Thacher recommended as "remedy for this fashionable folly" the method said to have been employed by Frederick the Great to check dueling, which was alarmingly prevalent in the Prussian army. When the King knew that two officers of high rank were committed to a meeting, he commanded that they fight in his presence. Not only that, when they arrived they found the whole army paraded to witness the combat, and in plain view were a gallows, halter, and coffins prepared. When the King explained that the survivor was to be immediately hanged, the intending antagonists implored his majesty's forgiveness.

Of course the duels of the Revolution did not always result in a death or even the drawing of blood. Often the combatants were not of the steady nerves they pretended, or were worse shots than officers should have been. Numerous times when powder and ball had been wasted, the seconds called a halt and induced satisfactory apologies.

Lieutenant Krafft of the Hessian troops, in the course of his military career, most of which he spent in America, was the principal in twenty duels. He would have been engaged at other times except that his opposite number was not so demanding of satisfaction. In his American diary he speaks of his encounters casually. Thus, "7 May, Tues. [1782] At noon, after work, I went out with Ensign Biskamm, with whom I had disagreed a few days before, and wounded him slightly on the right hand." The duels among the German soldiers were with swords rather than pistols; while a participant might be sliced, he was not killed.

The Hardest Winters

VALLEY FORGE IS TODAY A GOVERNMENT PARK, WITH FEW REMINDERS OF THE FORESTED WILDERNESS OF THE FAMOUS ENCAMPMENT. THE HILLSIDES ARE EXTENSIVE lawns, and graceful, curving highways offer no hint of the old roads which were alternately frozen ruts or slush and mud. Only the contours of the terrain, the heights to east and west of the creek that flows northward into the bordering Schuylkill, are the same.

The Pennsylvania Council and Assembly, in a formal resolution passed on December 17, 1777, remonstrated to Congress "against the Propos'd Cantoonment of the Army . . . under command of his Excelly. Genl. Washington." Four complaints were set forth. (1) By removal to the west side of Schuylkill—Valley Forge —part of Pennsylvania and all of New Jersey were left subject to ravages of the enemy. (2) Pennsylvania taxes, including those for support of the war, "must infallibly fail, provided the Army go into Cantoonment, at such a Distance as will prevent their covering the Country from the Depredations of the Enemy. . . ." (3) If the army were inactive it would be impossible to recruit troops in

Pennsylvania. (4) "The Army removing at a Distance from the Enemy must give a fatal Stab to the Credit of the Continental Currency throughout the State."

They protested that the army should be kept in fighting fettle, that it should engage in a winter campaign.

Washington explained to Congress "there was choice of difficulties." The army could not keep to the field owing to the naked condition of the troops. To retire to interior towns would mean exposing a large extent of country; also, if the troops were divided, any one of the cantonments might be cut off by the enemy. "Under these Embarrassments, I determined to take post near this place [Valley Forge], as the best calculated . . . to secure the Army, to protect our Stores and cover the Country; and for this purpose we are beginning to hut. . . ."

The General went on to deliver a telling reproof to his critics: ". . . finding that the inactivity of the Army . . . is charged to my Acct., not only by the common vulgar, but those in power, it is time to speak plain in exculpation of myself." The army was incapable of movement due to a desperate lack of food. The day before (December 22, 1777), he had received information that the enemy had left Philadelphia in force for Derby, to forage. "I order'd the Troops to be in readiness, that I might give every opposition in my power; when, behold! to my great mortification, I was . . . informed . . . that the Men were unable to stir on Acct. of Provision, and that a dangerous Mutiny begun the Night before . . . with difficulty was suppressed by the spirited exertions of some officers." He described vividly the afflictions of the half-starved, ragged, shoeless men, every day hundreds more of them down with sickness.

In spite of this picture of distress, the gentlemen of the Pennsylvania legislature were reprobating winter quarters "as if they thought Men were made of Stocks and Stones and equally insensible of frost and Snow. . . ." How could a winter campaign be urged as practicable? "I can assure these Gentlemen that it is a much easier . . . thing to draw remonstrances in a comfortable room by a good fire side than to occupy a cold bleak hill and sleep under frost and Snow without Cloaths or Blankets; however, although they seem to have little feeling for the naked, and distressed soldiers, I feel superabundantly for them, and from my Soul pity those miseries, wch. it is neither in my power to relieve or prevent." That rebuke must have set the gentlemen back on their haunches.

The December tramp from Whitemarsh to Valley Forge, though only a dozen miles, was one of the severest and slowest of the war, due to cold, hunger, and lack of covering. Some sympathetic narrators of the soldiers' sufferings may have exaggerated, but not Washington, who recorded that "you might have tracked the army from White Marsh to Valley Forge from the blood of their feet." Dr. Waldo committed to his diary his complaints of that trek: "The Army who have been surprisingly healthy hitherto now begin to grow sickly from the continued fatigues they have suffered this Campaign. I am Sick . . . discontented . . . and out of humour. Poor food . . . hard lodging . . . Cold Weather . . . fatigue . . . Nasty Cloaths . . . nasty Cookery . . . Vomit half my time . . . smoak'd out of my senses . . . the Devil's in't, I can't Endure it. Why are we sent here to starve and freeze." However, being a physician, he blamed his gloom on his upset stomach.

At Gulph Mills, just before reaching Valley Forge, Washington, in general orders, gave his directions to the soldiers for constructing the huts. The dimensions should be fourteen by sixteen feet, the sides, ends, and roof made with logs, and the roof, in order to be tight, covered with split slabs, "or in some other way." Gaps between the logs should be filled with clay. The fireplace, in the rear wall, should be "stick and dirt," with billets of wood plastered on the inside with clay to the thickness of eighteen inches. The door, in the end fronting the street, should be of split oak slabs, unless boards could be procured; the side walls should be six feet, three inches high.

The troops should be divided into squads of twelve men each, given tools, and "set about a hut for themselves." The General, "as an encouragement to industry and art . . . promises to reward the party in each regiment, which finishes their hut in the quickest, and most workmanlike manner, with *twelve* dollars." Also, as boards were scarce, he would give $100 to any officer or soldier who would substitute some other roof covering, cheaper and more quickly made, that would serve in all respects.

The prospect of being housed was never more welcome. The men had bivouacked at Gulph in the snow for four days before the tents and baggage reached them. Certainly they foresaw that they would not shelter themselves without pain. Not that felling trees, cutting the trunks to length, dragging them to the spot, and lifting them into position was unfamiliar work for countrymen, or that a dozen laboring together would be long about it. There would be no problem for men warmly clad and well fed. But the building job was severe hardship for men who were shivering and weak from hunger. Washington complained to Congress on December 23 that of the 11,000 men in camp, nearly 3000 were unfit for duty "because they are bare foot and otherwise naked." Soap— they had seen none since Brandywine—"we have now little occasion of [,] few men having more than one Shirt, many only the Moiety of one, and Some none at all." For want of blankets, the troops were compelled to "set up all Night by fires, instead of taking comfortable rest in a natural way."

While the troops chopped and rived logs, hoisted them on the walls, and daubed the openings with clay, they lived in tents. The Commander in Chief refused to quit his marquee for his stone headquarters house until the men were hutted. He urged officers of all ranks to spur the work. The builders were encouraged by generous issues of rum. Riding through the camp on January 6, Washington observed that many huts were covered with tents. He cautioned the men that they had only that week to complete the huts. As construction progressed, the tents disappeared; they were cut up for clothing and wrappings for frosty feet.

The huts were regularly spaced, fronting on regimental streets, but they were uncomfortable. In spite of inspections to ensure that roofs were tight, they leaked, so the dirt floors were damp. A fireplace is a tricky thing, no matter the perfect measurements recommended by Dr. Franklin and Count Rumford. Those cobbled at Valley Forge made the huts resemble smokehouses as often as not. "My Skin & eyes are almost spoil'd with continual smoke," wrote Dr. Waldo, "my eyes are started out [of] their Orbits like a Rabbit's eyes by a great Cold and Smoke." The dozen men assigned to a hut lay on straw, when it was to be had. Officers' cabins, ranged behind their respective regiments, were of the common pattern, only less crowded. Major Generals were each given a private hut, but they preferred to lodge in farmhouses in the vicinity.

The camp at Valley Forge in the winter of 1777–78 was threatened with starvation because the service of supply, previously limping, almost broke down. Commissaries, whose duty was to purchase and issue food, resigned, as did the Quartermaster General, who was responsible for providing wagons and teamsters. Not until spring, when Nathanael Greene accepted the post of Quartermaster and Jeremiah Wadsworth that of Commissary, did the work of these departments become efficient. The companion of hunger was nakedness. James Mease, a Philadelphia merchant, had sought his appointment as Clothier General, but after eight months Washington asked Congress to dismiss him as unfit for his office. He took a while to resign, then one after another declined to be his successor. In intervals of vacancies, Washington, in addition to all else, had to be camp provider.

Supplies for Valley Forge, except for droves of animals to be slaughtered, came by wagon. A few public teams were attached to the magazines, but main reliance was on hiring. Congress set 30s. a day for a wagon, driver, and four horses, but the private owners could get £3 or £4 from merchants. The only means of overcoming the preference for private employment was to authorize quartermasters and commissaries to impress wagons. Where possible, farmers evaded these orders by hiding their wagons. Others would have hauled their own produce to the camp but were afraid their teams would be detained indefinitely for government service. This cut down on delivery of the 400 barrels of flour needed every week from Lancaster, Reading, and York. Impressment bore heaviest in the vicinity of Valley Forge until, in fairness, parts more distant were compelled to contribute teams.

The private owners, when they chose, would disobey army commands. In February 1778 a score of wagons came to Valley Forge from Northampton County, Pennsylvania. By orders of the wagonmaster they made one trip to Head of Elk for provisions, then decamped; some of the horses, and drivers too, were lost in crossing the Schuylkill. When carting was hard over hilly roads deep in snow or mud, or became impossible, loads were dumped by the wayside and wagons were abandoned. The troops would be on short rations while food was spoiling fifty miles away because it could not be hauled. A committee of Congress found that public property was dispersed through the country, "not an encampment, route of the army, or considerable road but abounds with wagons, left to the mercy of the weather, and the will of the inhabitants." In the worst of the winter at Valley Forge, the Quartermaster's department, which was charged with furnishing transport, was without a head.

An idea of the toil of a faithful wagoner and his oxen in continental service is offered by the entry of Joseph Joslin in his diary for February 12, 1778: "it is Exceeding Stormy Snow North wind and very hard & we heard they ware a Suffering for hay at Danbury & So we must go and we set out about 10 o'clock and got a littel way and my Cart one wheel Sunk So far down in a hole that it Over Set the load the Snow was full of warter & the wheels would Sink into the [mud] and very heavy Carting indeed and we must waid almost knee Deep the Chief of the way. With 10 Cattel we got to Danbury just Dark 7 mild [miles] and then I went to Capt hays & laid in a bed it has been a very tedious day."

The pork that was to have reached Valley Forge from Virginia and Maryland by vessel did not arrive because the British held the Delaware River.

Within the camp "almost every species of . . . transportation," said visiting congressmen, "is now performed by men who without a murmur, patiently yoke themselves to little carriages [sledges] of their own making." Except for those near the Schuylkill River, the soldiers had to carry water half a mile, from Trout Run. Snow could be melted, but little liquid resulted in the bottom of the kettle. The difficulty in getting water was an obstacle to personal cleanliness, so important to a fixed camp. The problem of washing was worse because only three ounces of soft soap, or one ounce of "hard," cake soap, was issued per man per week. These morsels had to do for every purpose of bathing and laundry. Washington said what has been observed of all armies: "If a soldier cannot be induced to take pride in his person he will soon become a Sloven, and indifferent to every thing else."

Washington struggled in vain to procure clothing for the troops. Six months prior to Valley Forge he begged the "particular immediate attention" of Mease, the Clothier General, to the supply of shoes; "the army is in great distress. Some Corps are almost entirely incapable of doing duty for want of them. You cannot procure too many . . . the sizes should be much attended to. There have been many complaints . . . that in general they have been made too small, and of consequence of little use." Shoes made from green hides quickly wore out. When clothing was delivered, it too was on the small side. Company officers were cautioned to be more careful in the distribution of what was available. Often a small man was enveloped in a coat too big for him, while a "lusty fellow" would be bursting the buttons of a garment too small. At one point Washington complained to General Lincoln: "What makes the matter more mortifying is that we have, I am positively assured Ten thousand compleat suits ready in France & laying there because our public agents cannot agree whose business it is to ship them . . . a quantity has also lain in the West Indies for more than eighteen months, owing probably to some such cause."

The winter frosts and deep drifts of snow caused suffering in the huts, but worse misery for the unprotected men on sentry duty at all hours. In one respect the low temperature was beneficial: it froze the filth of the camp. Every effort was made by the doctors and other officers to police the place, but to small effect. The men were sternly ordered to relieve themselves at the latrines only, but the temptation to stop short was hardly to be overcome. Waste was strewn near the huts. The officers were admonished to keep no horse unless essential, but many insisted on retaining several. The result was that 1500 mounts died of starvation, and their corpses lay about. When a thaw came these made an intolerable stench, only tardily removed when the weak soldiers were called on to bury them.

The army ration was supposed to be a pound of bread, the same of meat, a pint of milk, a gill of peas or beans, a small quantity of butter, and a pint of beer. At Valley Forge in the lean months vegetables and milk were cut out and vinegar, which was used to prevent scurvy, was scarce. Farmers who brought milk to the camp wanted exorbitant prices. The men at Valley Forge did not employ General Putnam's corrective at Peekskill; there, when milk could not be had at sixpence the quart, thirty men from each regiment collected cows sufficient to supply the needs of the camp, then the owners came to terms.

[136]

Supply wagons frozen in the roads near Valley Forge were freed by a thaw in January, but when they were brought into camp the casks of herring, alas, were so spoiled that they "had to be shovelled up en masse." Dr. Waldo recorded the sense of humor that lightened the privations. "A general cry thro' the Camp this Evening among the Soldiers, 'No Meat! No Meat!' . . . What have you for Dinners Boys? 'Nothing but Fire Cake & Water, Sir.'" (Fire cake was a paste of flour, salt, and water, cooked on a hot stone in the embers). The surrounding countryside had been practically exhausted of food. To protect the inhabitants against plundering, the troops were forbidden to go more than a half-mile from camp. But now and then bold ones defied the order in darkness and gleaned with success. The companions of one campfire gave thanks for "a Roasted Pig at Night." Another time, after lean pickings, they got hold of some mutton, and though it was midnight they forthwith made a savory stew.

Dr. Waldo, who was as good with his pen as with his pills, gave a classic description of how the trials of Valley Forge reduced the soldier in body and spirit. "See the poor Soldier, when in health with what cheerfulness he meets his foes and encounters every hardship, if barefoot he labours thro' the Mud & Cold with a Song in his mouth extolling War & Washington, if his food be bad, he eats it notwithstanding with seeming content, blesses God for a good Stomach . . . and Whisles it into digestion." This of the well men. "But . . . There comes a Soldier. His bare feet are seen thro' his worn out Shoes, his legs nearly naked from the tatter'd remains of an only pair of stockings, his Breeches not sufficient to cover his Nakedness, his Shirt hanging in Strings, his hair dishevell'd, his face meagre, his whole appearance pictures a person forsaken & discouraged. He comes and crys with an air of wretchedness & despair, I am Sick, my feet lame, my legs are sore, my body covered with this tormenting Itch, my Cloaths are worn out, my Constitution is broken, my former activity is exhausted by fatigue, hunger & Cold. . . . I fail fast I shall soon be no more! and all the reward I shall get will be . . . 'Poor Will is Dead.' "

Baron von Steuben gave the true condition of the soldiers at Valley Forge when Washington requested him to undertake the training of the troops. Accustomed though he was to the regularity of European armies, von Steuben viewed the scene not with scorn, but with compassion. "The men were literally naked, some of them in the fullest extent of the word. The officers who had coats had them in every color and make. I saw officers mounting guard in a sort of dressing-gown made of an old blanket or woolen bed-cover. With regard to military discipline, I may safely say no such thing existed. . . . There was no regular formation. A so-called regiment was found of three platoons, another of five, eight, nine . . . their mode of drill consisted only of the manual exercise. Each colonel had a system of his own, the one according to the English, the other according to the Prussian or the French style. . . . The greater part of the captains had no roll of their companies and had no idea how many men they had. . . . When I asked a colonel of the strength of his regiment, the usual reply was, 'Something between two and three hundred men.' " One regiment had only thirty men; one company consisted of a lone corporal. "The arms," von Steuben found, "were in a horrible condition, covered with rust, half of them without bayonets, many from which a single shot could not be fired . . . muskets, carbines, fowling-pieces and rifles were seen in the same company."

"Cabin fever" was bound to develop in the confined winter camp. Hardships endured by all intensified the mutual dislikes of militia and continentals, Pennsylvanians and New Englanders. Many who could have helped to harmonize, if not cheer, the troops saw fit to quit the scene. Officers resigned or went on furlough; chaplains and physicians, particularly needed, deserted their posts.

The Pennsylvania legislature itself confessed that "too many of our People are . . . disaffected." In New Jersey the case was no different. This lack of commitment to the patriot cause took various forms, though all short of outright enlistment in enemy ranks. The mildest obstruction was price gouging. "I am pleased to find that your legislature," Washington wrote to Governor Livingston of New Jersey in January 1778, "have fixed a price circumscribing the avarice of your farmers, who like their neighbours are endeavouring to take every advantage of the necessities of the Army." Others drove off their stock on the approach of American commissaries.

Worse was the carrying of flour, meat, and other foodstuffs and supplies to the British occupying Philadelphia. Of course this was in defiance of resolutions of Congress, but the risks seemed worth running for the sake of payment in hard money instead of in depreciated continental paper. This was galling to the hungry American camp, as shown by the punishments dealt out by courts-martial to those of the guilty who were caught. Thomas Butler, an inhabitant of Pennsylvania, for attempting to carry flour into Philadelphia on the night of January 13, 1778, was sentenced to 250 lashes on his bare back. His companion, Thomas Ryan, had tried to deliver eight quarters of mutton and a bull beef; he was confined in the provost guardhouse until such time as £50 was paid to the adjutant general for the use of the sick in camp. Others were bolder, being taken with droves of cattle destined for the enemy-held city. William Maddock was held in the guardhouse until he paid £100 for the benefit of the sick, besides, of course, forfeiting his animals. Joseph Edward for the same crime received the same sentence; in his case $20 of the fine was awarded to each of the lighthorsemen who had arrested him, as an encouragement to their activity.

The camp guardhouse was burdened with such civilian prisoners, who had to be fed over long periods. This was avoided in the case of Philip Kirk, another who was driving in cattle; he was to be jailed somewhere in Pennsylvania during the enemy's stay in the state, and his real and personal property were confiscated by the United States. John Williamson and David Dunn lost their cattle and got 250 lashes each. All of the above were Pennsylvanians; Washington's patrols were similarly exhorted to put a stop to "the Trade carried on from Jersey to Pahiladelphia."

Four years later, when Washington's headquarters were at Newburgh, he was directed "to suppress the pernicious, clandestine Commerce" from New Jersey to the enemy in New York. He wrote to the Secretary of War: "The allotment of the whole Continental Army to that duty would not prevent the practice. It will never be checked unless the States contiguous to N.Y. will pass laws making such commerce punishable with death upon conviction." This was the penalty enacted by other nations at war, but his repeated recommendation to Congress and of Congress to the states had been without effect. (Incidentally, this was an early illustration of the need to confide authority over interstate commerce to Congress alone). Guarding New Jersey's extensive frontier was beyond Washington's power. Small parties risked being cut off by the enemy, and sentinels were apt to yield to bribes.

The winter at last gave way to spring. Efficient management by the recently appointed Quartermaster and Commissary (Greene and Wadsworth) summoned wagons with supplies. A farmers' market twice a week at three locations in camp offered produce of dairy and garden; soldiers with money could buy at prices less than prevailed in Philadelphia. Spawning shad were running in the Schuylkill; horsemen hurried them up the stream into nets, and for weeks the camp enjoyed a fish feast.

Valley Forge, in American history, has become the symbol of patriot suffering during the Revolution. Actually, the encampment of Washington's army near Morristown, New Jersey, in the winter of 1779–80 was in most respects more distressing. True, there was not the galling close proximity of the enemy, snug in the capital city of Philadelphia. That was a psychological more than a military pain, for there was little danger of either army moving against the other. The supply of food for Morristown was worse paralyzed than at the earlier camp, and the winter was more bitter and snowy. Baron de Kalb wrote, "Those who have only been in Valley Forge and Middlebrook during the last two winters but have not tasted the cruelties of this one, know not what it is to suffer." Dr. Thacher marched from Danbury to Morristown in mid-December 1779. "The snow," he wrote, "is about two feet deep and the weather extremely cold; the soldiers are destitute of both tents and blankets and some of them are actually barefooted and almost naked." James Wilkinson, then the Clothier General, could not deliver garments for lack of transport; when small stocks did come in now and then, they had to be prorated to the different units.

Snow made the roads impassable, not only for wagons, but for cattle. In one ten-day stretch the troops received only two pounds of meat per man. Often they were without any meat for four or five days together, they were destitute of bread for a similar period, and once or twice they went two days without meat or bread. To prevent plundering by the desperate soldiers, the magistrates of the neighborhood bestirred themselves to collect food, so that by the end of January 1780 the army was better provided. Then, in a sudden thaw, the roads became mire. In the middle of March there was only a five-day supply of bread for 10,000 troops, and three weeks later there was only a four-day stock of meat. When the states failed to forward their quotas of food, the commissaries were met by soaring prices. Congress was obliged to limit the commissaries to offering—in paper money, of course—twenty times the prices that had prevailed in 1774. This camp, in a forested area of hills and dales, was the scene of the most formidable mutiny of the war.

The arrival of spring found the camp still enduring privations.

THE PRICE OF INDEPENDENCE

The resident committee of Congress, on May 25, 1780, reported that the army contained fewer than 4000 effectives; all were five months in arrears of pay; the soldiers had been on half and quarter allowance of food for some days, and were at present without meat; the sick in hospital lacked medicines. Every department of the army was without money, "and not even the Shadow of Credit [is] left, consequently no article however necessary can be produced." Transport was at a standstill.

The Sick and Wounded

AT THE BEGINNING OF THE REVOLUTION, THERE WAS NEXT
TO NO PROVISION FOR MEDICAL SERVICE IN THE AM-
ERICAN ARMY. LIKE EVERY OTHER MILITARY NECESSITY,
this had to be improvised as the struggle proceeded. Later, organization and facilities improved, but care of the sick and wounded,
even by the standards of that day, remained a reproach. Knowledgeable physicians frequently said that patients would have been
better off without the kind of attention they received in the hospitals.

For the thousands of troops hastily assembled at the siege of
Boston in 1775, the Provincial Congress of Massachusetts set up
four small hospitals, staffed by qualified doctors but lacking medicines and other supplies. Most of the regiments had brought along
whatever medical man the colonel chose, without respect to his
professional competence, but in other cases they had no one.

General Washington had scarcely taken command at Cambridge when he inquired into the medical establishment and informed Congress that he found it "in a very unsettled condition.

There is no principal director, nor any subordination among the surgeons; of consequence, disputes and contention have arisen, and must continue until it is reduced to some system. I could wish it were immediately taken into consideration, as the lives and health of both officers and men depend upon the regulation of this department."

Not until then (July 1775) did the Continental Congress resolve on "an Hospital for an army . . . of 20,000 men," by which was meant a medical service. A Director General and chief physician at $4 per day was to have under him four surgeons at $1.33 each, an apothecary at similar pay, twenty mates at 66¢, one nurse to every ten sick, at $2 a month, besides storekeepers, a clerk, and occasional laborers. If fewer than twenty mates were required at any time, those not needed were to be dismissed. The professional men were assigned no military ranks.

Through the war years Congress increased the medical establishment, and more elaborately defined the duties of its members, but these well-meant plans were chiefly on paper; they had little to do with the conditions that actually prevailed.

The management began in controversy and discredit. Dr. Benjamin Church, the first Director General, though of high reputation for his medical ability and patriotism, was convicted by court-martial and Congress of an improper correspondence with the enemy. He protested his innocence, but was jailed from October 1775 until the following spring. He was released to take himself to the West Indies, but the vessel on which he sailed was lost at sea. His successor was Dr. John Morgan, professor of physic in the College of Philadelphia and a founder of the Pennsylvania Hospital. On him fell continued care of patients in the Boston area after the army moved to New York, then the much heavier demands following the battles of Long Island and White Plains. In the face of crying shortages, with little aid from Congress, Dr. Morgan assiduously collected medicines, instruments, lint, old linen for thousands of bandages, and bedding. He insisted on examinations before appointing his medical subordinates. He took too much on himself, which contributed to the active jealousy of Dr. Samuel Stringer in the Northern army, Dr. William Shippen, Jr., on the west of the Hudson, and the body of the regimental surgeons. The result was that Dr. Stringer and Dr. Morgan were removed and Dr. Shippen was made Director General and physician in chief. Dr. Morgan was exonerated by Congress more than two years afterward, but it was too late to prevent injustice and ill feeling.

Meantime, new appointments in the service placed Dr. John Cochran in charge of the middle department and, under him, as Surgeon General, Dr. Benjamin Rush. Dr. Cochran, brother-in-law of General Philip Schuyler, was a calming influence, and in 1781 he became Director General. Dr. Rush, probably the best known American physician of his day, could be as wrongheaded and stubborn as he was inventive and versatile. He accused Dr. Shippen of malpractice and soon resigned his post.

Positive disorganization, and in more than the medical department, resulted from the practice of allowing sick and convalescent soldiers to go into the country under the care of surgeons and mates of their regiments. From the standpoint of recovery, escaping crowded and unsanitary camp conditions was desirable, but discipline was so poor that those on leave, both men and medics, threatened to disappear from the rolls. General Washington, early in the war, declared that many of the regimental surgeons were "very great rascals, countenancing the men in sham complaints to exempt them from duty, and often receiving bribes to certify indispositions with a view to procure discharges or furloughs." From White Plains in November 1776, Washington ordered Dr. Morgan to call on absent surgeons and mates to account for their patients. Which had died, which had been released from care? Those still sick must be brought to the general hospital, unless so disabled as to warrant their discharge. Others must return to their commands or be looked upon as deserters. If surgeons and mates were remiss in obeying this order, their conduct would be subject to inquiry. Those needed at the general hospital would be detained there, others must resume duty in their regiments.

Throughout the war, regimental surgeons were prone to wangle furloughs, increasing the chronic shortage of doctors. They resented the discipline imposed by the general medical authorities, who in turn accused them of insubordination and unreasonable demands for supplies. This mutual and open distrust was sharpened by a genuine difference of policy in care of the sick and wounded. Physicians in the headquarters establishment, for convenience of administration and other reasons, were apt to favor putting patients in general hospitals. Doctors in the regiments, on the other hand, contended that these large collections of sick were breeding places of contagion, and that treatment in smaller units favored recovery. Experience bore out the latter view.

In spite of the efforts of Dr. Morgan, Dr. Shippen, and others to screen those offering themselves as physicians and surgeons, and though men best reputed in the profession were distinguished for their military service, many unfit were employed. Of some 3500 doctors in practice in America, only about 200 had earned medical degrees. Some of these had studied in this country, at the College of Philadelphia or at King's College in New York, and more in Edinburgh, London, or on the continent of Europe. The best of the remainder had served full apprenticeships of seven years with capable and conscientious practitioners, but others were certified by their mentors with less warrant, or simply presented their claims orally. In the dire need of the hospitals and camps, especially in periods of epidemics or following battles with many casualties, pretenders to knowledge and skill were accepted with little or no inquiry. Mates, junior to physicians and surgeons, were pressed into senior duties and station. In extreme cases, mere orderlies, who might be in their teens, became mates and were a peril to patients.

The movement, already on foot, to distinguish physicians from both apothecaries and surgeons was slowed by emergency demands of the war. The most professionally conscious doctors were implying that those who furnished drugs as well as prescriptions, unless compelled to do so in isolated localities, partook of the business of tradesmen, making profit on the wares they peddled. Surgery, as such, had not yet become a specialty, but was practiced incidentally along with medicine. Prevailing theory allowed little place for the curative services of surgery. Amputations, the remedying of dislocations, and the removal of external growths were more eligible operations than those which "invaded the chief body cavities." The latter aroused the objections, before and during surgery, of the conscious patient and were followed by "the near-certainty of fatal infection." * Toward the end of the war it was observed that military surgeons were resorting to amputations less than before; even in gunshot wounds in the joints, recovery without sacrifice of the limb was not despaired of.

The later description of "fresh air fiend" could be applied to the most aware of the doctors of the Revolutionary war. In the absence of bacteriological knowledge, climatic environment, particularly *miasmata* from swamps and rotting matter, held attention. Thus, in the handbook of Dr. John Jones, *Plain Concise Practical Remarks on the Treatment of Wounds and Fractures* (1775), "it appears how essentially necessary pure fresh air is to the cure of diseases, in general, and particularly those which arise from putrescent causes. . . . It is computed that a gallon of air is consumed every minute by a man in health, and much more must be necessary to one who is sick—as the morbid effluvi, which are continually exhaling from all parts of the body . . . must contaminate a larger portion of the surrounding atmosphere." Sir John

* See Richard Harrison Shryock, *Medicine and Society in America, 1660–1860*, pp. 132–33.

Pringle, in *Observations on the Diseases of the Army* (London, 1752), assigned as the principal source of diseases "changes in the sensible qualities of the air."

The insistence on pure air led these and others giving advice on military medicine to contemn crowded hospitals. Sick soldiers should never be treated in confined quarters. For hospitals take churches, barns, or other large buildings, not private houses. If a ceiling is low, remove parts of it; against the likely complaints of nurses and patients, open windows and doors for ventilation. No sickroom should lack a fireplace to give an escape for bad air. The contagion of typhus adhering to the walls and beams of a hospital could be destroyed only by whitewashing. Floors should be scrubbed and abundantly sprinkled with vinegar. By way of bad example, Jones described the Hotel Dieu, in the heart of Paris: "The beds are placed in triple rows, with four and six patients in each bed; and I have more than once in the morning rounds, found the dead lying with the living." Rush styled the general hospitals "Sinks of Human Life in an army . . . they robbed the United States of more citizens than the sword."

Bethlehem, Pennsylvania, the main village of the pacifist Moravians, was twice practically taken over for the general hospital. The first occupation took place from December 1776 to April 1777; it had been determined to move all of the 1000 sick at Morristown, New Jersey, to Bethlehem, but despite the best hospitality of the Moravians it was still necessary to open other hospitals at Easton and Allentown. Many of the deaths at Bethlehem were attributed to the winter transfer of patients in rough wagons. Joseph Kimmel of Ephrata testified before a court-martial "that a great number of sick soldiers were brought to that town about Christmas, 1777, in open waggons in the night time, almost naked; many of them without shoes, stockings, or blankets to cover them; neither were they accompanied by nurses or other attendants, and [they were] left there by the waggoners without orders what to do with them; that the sick crept into his and his neighboring homes in a piteous condition . . . that many died from the effects of the journey."

The second time Bethlehem was occupied was after the battle of Brandywine in September 1777. Dr. Shippen apologized to the Brotherhood for this new invasion by the sick and wounded. He needed not only the Single Brethren's house, as before, but more space; however, he was prevailed upon not to commandeer the women's quarters.

After three weeks in October, 450 patients filled the hospital; then came orders to find room for 100 more. In the next weeks the Single Brethren's house, crowded above capacity with 400, held 700. It had been computed that, allowing four feet to a patient, the building could contain 360. The crowding was increased because many of the men who had recovered could not be sent back to the army; they were naked. It was impossible to ventilate the filthy place, or even to sweep the floors until brooms were seized from people in the village. "Putrid fever" (typhus) broke out, and 500 died; the infection and mortality were high among the medical attendants. Dr. William Smith "had known from four to five patients to die on the same straw before it was changed, and . . . many of them had been admitted only for slight disorders."

Dr. James Tilton was a prescribing physician in the hospital in the college building at Princeton. After the battles of Brandywine and Redbank, "the sick and wounded, flowing promiscuously without restraint into the hospital, it soon became infectious and was attended with great mortality." Dr. Tilton caught jail fever and narrowly escaped with his life. In convalescence he was given leave to go to his home in Delaware, but in his circuitous route he stopped in the hospital at Bethlehem. This he found more deadly than the one at Princeton. Hardly an orderly or nurse and but few of the doctors had escaped illness.

Forty men of a fine Virginia volunteer regiment had come to

the Bethlehem hospital. Asked how many of these he supposed returned to service, Tilton guessed a third or a fourth. The Bethlehem surgeon "declared solemnly that not three would ever return, that one man had joined his regiment; that another was convalescent and might possibly recover; but that the only remaining one besides, was in the last stage of a colliquative flux and must soon die."

The Bethlehem hospital was evacuated in the spring of 1778, but not before many of the Moravians had been prostrated by illness; seven of the Single Brethren and a son of the pastor died.

The distresses at Bethlehem were repeated on a smaller scale at the same time at Lititz, Pennsylvania, where the Moravians again were hosts. The Single Brethren surrendered their house to the sick and wounded soldiers; only by imploring that the wagons bring no more than 250 patients was the whole little community saved from evacuation of civilians to accommodate a larger general hospital. Almost at once typhus broke out, the two doctors were down with it, seven soldiers died in ten days, and in January 1778 five Moravians who were serving as volunteer nurses and the assistant pastor of the flock joined the death list. By September 1778, when the last patients were removed from the Single Brethren's house, 120 of a total number of fewer than 300 had died there.

Dr. Shippen did not deny that there was much suffering in the hospitals after the battles of Brandywine and Germantown, but it was not owing to his neglect. Clothing and covering for the wounded were not procurable; "our army was raw, unused to camp life, exposure, fatigue . . . obliged to fly before an enemy in a cold and inclement season." Under such conditions the sick and wounded had to be moved great distances in open wagons. Dr. Shippen defended himself against many charges of dereliction and was pronounced not guilty by the court.

Many times the hospitals, both general and regimental, lacked the medicines, instruments, supplies, even the food necessary for care of the patients. In July 1776, Dr. Morgan, the Director General, ordered regimental surgeons to report their stocks. Only fifteen responded. Among them were six sets of amputating instruments, two for trepanning, fifteen cases of pocket instruments, seventy-five crooked and two straight needles. There were only four scalpels, three pairs of forceps for extracting bullets, half a paper and seventy pins, with a few bandages, ligatures, a little lint, and two ounces of sponge. The instruments were all the private property of the surgeons. A doctor sent from New York to Philadelphia to procure instruments reported that none could be had, as all of the fit workmen were making firearms. In the winter of 1778, Dr. James Hutchinson wrote, numbers of the regimental surgeons had no lancets. Four days before the battle of Long Island, Dr. Morgan feared the surgeons had no scalpels; he was sending two; if more were needed he recommended that they "use a razor for an incision knife." A pocket case of instruments, used by Dr. John F. Vacher in 1780 and now in the New York Academy of Medicine, contains a small razor.

Dr. John Bartlett, in July 1777, was called to the scene of the killing and wounding of American sentries, and the murder and scalping of Jane McCrea near Fort Edward. He summoned regimental surgeons, but none was to be found, "except three mates, one of whom had the squirts; the other two I took with me. There is neither amputating instruments, crooked needle, [n]or tourniquet in all the camp. I have a handful of lint, and two or three bandages, and that is all. What I am to do in the case of attack, God only knows; without assistance, without instruments, without everything."

Dr. John Cochran lamented the exhaustion of hospital stores at Morristown. They had all been expended two weeks before, so that "600 Regimental sick and lame . . . are languishing and must suffer. . . . It grieves my soul to see the poor, worthy brave fellows pine away for want of a few comforts which they have dearly earned." He would represent the situation to the Commander in Chief, but "what can he do? He may refer the matter to Congress, they to the Medical Committee, who would probably pow-wow over it for a while, and no more be heard of it. Thus we go before the wind."

"The hospitals are all suffering for want of stores," Dr. Thomas Bond, Jr., complained to the Deputy Director General at Philadelphia, "particularly wine, spirits, tea, coffee, rice, and molasses." The commissaries did not have cash to buy milk and vegetables. "God! 'twould rouse every pulse within you to see a fine brave fellow who has been dangerously wounded" suffering for the want of the most ordinary remedies.

Medicines and instruments came irregularly from France and the West Indies. Before the American army evacuated New York, there was neither jalap nor rhubarb, and "sal. cath. [cathartic salts] became a substitute." Dr. John Warren, senior surgeon in the general hospital in Boston in 1778, wrote to the Governor and council of Massachusetts, deploring the miseries of the patients. "For some days they have not had an ounce of meat; not a stick of wood but what they have taken from the neighboring fences; for near a week not a vegetable; and scarcely any medicine for above a year. . . . [T]he sick and wounded, many of which are exceedingly dangerous, and some of them in a state which requires immediate amputation, are not furnished by the public with a single article of sustenance except bread alone, and must have perished ere this had not the charitable donations of a few individuals . . . contributed to their relief." He had besought all departments of the Continental government in vain.

On August 10, 1776, the hospital at Fort George was in a plight. Dr. Jonathan Potts informed Dr. Morgan, "we have at present upwards of one thousand sick crowded into Sheds & laboring under the various and cruel Disorders of Dysenteries, Bilious Putrid Fevers and the effects of a Confluent Smallpox; to attend this large number we have Four Seniors and Four Mates, exclusive of myself, and our little [apothecary] Shop does not afford a grain of Jalap, Ipecac, Bark, Salt, Opium and Sundry other Capital Articles and nothing of the kind to be had in this Quarter." Their invention in contriving substitutes was exhausted. Dr. Stringer was sent to secure supplies in New York. Two weeks later General Gates confirmed this report, with a dig at Dr. Stringer, who had been the choice of General Schuyler. "Dr. Stringer instead of fulfilling his promises and returning with all dispatch to his Duty, is gone Preference Hunting to the Congress . . . while the Troops here are suffering inexpressible distress for want of Medicine."

The plaints of the hospital doctors that their medicine chests were empty and they were shorthanded were unceasing. Dr. Bodo Otto informed the medical committee of Congress of conditions at the Yellow Springs, Pennsylvania, hospital in May 1780: ". . . our necessary stores for the sick are entirely exhausted. There is no money in the hands of the Commissary to purchase fresh provisions. . . . There is but six days' supply of bread on hand, and the gentlemen who have furnished us that article as well as meat for the past two years now refuse to supply us any longer." The assistant physicians had been unpaid for the preceding seven months and needed clothing. "The nurses and orderlies refuse serving any longer, as they have received no pay."

Ocassionally, medical supplies were captured from the enemy on land or in prize vessels, and they were eagerly welcomed. When the British evacuated Boston, they left behind some hospital stores which were promptly appropriated by the American physicians. However, Dr. John Warren made oath, on April 3, 1776, to an act of spoilage, or worse, which could not be attributed to any responsible Englishman. "I found a great variety of medicinal articles lying upon the floor, some of which were . . . secured in papers, whilst others were scattered . . . loose. Amongst these medicines, I observed small quantities of . . . white and yellow arsenic intermixed." He then learned that his colleague, Dr. Daniel Scott, had collected twelve or fourteen pounds of the arsenic. The medicines thus rendered lethal were "chiefly capital articles, and those most generally in demand."

The feeling of revulsion at the sight of the hospitals was much the same from place to place and year to year. Joseph Wood wrote from Ticonderoga in December 1776 that a third of the "poor wretches" were barefoot, but were obliged to do duty; lying on the cold ground in thin tents or with no covering, many had pleurisy. "No barracks, no hospitals to go in . . . I paid a visit to the sick yesterday in a small house called a hospital. The first object presented [to] my eyes, one man laying dead at the door; then inside two more laying dead, two living lying between them; the living with the dead had so laid for four-and-twenty hours." At the same time Wayne wrote to Gates, "Our hospital, or rather house of carnage, beggars all description, and shocks humanity to visit . . . no medicine . . . no regimen suitable for the sick: no beds or straw to lay on: no covering to keep them warm, other than their own thin wretched clothing." The living got tired of digging graves.

Amidst all the tales of miseries of the sick, it is pleasant to find some favorable comments on the hospitals. Dr. James Craik, Washington's own physician, in April 1778 visited the Yellow Springs amd Red "Lyon" hospitals, "which I found in excellent order and have but few sick at present." William Bell of Lancaster that same month notified Dr. Potts at Yellow Springs that he was delivering two barrels of lime juice and held five more barrels subject to order. Dr. James Tilton was sending fifty lancets. The Rev. Dr. James Sproat, chaplain to the hospitals in the middle department, eighteen months later preached at Yellow Springs, where "the hospitals [are] well provided for, and the gentlemen take good care of the sick." In March 1778 the hospital stores at Manheim, Pennsylvania, included a pipe and a half of Madeira wine, two barrels of port, 220 gallons of molasses, three and a third hogsheads of spirits, 250 pounds of coffee, three barrels of salt, seven barrels of herrings, fifteen barrels of sweet oil, 250 shirts, 170 pair of stockings, other clothing and blankets, and tierces of rice and sugar. However, bad roads and high water had prevented prompt delivery from this depot. Also the Apothecary General of the Middle Department complained of deficiency of some of the most used medicines. Some of the boldest of the doctors thought the absence of medicines not a misfortune if they could induce sanitation in camp and hospital and furnish nourishing food to their patients.

Baron Gerard Van Swieten's *Diseases Incident to Armies, with the Methods of Cure,* translated by John Ranby, surgeon general of the British army, was a work available to American military physicians, though how far it was used is not known. It gave treatments for twenty-one complaints, ranging from nosebleed to "phrenzy." Judging from allusions made by American army doctors in letters and diaries, the afflictions with which they chiefly wrestled were fevers (variously but vaguely described), diarrhea, dysentery, "Peripneumony," jaundice, rheumatism, venereal diseases, and, omnipresent, "the Itch." Van Swieten did not include what plagued the American camps, smallpox. Diarrhea and dysentery were among the most common though not most dangerous conditions; they were not to be cured, some physicians thought, except by furloughing the patient to a country location where he could get a milk diet.

Jail, or hospital, fever (actually, typhus) was both prevalent and perilous. Dr. James Tilton, who had the best means of knowing its symptoms, if not its treatment, wrote that this disease "gave notice of its approach by a langour of the whole body and the feeling that the head was compressed in a hoop.'" High-running symptoms warranted bloodletting and an antiphlogistic course. "But after some days the pulse begins to sink; a dry tongue, delirium and the whole train of nervous and putrid symptoms supervene." After bloodletting, which was used only with caution after commencement of the disease, a vomit was "deemed of excellent use, by opening and squeezing all the glands of the body, and thus shaking from the nervous system, the contaminating poison, before its impressions are fixed." However, when "the fever is formed, mercury is of the greatest importance. . . . This remedy has the power of subduing all manner of contagion and infections that we are yet acquainted with. Thus, besides syphilis, itch &c. without fever, it is regarded as specific in small pox, measles, scarlatina, influenza, yellow fever &c."

His prescription was two drams of calomel, one of opium, fifteen grains of Tartar Emetic, and syrup enough to make sixty pills, one or two to be taken daily. The "neutral draught" was always "a good adjutant remedy," but it was idle to talk of lemon juice in a camp, even good vinegar was not easily obtained, and cream of tartar answered as well or better than either. As soon as the pulse sank and dry tongue, delirium, and other typhous symptoms predominated, he recommended recourse "to bark, wine, volatile salts, blisters &c."

In his own case of jail fever, Dr. Tilton had an obstinate delirium and "a crust on my tongue as thick as the blade of a knife, and black as soot. The skin was worn off my hips and dorsal vertebrae, so as to make it necessary to patch those parts with common plaister. At the acme of my disorder, eleven surgeons and mates . . . all gave me over, and only disputed how many hours I should live." What with Dr. Benjamin Rush's attentions, and the drinking of some gallons of wine, his tongue "began to moisten on the edges; and in the course of some days, the whole crust fell off and left it so raw . . . that I was obliged to hold skinned almonds in my mouth to abate the irritation." When at last he could stand, he could hardly walk from the soreness of his feet. Cuticle scaled off his skin, all of his hair combed out, "so that"—one happy result—"instead of my former straight hair, I had an entire new suit that curled beautifully." In spite of a voracious appetite, it was nine months before the elasticity of his muscles was restored. A soldier thus afflicted "cannot be fit for duty, afterwards, during the campaign."

"Fluxes," while better treated in the regimental hospitals than in a larger general hospital, were often attributed to careless policing of the camp. Wise warnings of doctors and commanders to keep stationary camps clean went unheeded. Directions were to place the latrines downwind of the camp, dig the pits deep, and cover the fecal matter daily with a sufficient layer of earth. Penalties were imposed for a man "easing himself except in the privies." Even so, "particularly during the dysenteric season . . . the effluvia arising from the discharges of the sick render the air of a camp almost pestilential."

In a young and inexperienced army, the officers were too apt to consider military duty their only obligation. They did not attend to the condition of their men, and when a soldier fell sick, he was turned over to the surgeons without further thought. The officers, Dr. Tilton admonished, should have a care to combat the ignorance and irregularities of the men in a new scene of life. The camp at King's Bridge in 1776 "became excessively filthy. All manner of excrementitious matter was scattered indiscriminately . . . insomuch that you were offended by a disagreeable smell, almost every where within the lines. A putrid diarrhoea was the consequence. Many died, melting as it were and running off at the bowels. Medicine answered little or no purpose." When the army moved to White Plains, it left the prevailing camp sickness behind. The troops were always healthiest when shifting from place to place.

Dr. Tilton had no register of deaths, but he had "no hesitation in declaring . . . that we lost no less than from ten to twenty of camp diseases, for one by weapons of the enemy." He noted that, in proportion to their number, more physicians and surgeons were fatalities than field officers were, but he forgot that the doctors were far more constantly exposed to danger.

Dysentery, besides being treated with bloodletting, frequently required a vomit; afterwards the bowels were kept open with small drops of calomel and repeated doses of Sal. Cath. Amarum (Epsom salts) until the griping abated. Then treatment was completed with gentle astringents and anodynes. When dysentery was complicated with jail fever, it became dangerous.

Of all the diseases in the Revolutionary army, putrid diarrhea was the most intractable. While sufferers remained about the hospital, nothing had more than a palliative effect. Multitudes died of the complaint. The only expedient was to send patients to the country for the benefit of pure air and superior food.

Tilton was convinced that army diseases were worst in winter. "Then the foul air is pent up in the hospitals, and becomes exalted to such a poisonous malignancy as to make all approach to them hazardous." The potter's field of Philadelphia gave evidence of the fatal effects of cold weather in military hospitals in 1776. "Instead of single graves, the dead were buried in large square pits, in which the coffins were placed in ranges, cross and pile, until near full and then covered over." Whether done to save labor or save ground, this method witnessed to great mortality.

The same physician observed that tents were preferable to buildings for hospitals when the weather permitted. Musty old barns were the most dangerous, but all wooden structures retained infection. If there had to be wooden hospitals, he recommended the design of that erected at Morristown in the hard winter of 1779–80. (It has since been duplicated there and is an exhibit.) Of rough logs chinked with clay, the central section was thirty-one feet, six inches long by nineteen feet, six inches wide, while the two flanking rooms were slightly smaller. The larger ward was occupied by the wounded in twelve bunks, the end wards, with eight bunks each, by patients with fevers. The floors throughout were earth. There were no chimneys; smoke found its way out through holes in the roof. As the rooms were well ventilated, the smoke did not trouble the patients, but helped to purify the air. Dr. Tilton hoped that this type of hospital would prevent what he lamented in others. "Many a fine fellow have I seen brought into the hospital, for slight syphilitic affections and carried out dead of a hospital fever."

After the siege of Yorktown, Dr. Tilton was left in charge of the American sick and wounded at Williamsburg. Though the French physicians and surgeons, in the main building of the College of William and Mary, prided themselves on the care of their patients, even supplying them with nightcaps, the death record there was no better than that in the American wards. Dr. Tilton blamed the French because they "contrived a common necessary, for their whole hospital . . . three stories high, by erecting a half hexagon, of common boards, reaching from the roof down to a pit in the earth. From this perpendicular conduit doors opened upon each floor of the hospital: and all manner of filth and excrementitious matters were dropped and thrown down this common sewer into the pit below. This sink of nastiness perfumed the whole house . . . and vitiated all the air within the walls."

Dr. John Jones was realistic. In addressing his directions to "young Military and Naval Surgeons in North America," he recognized the limitations of those he sought to help. "In new settled countries," he said, "where opportunities of improvement are not within reach of every student, many gentlemen are obliged to set out in practice, with such a stock of knowledge as they are able to acquire under the tuition of a single master, who may, himself, too often stand in need of instruction." Bearing in mind the progress that medicine is constantly making, the omissions in Dr. Jones' teaching two centuries ago are not surprising. Nothing was said of asepsis, let alone disinfectants, aside from a liberal sprinkling of the premises with vinegar. Surgeons and their mates, in contact with tissues, muscles, and bones, were not so much as admonished to wash their hands before an operation. Instruments were not directed to be boiled, and some of the materials used, not only old linen, lint, and tow, but leather for ligatures, might promote infection. In fact, infection itself was not always deprecated. Thus, of a wound in a visible place in a healthy body, "About the fourth day a white, pinguidous equal matter, called pus, is generated in the wound; and this produces very happy effects, by separating the lacerated vessels and extravasated fluids from the sound parts which then grow up a-fresh. Hence laudable pus is esteemed by Surgeons the best of signs." In suturing, the needle was previously to be dipped in oil. Nothing was said of sedatives for the patient who had to submit to the operation.

Dr. Jones described apparatus for an amputation, mercifully to be prepared in a separate room so the patient would not be notified of what was in store for him. The reader may be spared the step-by-step directions for severance of a leg. When the ordeal was over, and the knitted woolen cap was drawn over the stump, the patient, laid in his bed, was immediately given "a sudorific [sweat-producing] anodyne, to quiet pain, and dispose him to a gentle diaphoresis."

Another writer cautioned the young surgeon, in amputating a limb, not to be affected by the groans of his patient, but, at the same time, to avoid giving unnecessary pain. The assistants in such an operation had to be men of muscle as well as of nerve, for they had to hold immobile the part undergoing inevitable torture. A most delicate procedure was the application of the trephine (trepanning instrument) to a fractured skull. The appearance of the diploe (the light bone tissue lying between the inner and outer tables of the skull) was "not to be depended on, as a guide to ascertain the thickness of the skull," as this differed in individuals. Otherwise the surgeon "might fatally plunge the crown of the trephine into the patient's brain; an accident, which has happened to some incautious operators."

Especially in compound fractures from gunshot or shell fragment, the dreadful march of gangrene was detailed, with little hope of arresting it. A cannonball severing a limb left the bone ragged, but at least there was no problem of setting and knitting.

Dr. John Jones was ahead of his time in urging the student of surgery "to make himself thoroughly acquainted with most of those branches of medicine, which are requisite to form an accomplished Physician." (His little book, prompted by the emergency of the Revolutionary War, was the first medical work by an American published in this country.) Those who gave advice for care of sick and wounded soldiers were not perfectionists; they tried to allow for the actual conditions under which their directions had to be applied. Still, the medical manuals were ideal compared with the limitations of all sorts that existed.

Baron Van Swieten's *Diseases Incident to Armies,* besides giving physicians instructions for the treatment of complaints, also gave a straightforward description of soldiers' ailments, with medicines for their treatment, designed for attendants with no medical knowledge. When there was no doctor present, which was often the case, the enlisted man assigned as an orderly, if he could read, by consulting this medical primer might be able to identify a patient's complaint and dose him suitably. Thus, in "peripneumony," "an inflammation of the lungs," the symptoms were listed, then the direction was "Let the common drink be the decoction No. 1. . . . While the patient is awake, let him take every half hour a spoonful of No. 13. . . ." Recipes were given for two score drinks, pills, and ointments, though these would have to be compounded in advance by an apothecary, one who was resourceful in collecting strange substances, including crabs' claws.

For the novice nurse, diarrhea was distinguished from dysentery, and an attempt was made to differentiate intermittent fevers. No definition was needed for the Itch, always and properly capitalized, Treatment of this torment was to keep the body clean, fumigate clothes with brimstone, every eight days take the purging powder

No. 8 (scammony; Ethiops mineral, which was black sulphide of mercury; diaphoretic antimony), on intermediate days take No. 69 (flower of sulphur, Ethiops mineral), and every night smear on ointment No. 70. This last was the sovereign Ethiops mineral in hog's lard. Actually, the American hospitals, general as well as regimental, were often deviod of the medicaments so precisely prescribed in the printed pages.

Sergeant Joseph Martin and his companions, at Peekskill in the summer of 1778, caught the Itch, they supposed, when they were inoculated against smallpox. They had to endure its agonies the whole season without medical relief. "I had it to such a degree," said Martin, "that by the time I got into winter quarters I could scarcely lift my hands to my head." Some in his foraging party had friends in the artillery from whom they secured some sulphur. They mixed "a sufficient quantity of brimstone and tallow, which was the only grease we could get, at the same time not forgetting to mix a plenty of hot whiskey toddy, making up a hot blazing fire and laying down an oxhide upon the hearth. Thus prepared with arms and ammunition, we began the operation by plying each other's outsides with brimstone and tallow and the inside with hot whiskey sling. . . . This was a decisive victory." However, a couple of the attackers of the animalcule of the Itch were so overcome by their internal emolient that "they lay all night naked upon the field."

General Washington had had smallpox himself "in the natural way," and he was a believer in the benefits of inoculation, which greatly reduced the severity and danger of the disease to the patient. Mrs. Washington was inoculated, and in the spring of 1777 the General ordered inoculation for all of the troops in camp and also for recruits arriving in Philadelphia if they were not "over the smallpox." He arranged for several houses in the vicinity to be equipped for the purpose, and, furthermore, secured the cooperation of clergymen of the village of Morristown in having most of the civil population inoculated. A church was used as an isolation hospital for those who contracted smallpox otherwise.

Exercise of his authority in favor of inoculation required courage on Washington's part, for there was still opposition to the practice in many quarters. A deliberate corruption of the blood of a well person with pus from a sufferer with the foul disease was declared to be against nature, and distrustful of God. The fact is that there was some danger to the inoculated patient, for one in fifty or sixty died, but this was minimal compared with the mortality rate among sufferers in a smallpox epidemic. Also, unless the inoculated were isolated, they could spread the disease in the general population, as had frequently happened. Vaccination, equally preventive as inoculation and not dangerous at all, was not known until some twenty years after the Revolution.

In spite of inoculation at particular times and places, smallpox was a frightful affliction in the American army. To escape its ravages, especially in prisons, if a doctor was not available, some men inoculated themselves. This simple expedient seems to have been as effective as when a patient, if he could afford it, paid for elaborate preparatory treatment by physicians who charged high fees for unnecessary conditioning of their dupes.

On the withdrawal of the Americans from Canada, General Arnold ordered the inoculation of the troops at Sorel against smallpox. Porter's regiment was inoculated, but then General Thomas arrived from Quebec and canceled Arnold's direction: "it should be death for any person to inoculate," and those already inoculated should be sent immediately to Montreal. Thomas, fifty-one at the time, had practiced medicine in Massachusetts, and he was of the school that believed, against the evidence, that inoculation invited fatal results. Thomas promptly complained of feeling unwell, in a few days he was moved to Chambly with smallpox, and within two weeks after appearance of the eruption he was dead.

Dr. Lewis Beebe, who had attended General Thomas, was next

at St. John's. He recorded that "here in the hospital, is to be seen at the same time some dead, some Dying . . . some Whistleing, some singing & many Cursing & swearing . . . poor Distressed Soldiers, when they are taken sick, are thrown into this dirty, stinking place, and left to take care of themselves. No attendance no provision made, but what must be Loathed & abhorred by all both well & sick." He was soon at Ile-aux-Noix, the worst pesthold of the unfortunate campaign. "Language cannot describe the misery and distress the soldiery endure. . . . The most shocking of all Spectacles was to see a large barn Crowded full of men with this disorder [smallpox], many of which could not See, Speak, or walk—one nay two had large maggots an inch long, Crawl out of their ears, were on almost every part of the body."

All of the sick were removed to Crown Point, where smallpox raged among four or five hundred of Beebe's regiment. Across the narrow water from the camp more than a hundred were buried in eight days. So much, though Dr. Beebe did not say so, for General Thomas' refusal to have the troops inoculated. At Ticonderoga, Beebe thought the "dirty, Lousy, stinking Hospital" was "enough to kill well men." He had "not one article" for the assistance of those who suffered from dysentery.

"Left for dead on the battlefield" was the expression used to describe a soldier, abandoned, who miraculously survived wounds supposed to be fatal. In most cases the words should have been, "left to die." The losers in a fight had no say in the matter, and the victors left too fast to be burdened with the worst hurt friends or foes. This was what happened at King's Mountain; only the prisoners who could walk were sent away under guard, and there were no facilities for caring for those of the winning side who could not ride. In Arnold's march to Quebec, when the food was all but exhausted, a man who could not struggle forward was left to perish in the wilderness. Frontiersmen who were victims of Indian ambush could expect no mercy, unless by a blow from a tomahawk

THE SICK AND WOUNDED

before wolves visited the scene. After Benedict Arnold's attack on New London, the raiders, intending to blow up Fort Griswold, moved the severely wounded to a safe distance; that was the limit of their care. They hastened off, and it was hours before American civilian doctors appeared to give first aid.

Following Saratoga, no fewer than a thousand sick and wounded soldiers, British, German, and American, were in Albany, where the Dutch church and private houses became hospitals. The patients of the enemy were tended by their own surgeons. Dr. James Thacher was one of thirty American surgeons and mates on duty for long hours. He observed that in their "capital operations" (amputations mostly), the British surgeons were dexterous, but the Germans, with few exceptions, "do no credit to their profession; some of them are the most uncouth and clumsy operators I ever witnessed." Nor did they show sympathy for their suffering patients.

Thacher had twenty wounded under his care; the hurts of some are illustrative. A young man had received a musket ball through his cheeks, "cutting its way through the teeth on both sides and the substance of the tongue; his sufferings have been great but he now begins to articulate tolerably well. Another had the whole side of his face torn off by a cannon-ball, laying his mouth and throat open to view." Wounds might testify to the courage or cowardice of a soldier. A musket ball in the forehead of one did not penetrate deeply and appeared to have rebounded and fallen out. Later examination revealed the ball "laying flat on the bone, and spread under the skin." It was removed with the praise, "No one can doubt but he received his wound while facing the enemy." Derisive laughter was the portion of a fellow whose wound was in the bottom of his foot!

On the battlefields of Saratoga, it was said, the Indians, auxiliaries of the British, made a harvest of scalps from the dead. As they also stripped many bodies of every article of clothing, it was

[165]

impossible for the burial details to tell whether the corpses were English, German, or American.

The next year, Dr. Thacher was assigned to the punitive expedition of General John Sullivan against the Indians of the Six Nations (actually five, as the Oneidas were neutral). He related the singular and terrible case of Captain Gregg, who was brought to his hospital. The Captain, stationed at Fort Stanwix (Rome, New York) had gone into the woods with two companions to shoot pigeons. There they were surprised and shot down by a party of Indians, who scalped them and left them for dead. After a time Gregg revived enough to stir a little, which attracted his faithful dog to lick his wounds. On command, the intelligent animal ran off for help. By dint of whines and tugging at their clothing, he brought back some fishermen from the river, a mile away. They got the poor fellow to the fort and so to the doctor's care. "He was a most frightful spectacle, the whole of his scalp was removed, in three places on the fore part of his head, the tomahawk had penetrated through the skull; there was a wound on his back with the same instrument, besides a wound in his side and another through his arm by a musket-ball." The modest doctor further recorded only that "This unfortunate man, after suffering extremely for a long time, finally recovered."

Thacher gave what was evidently an eyewitness account of the Indian mode of scalping: "they make a circular cut from the forehead, quite round, just above the ears, then taking hold of the skin with their teeth, they tear off the whole hairy scalp in an instant, with wonderful dexterity." He went on to say how, by painting certain symbols and colors on the dried skin, a savage indicated age and sex of his victim, and the circumstances under which he obtained his trophy.

Prisoners of War

PRISONERS SUFFER IN ALL WARS. THE MAIN ADVANTAGE THEY REPRESENT TO THE SIDE HOLDING THEM IS ACCOMPLISHED AT THE TIME OF CAPTURE. THEREAFTER, UNLESS EXchanged, they must be burdensomely maintained and guarded, which does not encourage good treatment. The prisoners themselves chafe at their idleness or under forced labor for the enemy.

The Americans taken prisoner in the Revolution experienced peculiar hardships. The British did not control interior areas for any length of time, only particular coast cities: New York throughout the war, and Newport, Philadelphia, Charleston, and Savannah for shorter periods. Thus they were obliged to confine their prisoners in quarters already cramped by their own troops. Batches of prisoners were exchanged from time to time, but no general cartel was ever agreed to. This was due partly to British objection, but more to American disinclination. If exchange were on the basis of soldier for soldier and sailor for sailor, the enemy, the Americans felt, would be the net gainer; the British would retrieve men better disciplined and equipped, whose places it was difficult to fill from Europe. The Americans, by contrast, had the native population on which to draw for troops. Grieved as he was by the plight of his soldiers in enemy hands, General Washington was reluctant to liberate enemy prisoners in good health and receive in return Americans who were ill, emaciated, and, typically, unfit for duty.

American prisoners of war were held principally in New York City. That was the chief British post, and the largest numbers of prisoners were taken by the British in the Battle of Long Island and in the capture of Fort Washington on Manhattan. These hauls, together with civilians held to be obnoxious, gave a total of about 5000. Besides, American privateersmen captured at sea were generally brought to New York and imprisoned in a dozen old ships. The other big bag of prisoners was at Charleston in the spring of 1780; of these, the militia were paroled to their homes, but the continentals were penned at Haddrell's Point on the opposite side of the Cooper River. However, other Americans, mostly sailors, were held at widely scattered places—Halifax and Antigua in the New World, and Dartmoor, Plymouth, and Portsmouth in England.

The problem of where to confine prisoners in New York was complicated by the great fire of September 21, 1776, which burned a third of the town. Warehouses, jails, churches, the King's College building, and hulks were used as prisons. There were but two jails. That used as the provost (headquarters of the military police, presided over by Cunningham and his deputy, O'Keefe) was a small stone building of three stories in "the fields" (now City Hall Park); on the upper floors were confined officers and prominent Whig civilians. The Bridewell, which, before the war, had been tenanted by debtors, was near by and larger. The prison ships were reserved primarily for sailors, but at times contained soldiers as well. To supply enough vessels it was necessary to strip some; their sails, spars, and rigging were advertised for sale. While there was foraging for meat, grain, and wood, and loyalists and others sold sup-

plies to the British camps, most of the food for the army and the
prisoners had to come from Europe. Quantity and quality were poor,
and fresh vegetables, fruit, and dairy products were lacking.

The conditions of cold in winter, stifling heat (especially 'tween
decks of the hulks) in summer, bad and scanty food, filth, sickness,
and death were as related. At the same time, mistreatment of the
prisoners lost nothing in their telling of it. Their keepers were their
enemies, against whom they had fought and might fight again. They
saw no friends except the American Commissary of Prisoners, or
his deputy, on occasional visits. With nothing to do in the endless
days and nights except be miserable in body and mind, they nursed
their grievances into premeditated abuse by the British authorities,
from the commanding general down. They were starved, beaten,
poisoned, or otherwise killed; their collected corpses were dumped
into boneyard pits or into the rivers.

The imprecations applied mostly to underlings who ought never
to have been allowed power over their helpless charges. In New
York the accusations went higher, against Captain William Cunningham, the Provost Marshal, and Sergeant O'Keefe, his minion.
Cunningham was born in Dublin in 1738. He became a sergeant
of dragoons and, later, recruited Irish immigrants, whom he is said
to have deceived, for the colonies. He accompanied a batch of his
clients to New York in 1774, sought work as a horse-breaker, and
for his Toryism was mobbed. He took refuge on the warship *Asia*.
From thence he went to Boston, where General Gage appointed
him Provost Marshal. In that office he came, with General Howe,
to New York in 1776, bent on revenge. By all accounts he was a
first-class villain, arbitrary and viciously cruel. Elias Boudinot,
American Commissary General of Prisoners, was directed by
Washington, under agreement with the British authorities, to investigate complaints. Cunningham insolently confirmed his mistreatment of his prisoners.

For trifling infractions of his rules he had consigned prisoners to the "dungeon" of the provost and kept them there for weeks. Drinking water was sometimes supplied to the prisoners in latrine tubs. Cunningham beat prisoners with his cane and knocked them down with his fists. General James Robertson, Commandant of the city, was reluctantly obliged to believe the evidence. He admitted that General Howe was culpable for his negligence in allowing such vindictive tyrannies. Robertson promised that Cunningham and O'Keefe would be punished, but the only result was that Howe took Cunningham to be Provost Marshal at Philadelphia. Cunningham returned to New York under Sir Henry Clinton. Charges were freely made—but were unsupported—that he burned prisoners with hot irons, poisoned their food, and, with no trial, hanged them at midnight to the number of 250 during his reign.

However, prisoners in the provost from April 1777 to October 1778, for which there is a record, received more aid from the American Commissary and better attention from the British authorities than the men in the other jails did. There are several explanations: they were fewer in number, they were officers or prominent civilians, and, during most of the period, Captain Cunningham was practicing his meanness in Philadelphia. In the jottings, not daily, but frequent, of John Fell, a committeeman of Bergen, New Jersey, are a score of mentions of visits of inspection or outside supplies furnished. Thus: "July 6. Received of E. Boudinot per Pintard [deputy commissary of prisoners in New York] ten half Joes." "Aug. 6. Mr. Pintard came to supply prisoners of war with clothes." "Sep. 6. Lewis Pintard brought some money for the officers." "Oct. 10. Mr. Pintard sent up blankets, shoes, and stockings for the prisoners." "Nov. 5. Gen. Robertson's Aid-de-camp came to inquire into grievances of prisoners." "16. Mr. Pintard came for an account of what clothing the prisoners wanted." Later he noted that six tailors were brought from a prison ship to make clothes for the provost inmates; General Robertson and the mayor examined the prisoners; Pintard furnished four cords of wood and, a few days later, a hundred loaves of bread and a quarter of beef. The diary ended when Fell was exchanged for Governor Skene at the end of October 1778.

Milder crimes than those charged against Cunningham were laid to David Sproat, the Commissary for Naval Prisoners at New York, and Joshua Loring, British Commissary General of prisoners, both of whom drew special venom because they were Americans in enemy service.

British officers of army and navy cannot be accused of intentional mistreatment of American prisoners. For several years they continued to believe that the rebellion would soon be crushed, and thus they did not undertake reforms ever more desirable in a protracted struggle. General Howe was neglectful of his prisoners, as of much besides; conditions did improve after Sir Henry Clinton took command in the summer of 1778.

In the absence of prompt exchanges, the British held out means of escape from the pains of imprisonment. They constantly urged captives, both seamen and soldiers, to enlist in King George's service. Soldiers were promised that they would not have to fight against their own country, but would be given garrison duty in Jamaica or elsewhere. Of course this would release troops for the American continent. Not even such indirect assurance could salve the conscience of sailors, who would be actively engaged on enemy warships. The vast majority of American prisoners rejected these overtures. They were rightly praised for choosing patriotism at the cost of confinement on a crust, in rags, amidst disaease, and the prospect of an early grave. However, a number did yield to the temptation of food, health, and survival. As stout a patriot as Ethan Allen, when he saw the miseries of prisoners in New York, advised this course. He added what many told themselves, that they should seize any opportunity to desert.

A more honorable practice of the British was to give officers their liberty on parole until exchanged. In prisons, officers were usually, but not always, kept separate from the rank and file. This was in obedience to military etiquette, which was observed even between enemies. At the same time, one does not read far in the history of the American Revolution without being impressed by social distinctions that were demanded by gentlemen and acquiesced in by those of the common clay. Class cleavage obtruded in all spheres of life, but nowhere more sharply than in the fortunes of prisoners of war. Often kind condescension of superiors was the substitute for democracy.

Of the buildings in New York in which soldiers were held, those bearing the worst reputation were three sugar warehouses —Van Cortlandt's, on the northwest corner of the Trinity Church lot, Rhinelander's, on William and Duane Streets, and that on Liberty Street, which was the longest used. They were of stone, five stories high; the windows had neither sashes nor shutters, and there was no provision for heat. Packed to utmost capacity, the rooms were stifling in summer. Messes of six prisoners took turns standing at the windows for ten minutes each. Parties of twenty were allowed half an hour each day in the cramped yards. Numbing cold was the winter ordeal. After long confinement, the captives, scantily clad to begin with, were in tatters. Few had blankets; sometimes in the morning prone forms near the windows were snow-blown. It was testified that one cause of death was frozen limbs that mortified.

The fullest knowledge we have is of the Liberty Street sugarhouse. Issues of food were minimal, and fire for the prisoners' cooking was allowed only at three-day intervals. The bread, one man recorded, was baked from ground wormy ship biscuit, and was offensive to the smell. Another described how "old shoes were bought and eaten with as much relish as a pig or turkey . . . a beef bone of four or five ounces, after it was picked clean sold for as many coppers." Jonathan Gillett, Jr., reported that prisoners ate mice, rats, and insects, and that the dry parings of a turnip, found in the prison yard, was a delicious banquet. A doctor discovered that some of his patients, starving when they were transferred to the hospital, had tried to satisfy their pangs of hunger with grit scratched from the walls and splinters of wood. These must have been extreme occurrences, even in that place of privation. The vermin—lice, bedbugs, fleas—were a constant torture. They infested the straw which was the only bedding. The men had small chance to keep either their bodies or their rags of clothing clean.

As a result of crowding, lack of sanitation, bad food, and dejection of spirits, disease was ever present. Jail fever was chronic and became epidemic at times. Victims of smallpox mingled with the other prisoners, who might choose to be inoculated when the doctor visited, or could inoculate themselves. The presence of yellow fever is often mentioned in the accounts. Dysentery and diarrhea ("flux") were common. These complaints caused disgusting filth on the prison floors, the only place the men could sit or lie down. Ethan Allen visited a church occupied by prisoners where he had to pick his way to avoid stepping in excrement. As no lights were allowed at night, sleepers stretched in close rows were stumbled over by afflicted companions making for the tubs. Pails and scrub brushes were furnished for cleaning the floors, but too few of the prisoners put them to use.

If men were to sleep they had to get used to the chorus of groans topped by the cries of delirium. Several churches were used as hospitals, but there seems to have been no compulsion to enter them. Many thought their chance of survival was better if they avoided a place where every man was diseased. Carts came to the prisons in the morning to collect the corpses, which were said to average seven or eight a day out of as many hundreds of inmates. The dead bodies were loaded like cordwood and buried without ceremony in trenches outside the city. The old fortifications which had been dug by the Americans before the enemy took New York became convenient mass graves.

In the cold weather, the prisoners in churches were better off

[173]

than those in warehouses, because the churches had window sashes, though no heat. The pews of the North Dutch Church went for firewood for cooking. To make room for 800 inmates, a second floor was built, at the level of the galleries. The Middle Dutch Church held hundreds of captives, and the "Brick Church" did too, for a time. The Presbyterian and Scotch churches and the Friends' Meetinghouse were hospitals.

William Slade, of New Canaan, Connecticut, was captured at Fort Washington on November 16, 1776, and he was one of few prisoners who was able, or cared, to keep a diary. At first held in a barn at Harlem and then marched to the North Church, he and his companions were without any food for four days. On the fifth day, "almost night . . . we got a little mouldy bisd. [biscuit] about four per man." Next day, "Wednesday, 20th. We was reinforced by 300 more. We had 500 before. This causd a continual noise and verry big huddle. Jest at night drawd 6 oz. of [salt] pork per man. This we eat alone and raw. Thursday, 21st. We passd the day in sorrow haveing nothing to eat or drink but pump water. Friday, 22nd. We drawd ¾ lb of pork, ¾ lb of bisd, 1 gil of peas, a little rice and some kittels to cook in. Wet and cold. Saturday 23rd. We had camp stews plenty. . . . Monday, 25th [no entry for Sunday] We drawd ½ lb of pork a man, ¾ of bisd, a little peas and rice, and butter now plenty but not of the right kind. Tuesday, 26th. We spent in cooking for wood was scarce and the church was verry well broke when done [evidently window facings and other trim were ripped out], but verry little to eat. Wednesday, 27th. We spent in hunger. We are now durty as hogs, lying any and every where. Joys gone, sorrows increase."

After this fast they got their two-day ration of two pounds of bread per man, three-quarters of a pound of pork, some butter, rice, and dried peas. So he continued in the North Church four days more until, with 300 others, he was "carried on board the shipping." A month later, after several days of feeling poorly, being "blooded," and complaining of "Stomach all gone," he broke out with smallpox.

Escapes from the prison buildings were accomplished, though they were hazardous because of detection in passing through the streets. Fugitives from the hulks ran less risk; if they were missed by the shots of the guards, they could swim to fairly safe shores.

The "Old *Jersey*" was the most infamous of the prison ships at New York. She was launched in 1736, a ship of the line with sixty-four guns and a crew of 400. She served in the Channel fleet, in the Mediterranean, and in the West Indies. Twice in fierce engagements with French men-of-war, she was once victorious and once the battered loser. Three times she was laid up, then in 1776 she was sailed to New York, without armament, to be a hospital ship. Anchored in Wallabout Bay in the East River from April 1777 to the evacuation, she was stripped of all rigging, had only a mast for signaling, and her bowsprit was used as a hoist. Her gunports were covered, but, to give some air, holes about twenty inches square were cut in her sides, and barred, four for each of the two decks. Appropriately, the hulk was painted black. She was anchored in the Wallabout about 300 yards from the shore, opposite a tide mill. To the south and east of her were salt meadows bordering higher sandy farmlands. Nearby were *Hope* and *Falmouth*, hospital ships, and others from time to time. Vessels first moored near the city had been brought to this out-of-the-way cove of Long Island for fear of infection. The effluvium arising from them, especially the Old *Jersey*, was thought to be noxious and was certainly disgusting, though prisoners confessed that with long exposure to the stench they smelled it less.

The Old *Jersey* usually contained 800 to 1100 prisoners, predominantly seamen captured from privateers. French and Spanish sailors were confined on the lower deck. Above, the ordinary seamen allowed officers (captains, mates) to have space to themselves in what was called the gunroom aft. The vessel had a captain, two mates, a steward, and a crew of twelve, no member of which had any responsibility for the prisoners. There were eighteen guards, taken for a week at a time from regiments on Long Island. The prisoners found the refugee guards the most obnoxious, the Scots not much better; repeated testimony favored the Hessians as more feeling than the others.

Even on a hulk like the Old *Jersey,* partly settled in the mud and put to an ignoble purpose, the tradition of cleanliness aboard ship was maintained. That is, cleaning the vessel itself, for the inmates had no effective way—nor had all of them the wish or the energy—to wash their bodies and clothing. Every day a working party was chosen from among the ablebodied, commanded by one of the imprisoned officers, to carry up the latrine tubs, return them below in the evening, and swab the decks and gangways. They also hoisted the food, wood, and water brought alongside. Their pay was a full, instead of a two-thirds, ration, and a half-pint of rum, but others were glad to help them for the sake of the exercise and something to do.

On a few occasions, the prisoner population was evacuated briefly to allow the ship to be drastically cleansed, so far as was possible in a spongy old bottom impregnated with vermin and contagion. Said one unhappy sufferer, "The whole ship, frrom her keel to her taffrail, was equally affected, and contained pestilence sufficient to desolate a world; disease and death were wrought into her very timbers."

The prisoners were allowed to be on the upper deck during the day. Due to the limited space, they walked around in platoons, all in the same direction. At sunset they were ordered below, and gratings were drawn over the hatches. No lights were permitted after nine o'clock. The weather did not have to be hot to make the holds stifling, especially for those with fever. As the only butt with drinking water was on the top deck, one man at a time was allowed up through a trap door in the grating, guarded by a soldier with fixed bayonet. By a rule of the prisoners themselves, no smoking was allowed below decks, for the sake of the sick, though this was a severe deprivation in the long wakeful night hours.

Anyone acquainted with institutions where meals are served to large numbers, short of an expensive restaurant or hotel, is familiar with complaints of the food, its quantity, quality, or how it is prepared. (Within recent memory the Queen of England found fault with the performance of the kitchens in Buckingham Palace!) Small wonder that the customers on the Old *Jersey,* which may be taken as a type, were loud against commissary and cook. Their clamors were just, for no matter how distasteful, the rations were so insufficient that they were devoured to the last crumb. The cook was himself a prisoner, who had either enlisted in the British service or enjoyed a privileged status. He presided in the galley over an enormous "copper," a cubical container divided into two compartments and set in a brickwork. On one side, in fresh water brought from Long Island or Manhattan, oatmeal or pea soup or pudding (flour and raisins) were boiled; on the other side, in brackish water dipped from beside the ship, salt pork or beef was cooked. The prisoners were divided into messes of six; a representative of each mess stood in line until his number was called, which might be several hours after distribution of the food started. The only bread was ship biscuit, hardtack.

The men declared that the food was what would not be issued in the British navy, that the meat was of venerable age or had been spoiled because the casks containing it had lain in bilgewater, and that the biscuit had to be rapped on the deck to dislodge the worms. The brackish water and the salt boiled out of the meat corroded the copper, which gave an unwholesome content to the food. The water dipped from the ship's side was the same in which the waste from the vessel was dumped. Some of the prisoners preferred to eat their meat raw. A few messes treasured splinters of wood and cups of pure drinking water and got permission to cook in their own kettles on the hearth of the kitchen. Captain Thomas Dring, of Newport, and his friends managed to secrete a large billet of wood from which they cut slivers with their jackknives for their fires; they were envied as the wealthiest persons "in all this republic of misery."

Prisoners who had a little money could supplement their Spartan diet by purchases from "Dame Grant," as she was called. Her boat was rowed to the foot of the accommodation ladder every other day; she sold small packages of tea, sugar, "soft bread," fruit, tobacco, combs, and other desirable items. However, "it was distressing to see the faces of hundreds of half-famished wretches, looking over the side of the ship into the boat, without the means of purchasing the most trifling article." After Dame Grant did not come for several days, it was reported that she had died of a disease contracted from her customers.

The prisoners' skin became parchment-like from bathing in salt water. Many had no soap, and they washed their clothes by wetting and treading them on the deck.

No feature of life of the Old *Jersey* was more desperate and dangerous than the cheek-by-jowl mingling of victims of smallpox and other contagious diseases in the mass of prisoners. A new tenant, on reaching the upper deck the first morning, encountered "a man suffering from small-pox; and in a few minutes I found myself surrounded by many others laboring under the same disease in every stage of its progress." He borrowed pus, scratched it into his hand, and got off with a light case. One prisoner said that he never knew an English doctor to visit the Old *Jersey,* nor any other doctor but rarely, except for an American, from Brooklyn, who volunteered his services until he contracted a disease of the ship and died. The sick, as a last resort, could go or be carried to a designated place on the upper deck to be taken to one of the hospital ships. There the death rate was high, for many patients on arrival were probably past recovery.

In February 1778, a New Hampshire paper reported: "A cartel vessel lately carried about 130 American prisoners from the prison ships in New York to New London in Connecticut. Such was the condition in which these poor creatures were put on board the cartel, that in that short run, sixteen died on board, upwards of sixty, greatly emaciated and enfeebled; and many who remain alive, are never likely to recover their former health." One who inquired particularly into the treatment of prisoners said that few of the Americans who had been taken at Fort Washington and who had survived their captivity were ever able to fight again. Washington wrote Howe, on January 13, 1777, that exchanged American prisoners gave "the most shocking account of their barbarous usage, which their miserable, emaciated countenances confirm. How very different was their appearance from that of your soldiers, who have lately returned to you after a captivity of twelve months. . . . If you are determined to make captivity as distressing as possible, let me know it, that we may be upon equal terms, for your conduct must and shall mark mine."

Many died on the Old *Jersey;* morning light would reveal that the body lying next one was a corpse. Captain Dring nursed his cabin boy, who was only twelve years old; though inoculated, the lad had smallpox in its most virulent form. "The night of his death was a truly wretched one to me; for I spent almost the whole of it in perfect darkness, holding him during his convulsions; and it was heart-rending to hear the screams of the dying boy, . . . calling in his delirium, for his mother. . . . But exhausted nature, at length, sunk under its agonies; his screams became less piercing. . . . In the midnight gloom I knew, by placing my hand over his mouth, that his breathings were becoming shorter, and thus felt the last breath as it quitted his frame." He sewed the little fellow's body in a blanket, to be carried on deck with others of the night's corpses.

Every morning a boat visited all the ships to take off the dead for burial. The bodies, if stiff, were lowered with a rope, if yet limp were fastened to a board. Those who died after the boat had gone were laid out on deck for the next day's load. One day, on a hospital ship, while "launching" the corpses sewed in hammocks, one of the sailors saw movement under the covering, and cried, "Damn my eyes! That fellow isn't dead!" His mates thought he was dead enough, but their impatience was overruled. The hammock was slit open, and, sure enough, the candidate for burial was alive. Rain during the night had refreshed him. A month later he was exchanged and was on his way to his home in Rhode Island.

A few prisoners were taken along, under guard, to bury the bodies on the shores of Wallabout Bay. The practice was to dig a shallow trench beneath the bank, place the bodies in it, and shovel down sand upon them. The work was so perfunctory that the first storm exposed arms and legs. All of the prisoners were anxious to be selected for the burial squads, for the sake of the feel of the ground beneath their bare feet. One man plucked up and brought back to the ship a clump of grass with earth adhering to the roots. This was divided and passed around for its unwonted fragrance.

It is the duty of prisoners of war to escape if possible. Many on the Old *Jersey* acted on ingenious plans. Officers held in the gunroom, with only a gimlet and their jackknives, cut a man-sized hole in the four-inch planking of the ship. One rainy night, four men, their clothes bundled and tied over their shoulders, dropped to the water. From the speed with which they were pursued by the guards' boat it was thought the escape was expected and purposely not foiled by closing the hole. In any case, the anxious listeners in the gunroom heard shots. Soon one Lawrence, who had been mate of a Philadelphia privateer, was brought in, almost insensible from bullet wounds and a cutlass slash on his arm. The guards left a candle beside him; by its light his friends did what little they could for him, which was not much more than to stare in pity at his bloody form. He died in a few hours.

An athletic prisoner, admitted one night through the trap door for a drink of water, suddenly felled the guard, and thirty men streamed up from below and dove overboard. An officer leaving the ship for exchange concealed a cabin boy in his sea chest. An informer alerted the guards and that night was nearly killed by his fellow prisoners. Profiting by the carelessness of the cook, two young Rhode Islanders stole a crowbar and axe from the galley. In the midst of a thunderstorm, they wrenched loose the bars over a gunport and made their escape. One day official visitors left their yawl beside the ship; a captain and four mates sprang into it and rowed off, to the accompaniment of musket fire from the guards and cheers of the prisoners. More escape attempts succeeded than failed. The prisoners could have taken possession of the ship at any time, but in a mass exodus to Long Island they would have been promptly recaptured and punished.

Beginning in January 1781, General Washington remonstrated with the British naval commanders against the reported "calamitous and deplorable" condition of American seamen confined in the prison ships in New York harbor. His proposal, that a trusted officer should visit the ships and discover the facts, was rejected. Washington was not deterred in his efforts for these sufferers, even though sailors did not come under his jurisdiction.

American seamen in British hands, the crews of captured privateers, were their own worst enemies, for this reason. Sailors were exchanged only for sailors. The active American privateers took many prisoners, but more often than not turned them loose to get rid of them; if they brought them to port, as they did at New London, the townsmen did not want to be burdened with them. Exchanges did take place and the British paroled some, but there was usually a heavy preponderance of American seamen in enemy hands over the number of British sailors taken prisoner by the Americans. The owners of vessels and their crews, mostly from New England, were motivated by a desire for private profit as well as by patriotism. In the whole period of the war, 1775–83, more than 1100 American privateers put to sea, with an average of 100 sailors each, and perhaps 20 guns each; they captured about 600 British vessels and realized in prize money some $18 million. Their cruises did not work entirely to the advantage of the United States; they sold to the highest bidder, often in Europe, and some of the cargoes were bought back by the British. The states issued the letters of marque and reprisal; there was no central organization, as with the army. The attractions of privateering drew off seamen from the Continental navy, which was thereby checked in its development. These circumstances account for, but do not palliate, the harder lot of American sailors, as compared with soldiers, imprisoned in this country. Washington said in December 1781 that for more than two years he had heard little complaint of the treatment of landsmen. American sailors held in prisons in England were few in number and were considerably relieved by the charity of local sympathizers and by the efforts of Benjamin Franklin in their behalf.

Congress directed Washington to renew his remonstrance against treatment of sailor-prisoners, with the threat of retaliation on enemy prisoners in American hands if cruelties were not corrected. Washington told Congress that the cure of wrongs of marine prisoners lay in obliging American privateer captains to turn over their captives to the Commissary General of Prisoners, then there would be a sufficient number to effect swift exchanges. The Commander in Chief would not agree to a British proposal to send in sailors if he would release soldiers. Most of the seamen held prisoner, Washington pointed out, were not in the Continental service. However, a committee of prisoners on the Old *Jersey* took it hard that General Washington would not accept their offer to enter the Continental army if they were released in exchange for enemy soldiers. The protesters were reminded of unhappy adherents of the British "languishing out [their] days" in the mines in Connecticut, a palpable touch. Finally, as peace negotiations progressed, complaints from the prison ships became fewer.

Elijah Fisher, captured on *Tartar,* a privateer, was one of the last to be held on the prison ships in New York harbor. On April 6, 1783, he wrote: "We had the proclamation of peace read on bord the old *Jersey,* and it was proclaimed through the British that all preasoners on both sides were to be desmest and no more hostaletys to be committed on either side, nether by see nor land, and all the preasoners gave three howzas on bord the preason ship." The remaining prisoners were evacuated from the Old *Jersey* in August 1783. Through the years, the old hulk sank deeper and deeper into the mud, until she disappeared.

It is not known how many Americans, soldiers, sailors, and civilians, were imprisoned in New York during the Revolution, or how many of them died in confinement. In May 1783, an anonymous contributor to a Fishkill newspaper offered the figure of 11,644 who breathed their last on the Old *Jersey* alone, but this exceeds by several thousand the total number of prisoners held on that ship, as revealed by British records. In 1808, the Tammany Society collected, it is said, twenty hogsheads of bones from the shores of Wallabout Bay and interred them in a crypt. For years after that, bones continued to be exposed by washing of the banks, and more were uncovered in digging foundations for buildings at the Brooklyn Navy Yard. Finally, in 1908, all were buried with proper ceremony under an impressive Prison Martyrs' Monument at Fort Greene, Long Island.

The treatment of war prisoners by the Americans was far superior to that practiced by the British, with the exception of the wretched confinement of some forty loyalists in the copper mine at Simsbury, Connecticut. The mine, which had been worked since early in the eighteenth century, was taken over in 1773 as a state prison for burglars, horse thieves, and counterfeiters, to whose ranks offending loyalists were later added. Two perpendicular shafts, one of twenty-five feet, the other of seventy feet, led to passages and galleries of varying depths. The committee of the Assembly reported that by blasting rock it had "prepared a well finished lodging room about fifteen feet by twelve in the caverns." The shallower shaft, which held a ladder, was topped by a hinged iron grating; the deeper one, which had water in the bottom, was left open for air.

At first the prisoners mined copper ore, always immured in damp darkness at the constant temperature of fifty-two degrees. Later they worked aboveground at nail-making; each was chained by the ankle to his station, and those considered most dangerous wore iron collars with chains fixed to roof-beams of the shop. At four o'clock in the afternoon they descended to the caverns for the night, to sleep on platforms provided with blankets and straw.

The dank hole and punishments were bad enough, but later descriptions managed to add to the manacles, vermin, dripping walls, and moldy rags of the sufferers. Though heavily guarded, half of the prisoners committed to the Simsbury Newgate escaped. A mass break occurred in May 1781, when twenty-eight prisoners, mostly loyalists, overpowered the guards, locked them in the caverns, and made off; few were retaken. Several times, incident to escapes, the prisoners burned some or all of the buildings aboveground. The last was in November 1782, after which the copper mine prison was not again used until some years after the war.

Treason

AT MIDNIGHT, SEPTEMBER 26, 1780, IN THE HUDSON HIGHLANDS AFTER A TUMULTUOUS DAY, GENERAL WASHINGTON HAD TO GET OFF TWO LETTERS. BOTH EXPRESSED deep mortification, and one was the shamed apology of America. Skillful writers worded these messages for the Commander in Chief; James McHenry penned the one to Congress, Alexander Hamilton the other, to Count Rochambeau. Both letters announced the treason of Benedict Arnold.

Attempts have been made to explain the startling contradiction in Arnold's character and conduct. How could a man go from acting with perfect valor on the battlefield to plotting the sacrifice of the cause for which he had fought? It has been pointed out that Arnold was restless, arrogant, vain, and avaricious, as well as possessing the admirable quality of magnetic leadership. The motives that have been given to explain his conspiracy to betray the fortress of West Point to the enemy seem unconvincing. In February 1777, nearly three years before the discovery of his treachery, he was bitterly resentful because five Brigadiers of less distinction had been promoted to Major General over his head. But that unfortunate neglect on the part of Congress was soon repaired by his advancement to the higher rank. It has been offered that he never liked the French alliance, also that his adored young wife, who had Tory connections, drew him to the British side. His own excuse, or boast, was that he aimed, by a military coup, to restore his country to its old, right allegiance.

Whatever Benedict Arnold's prompting, his career in faithlessness makes sorrowful reading. Sudden anger, flaring into a violent act, is better understood than long, premeditated crime. Sixteen months—Sir Henry Clinton said eighteen months—before the collapse of his scheme, Arnold made overtures to the British Commander, and during all this time he professed ardent patriotism to America.

One historian has suggested that, as the plot was exposed in time to avert the intended disaster, Arnold's treason had its beneficial effect. He had jeopardized not a local post, but the country's most crucial stronghold; thus the horror of his crime awoke national unity and nerved the people to win the war. Undoubtedly so, but, by the same token, Arnold's treason illustrated, as Washington confessed to Rochambeau, the danger that lurked in divided loyalties in America. Sincerity is the last quality that could be ascribed to Arnold, who, when bargaining with Sir Henry Clinton, argued that "£20,000 sterling . . . will be a cheap purchase" for West Point. That the British Commander took the offer seriously showed that he accepted as plausible the defection of a high American military officer. Of all the shortcomings of the effort for independence, Arnold's treason was the most spectacular reproach. The bungling of Congress, financial mismanagement, failure to support the army, disquieting internal jealousies, and battle defeats all could be better explained than Arnold's eagerness to put a price on infidelity.

Washington called the long-maturing negotiations by which the

British were to possess themselves of West Point "a conspiracy of the most dangerous nature." General Nathanael Greene thought that success of the plot "must have given the American cause a deadly wound if not a fatal stab." The stroke was averted barely in time, and by the merest accident, one which no one could foresee, even though for months Arnold had been using risky means of sending and receiving guilty messages through the lines. Ciphers were based on a volume of Blackstone's *Commentaries* and on various editions of Bailey's *Dictionary*. Each word in a message was indicated by three numbers—that of the page, the line, and the printed word in the line. This was a device commonly employed, the books were widely available, and a clever person bent on reading the secret writing could have discovered the code. Besides, long phrases or parts of sentences were frequently written in the ordinary way, in alphabetical characters. Some of the treason letters were not in code at all, but used the disguise of commercial correspondence, and were so crude as to arouse suspicion. Or innocent letters were interlined with invisible ink and marked to show by what "process" the secret writing was to be brought out: "F is fire, A acid." Letters of third parties, ignorant of their role, might be employed in this dodge.

Captain, later Major, John André, Sir Henry Clinton's aide, who had been promoted to Deputy Adjutant, conducted the secret correspondence for British headquarters. Loyalist go-betweens were Joseph Stansbury, a crockery dealer; the Reverend Jonathan Odell, a physician-clergyman; and Samuel Wallis, a Quaker merchant and land speculator. Couriers were deserters, real or pretended, prisoners being exchanged, private persons with passes, or—more reprehensibly—officials under flags of truce. Peggy Shippen Arnold, who was thought by Washington and most others at the time to be utterly guiltless, has since been proved to have been an artful dissembler, active in her husband's operation.

If Arnold had continued as a New Haven apothecary, merchant, and shipper, his sharp practices would have passed as business shrewdness. But he early volunteered in the patriot cause, where his succession of questionable dealings, along with his brilliant soldiering, brought him under public scrutiny. There were suspicions and investigations of him even prior to his grand coup. Always he was able to stand off accusations with more or less success, not omitting to plead that his blood spilled in America's defense wiped out alleged stains of peculation. In his daring—too daring— assault on Canada in 1775, he was obliged to be Quartermaster as well as Commander. He was afterward unable to account for large sums of public money committed to his charge. He could say, with truth, that the incessant dangers he encountered and the emergencies he was forced to meet in that expedition made record keeping uncertain. If that were not enough, he claimed that government clerks had lost vouchers that would prove him blameless. He denied that he had plundered the stocks of Montreal merchants.

These questions were pushed into the background by Arnold's brilliant exploits in the battles with Burgoyne in September and October of 1777. His severe wound, a broken thigh, added the touch of pity that carried admiration of him to a height. Along with Generals Gates and Lincoln, he was formally thanked by Congress for his "successful efforts in support of . . . independence" of the country. On order of Congress, Washington issued to Arnold a new commission which restored his seniority in rank. However, these sweets could not give him patience while he lay six months in hospital at Albany. There he abused the doctors "for a set of ignorant pretenders," not because they were at fault, but because he was irked by forced inaction. He hobbled out in March 1778, and was saluted by thirteen guns when he visited New Haven. Washington, anticipating Arnold's return to camp, presented him with epaulettes and a sword knot.

Arnold reported at Valley Forge in late May 1778. As his

wound prevented him from campaigning, Washington appointed him to the command of Philadelphia as soon as the British should evacuate the capital. He then took the newly required oath, which contained the words, "I renounce, refuse, and abjure any allegiance or obedience to [George the Third, King of Great Britain], and I do swear that I will to the utmost of my power support, maintain, and defend the . . . United States against . . . King George the Third . . . and will serve the . . . United States . . . with fidelity."

It was no surprise that he found the repossessed city full of tensions. The hard-core loyalists had fled with General Clinton, but the patriot returnees were suspicious of the majority of the inhabitants, who had accepted enemy rule. Nor were the proclamation of martial law and the closing of the shops for a week, while abandoned property was confiscated, welcome measures. Arnold might have composed these discontents had he not roused bitter protest by seizing opportunities to profit financially from his own orders. Public indignation finally resulted in the complaint of the Pennsylvania Council to Congress against Arnold on eight counts of malfeasance. The Pennsylvania protest was widely published.

Arnold declared his innocence of all charges. The most serious of them were that he had made private contracts by which he stood to gain by favors shown to shipowners and public purchasing agents. He was accused of using government wagons in a long-distance haul of his ill-gotten goods. Not least in stirring popular resentment, it was alleged, with truth, that, while the shops were shut to all others, he bought of their stocks for his personal benefit. It was demanded that he resign his command of the city.

Congress eliminated the less substantial counts in the indictment and referred the remainder to General Washington for court-martial inquiry. In the midst of this uproar Arnold had married (his first wife having died three years before) pretty Margaret, the daughter of Judge Edward Shippen, and settled on her the mansion he bought on the Schuylkill. Judge Shippen was politically neutral, but Peggy and her sisters had been favorites of the young British officers, including Captain John André. The aura of loyalism thus clinging about the Shippen family did nothing for Arnold's popularity with the returning patriots.

In mid-March of 1779, General Arnold resigned his command and cried loudly for a court-martial. Washington set it for May 1. When it was postponed for a month or more, Arnold's anger spilled over in a melodramatic plea to the Commander in Chief for swift vindication or, if guilty, execution. The turmoil of his letter reflected the resolve to which he had come: he would betray his country to the enemy.

Shortly before May 10 he called the London-born Joseph Stansbury from his china shop. Arnold, as Stansbury later told, "after some general conversation communicated to me, under a solemn obligation of secrecy, his intention of opening his services to the commander-in-chief of the British forces in any way that would most effectually restore the former government." He might either immediately join the British army, or cooperate "on some concealed plan with Sir Henry Clinton."

Arnold's confidant went by stealth to New York, where, on May 10, he had two interviews with Captain John André, General Clinton's aide, whom he had doubtless known in Philadelphia during the occupation. André wrote out a long memorandum of agreement which the British would enter into with Arnold. From the first André knew that it was Arnold with whom he was dealing, no matter what fictitious names the American assumed. Stansbury must have made this clear in the beginning, for André, in the original agreement, started to write the name Arnold, crossed it out and put "Monk," which was the pseudonym being used at that time. André told Sir Henry Clinton of the "Confusion" he felt at receiving such important "Sudden Proposals." He took time to reflect before committing a response to paper. He knew that he was in touch with no free-lance spy to be paid in shillings and pounds, but with a highly accredited American officer who enjoyed the reputation of a hero. André advised Arnold to remain in the patriot forces, where his assistance would be far greater than if he came over at once to the British army.

It was stipulated in the agreement that information leading to secondary or partial damage to the American cause would be paid for in proportion to the service. Such service would include the capture of dispatches, news of decisions of councils of war, the location of magazines that might be surprised, bodies of troops to be ambushed, "whence & what reinforcements are expected and when," or notice of a vulnerable seaport. But throughout the correspondence the British expressed the hope that Arnold would make possible "the most brilliant and effectual blow finally to compleat the overthrow of [the rebellion]." It was implied that such a "grand Stroke" would best follow from successive lesser injuries. If Arnold's assistance led to the American defeat, "then woud the generosity of the [British] nation exceed even his own most Sanguine hopes. . . ." Should his manifestly zealous efforts be foiled and his flight be necessary, "the Cause in which he suffers will hold itself bound to indemnify him for his losses and receive him with the honour his conduct deserves." André gave full assurance on the cardinal question which Arnold had made the condition of his cooperation. "S[ir] H[enry] C[linton] informs you with the Strictest Truth that the War is to be prosecuted with vigour and that no thought is entertained of giving up the dependency of America." The British would not yield the contest and leave Arnold abandoned in his treason.

On May 23, 1779, Arnold accepted these terms, including—this was always Arnold's care—Clinton's engagement "to answer my warmest Expectations for any Services rendered." He immediately offered a budget of confidential items: "Gen. W[ashington] and the Army move to the North River as soon as forage can be obtained. C[ongress] have given up Chs. Town if at-

THE PRICE OF INDEPENDENCE

tempted. They are in want of Arms Ammunition and Men to defend it. . . . No foreign loan obtained. . . . No Encouragement
from Spain. The french Fleet has Co[nditional] orders to return to
this Continent." There was more of similar sort, ending with repe-
tition of Arnold's reliance on "a revenue equivalent to the risk and
service done."

In the course of the negotiations, some forty-five letters passed
back and forth, with different persons serving as messengers, some
of them not knowing what they carried. Arnold's stark deception
in all this is shocking, the more so when taken in connection with
his professions of innocence before the court-martial that tried him
on the charges of the Pennsylvania Council. His was a consum-
mate Jekyll and Hyde performance. Meanwhile, the meetings of
the court-martial were delayed for six months. The verdict was not
reached until the end of January 1780, and Washington did not
get notice of its confirmation by Congress until a month after that.
The court-martial acquitted Arnold on two charges, but for his
fault in giving a sailing permit to the *Charming Nancy* and employing public wagons in a private service it sentenced him to a reprimand by the Commander in Chief. Washington delivered the
reprimand, regretfully but unmistakably, in general orders on
April 6. Arnold's resentment was the greater because at the same
period the treasury board, after a year's examination of his accounts on his Canadian expedition, refused to pay his claim of
£2000. He was living expensively in Philadelphia, other expedients for securing money had failed, and he coveted ever more a
handsome reward from the British for his treachery.

Arnold retracted his request for leave from the army. Through
General Schuyler, chairman of a committee of Congress to confer
with General Washington at Morristown, he inquired whether he
could be given the command of West Point. On account of his
wound, which made it painful for him to walk or ride, he would
prefer that station to a more active role in the coming campaign.

Washington felt that West Point, manned by invalids and sufficiently protected by the main army, was beneath Arnold's abilities,
and he would assign him there only if his wound forbade his service in the field. Arnold visited Washington at Morristown and
wrote the British that he expected soon to have the command of
West Point (though Washington had made him no such promise).

Surrender of this prime American stronghold to the enemy was
to be the "grand Stroke" in his treason which would justify the
high reward he sought. He took opportunity to inspect the works
and reported them to British headquarters as weakly held, badly
designed, and vulnerable to attack in ways that he particularly
pointed out. Next, a tentative arrangement was made for Arnold
to have a personal meeting with a British officer, General William
Phillips or Mayor André; this was deemed necessary to fix plans
for the capture of West Point.

On August 1, Arnold got a shock. He was ordered to command
the left wing of the army. He saw his climactic scheme crumbling.
He would have to appear incapacitated indeed not to accept this
prestigious assignment. He evidently convinced Washington that
he was on the invalid list, for two days later he was put in charge
of West Point and its neighboring posts. Like his predecessor, General Robert Howe, he established his headquarters across the river
from West Point, in the house of Colonel Beverley Robinson, a dis-
possessed Tory. Arnold's long-time aide, Major David Franks, was
with him, and he summoned as his secretary Lieutenant-Colonel
Richard Varick, whom he had known at Saratoga. For three
weeks, while puzzling how he could obey Washington's instructions for strengthening West Point and at the same time weaken it
for enemy attack, he did not know whether he was to be paid for
his pains. Then, in the last week of August 1780, Sir Henry Clinton agreed to his terms—£20,000 if the British seized the fort
through Arnold's complicity.

Franks set off for Philadelphia to fetch Mrs. Arnold and her infant son. Arnold gave solicitous directions for their stopping places on the way northward. The last was at the home of Joshua Hett Smith, on the Hudson between Haverstraw and Stony Point. Smith bore the reputation of a Whig, though his brother William was Royal Chief Justice in New York. Joshua Hett Smith had been in the confidence of General Robert Howe, from whose spies he had taken reports. Howe had commended Smith to Arnold for similar service. Smith fitted in with Arnold's need for a courier who would guide André to a meeting place. André was to be the British agent because General Phillips, on parole since his capture at Saratoga, was not available.

Arnold wanted André, using the name John Anderson, to come disguised within the American lines, either to South Salem or to North Castle on the east side of the Hudson, whence he would be conducted to Arnold. Sir Henry Clinton would not permit any of this—the disguise, the assumed identity, or the entering of the American lines—because, if discovered, his Adjutant would be in gravest danger as a spy. Instead, André came, on September 11, with Colonel Beverley Robinson under a flag to Dobbs Ferry. The pretense was that Robinson wanted to confer with Arnold about Robinson's house. Arnold's real talk, of course, would be with André. Arnold went down the river in his barge, but British gunboats, which had not been alerted to what was afoot, fired on the barge, forcing it to the west bank, and the intended interview did not take place.

Arnold then received a letter from Washington saying that he would be on his way to Hartford to meet General Rochambeau and Admiral Ternay, and would spend the night of Sunday, September 17, at Peekskill. Arnold was ordered to send down a guard of a Captain and fifty men, evidently to see the Commander in Chief and his party safely across King's Ferry (Stony Point to Verplanck's). Washington enjoined secrecy, but Arnold at once notified British headquarters in New York of Washington's journey to confer with the French and that he would be at King's Ferry and Peekskill. As this coded note did not go off until five days before Washington was to arrive, there was small chance that Sir Henry Clinton would have time to capture him. In any case, Arnold was not omitting to report the American Commander's movements.

Some days later the British armed sloop *Vulture* came up to Teller's (now Croton) Point on the east side of Haverstraw Bay, bringing Robinson. Robinson sent letters to General Israel Putnam and Arnold. If Putnam, who had formerly occupied Robinson's house, was not near, could Robinson see Arnold? Several of Arnold's officers were present, and, when told of Robinson's request, they strongly objected. Robinson's business, presumably private, should be taken up with the Governor or other civil authority. Arnold met Washington later that day, probably on the west side of the ferry, to accompany him to Peekskill, and referred to him Robinson's application. No, said the Commander in Chief, it should be refused.

The next day, Monday, September 18, Arnold sent an officer under a flag of truce to the *Vulture* with two letters for Robinson. The one that Varick saw was unexceptionable, explaining that Arnold could not meet Robinson on any private business. The other letter was secret, and enclosed in it was one for André. It informed that Arnold would send a confidential friend to the *Vulture,* with a flag, on the night of Wednesday, September 20, between eleven and twelve o'clock, to conduct André to a safe place of meeting. André had boarded the *Vulture* late that day. This was to be the frequently planned tryst with Arnold at which André would learn all that was needed for the British attack on West Point.

Joshua Hett Smith was to fetch André. Arnold gave Smith a pass for himself, passes for John Anderson (André) and two servants, and an order for a boat to be furnished by the quartermaster at Stony Point. But Smith could not persuade his tenant, Samuel Cahoon (probably a corruption of Colquhoun) to do the rowing, and Smith had not procured the boat. He coerced Cahoon into riding to Arnold's headquarters with a letter. When Cahoon arrived at sunrise, he was told that Arnold was still abed. Cahoon left the letter. Arnold had not made sure that Smith had a boat and willing oarsmen. He had assumed that André had been taken to Smith's house and was there awaiting him for their talk on Thursday, September 21. If this had been done, it would have been perilous for the British officer, for Smith's house was within the American lines.

When no boat came to the *Vulture* Wednesday night, André decided to wait until the next night, in the hope that he would be called for. On Thursday morning Arnold went to Verplanck's Point, where he received letters from the *Vulture*. That from the captain, Sutherland, in André's handwriting and countersigned "John Anderson," complained that one of the *Vulture's* boats, carrying a flag, had been fired on from Teller's Point. The other, from Robinson, said that he and his "partner" (André) were waiting.

Arnold then got busy. He sent his barge upriver to tow down a boat and leave it in a creek near Smith's house. He himself went to Smith's house to make certain there would be no further hitch. Again Smith could not cajole Sam Cahoon into doing the rowing. He had been up all the night before on his errand to Arnold's headquarters, and balked at the prospect of laboring at the oars in the twelve-mile round trip. Arnold urged him, but Cahoon still refused, pleading that he was afraid of guard boats. Arnold assured that Smith's pass would protect them. Then Sam said he could not row the boat alone. Directed to get his brother Joseph (who was also Smith's tenant), he came back explaining that he had stopped at his own house and that his wife objected to his going on the river that night. Arnold then declared that if Sam did not consent it would show he was not a friend of his country.

Sam Cahoon brought his brother, but now the two of them objected. Why was the trip, if under a flag, not made in the daytime? Wasn't there something "bad in it?" Pressure by Arnold and Smith did not move the brothers. It looked as though a Major General with a game leg and a plethoric squire would have to do their own rowing. Arnold saw months of anxious planning, on the eve of success, about to be canceled by a couple of stubborn countrymen. Finally the Cahoons agreed to go when Arnold threatened that otherwise he would put them under arrest.

Smith gave Sam and Joe each a dram and the three of them entered the boat at the creek, muffled the oars with sheepskins, and shoved off. It was after midnight when they were hailed by the *Vulture,* went alongside, and Smith was taken aboard. He told Robinson that he would deliver John Anderson at a point on the west shore called Old Road, where Arnold would be waiting with a spare horse; if Anderson did not return to the *Vulture* that night he would have gone to Smith's house.

Before stepping into the boat, André threw a blue cloak over his uniform. They touched the shore a couple of miles below Haverstraw and André climbed up the bank to a clump of firs for his meeting with Arnold. Around four o'clock, Smith warned them that it would soon be light. Whether it was Arnold or Smith who begged the Cahoons to row André back to the British vessel is not known. The Cahoons refused. If they had known André's errand —which they did not—they might have said that treason was all very well, but rowing two dozen miles, when Sam had had no sleep for two nights, was too much. The conspirators mounted to ride to Smith's house. On the way they passed a sentry, which gave André a turn, since Sir Henry Clinton had forbidden him to go within the American lines.

Daybreak brought André's doom. Colonel James Livingston had fetched a couple of guns to Teller's Point, and he fired on the *Vulture* with such effect that she dropped some miles down the river. When André, from his upstairs window, saw no vessel he must have been shaken, for he had expected to return to her that Friday night. After breakfast, Arnold left for King's Ferry and his headquarters, but not until he had penned three passes. One was for Smith to go with a boat and three hands to Dobbs Ferry. Another permitted Smith to pass the guards to White Plains. The third allowed "Mr. John Anderson to pass the guards to the White Plains, or below . . . he being on public business by my direction." Thus, whether André, escorted by Smith, went back by water or by land, he would be protected. Smith rode with Arnold to the ferry. It was probably then that Arnold told him that if the land route was chosen, "Anderson" must not go in the British officer's coat he had been wearing. Anderson was only a merchant, said Arnold, and he had borrowed the scarlet coat out of vanity. Afterwards, many thought Smith must have known that his charge was a British officer, that he was not fool enough to swallow Arnold's tale about the borrowed uniform.

During the day the risks of return by river or by the east shore were balanced. André preferred the river. If guard boats made trouble he would weight and drop overboard the packet of papers Arnold had given him for Sir Henry Clinton. He was obliged to accept Smith's decision for the land journey, though this made it necessary for him to shed his uniform coat and don a purplish civilian one and a round hat offered by Smith. Clinton had warned against assuming a disguise, but there appeared to be no alternative. André put Arnold's papers in his stockings.

At dusk they passed King's Ferry without incident, but they were stopped by militia eight miles along, at Crompond. Smith finally satisfied the Captain's questions, but, against his companion's wish, thought it best to take the advice to stop the night at a near-by farmhouse. If they rode at night past Croton River, the Captain warned, they might be pounced on by the loyalist irregulars who haunted that district. The travelers were early in the saddle next morning, Saturday, September 23, and after an hour they paused for breakfast at a farmhouse. A bit farther along, at Pine's Bridge, over the Croton River, Smith turned back. André, by accident or design, took the road near the Hudson instead of the easterly one to White Plains.

The area between the American lines on the north and the British on the south was infested by semi-military gangs bent mostly on thievery. The patriot parties were known as "Skinners," the loyalist marauders as "Cowboys." Just above Tarrytown, three volunteer guards issued from the woods and halted André. Supposing them to be loyalists, he said he was on their side. Actually they were Americans. They took him off the road to search him. When they found suspicious papers in his stocking feet, he produced his pass and offered them bribes. It did no good. The Skinners—John Paulding, Isaac Van Wart, and David Williams—were afterwards praised, especially by Washington, for their homespun honesty and patriotism, which were compared with the treachery of the highly placed General Arnold.

André's captors delivered him to Lieutenant Colonel John Jameson, who commanded the American post at North Castle (now North White Plains). Jameson has been blamed by historians for sending André to Arnold. But Jameson took André to be the "John Anderson" who, by Arnold's orders, was to be escorted into the American lines. As Anderson had been arrested going southward, Jameson conjectured that he had stolen the papers, "of a very dangerous Tendency," which he carried concealed. Jameson sent the papers to Washington, hoping the messenger would find the Commander in Chief on his return road from Hartford.

When Major Benjamin Tallmadge came by and heard the story, he was suspicious of Arnold, and he prevailed on Jameson to bring "John Anderson" back to North Castle. The next day, Sunday, André was taken to Lower Salem for greater safety. The officer who retrieved him went off again with Jameson's letter to Arnold. The captain who had been sent with the incriminating papers had

THE PRICE OF INDEPENDENCE

missed Washington, but now he started off the second time. He was sure he would find the General at Arnold's headquarters. He also carried a letter from André, confessing to Washington that "the person in your possession is Major John André, Adjutant General of the British army." Without naming Arnold, he declared that he had been "betrayed . . . into the vile condition of an enemy in disguise within your posts." He begged not to be considered dishonorable, as he was "involuntarily an imposter."

On Monday morning, Washington and his party were expected for breakfast at the Robinson house. But the Commander in Chief, Lafayette, Knox, and Hamilton turned off to examine some redoubts while two aides, McHenry and Shaw, went ahead to give notice of the delay. Arnold and Franks were at table when Jameson's messenger arrived with the letter to Arnold. (Varick was in bed with a fever.) A glance at the staggering contents—"John Anderson" had been captured with his papers—left Arnold outwardly calm. He needed only a few minutes to collect himself, then went up to Mrs. Arnold. She probably knew before he spoke that their plot had collapsed.

In two minutes Washington's servant came with word that the General was near. Told of this by Franks, Arnold rushed down, ordered a horse, said he was going to West Point but would be back in an hour, and took the shortest way to his barge. Washington arrived, had breakfast, and crossed to the fort. Soon shrieks came from Mrs. Arnold's bedroom. Varick found her "raving distracted." Scantily clad, her hair disheveled, she exclaimed wildly of hot irons on her head, accused Varick of ordering her baby killed, and entreated him on her knees to spare the infant's life. The aides and Dr. William Eustis, the headquarters physician, assured her that all were her friends and that her husband would soon be there. "No, no," she cried, "he is gone forever." She burst out in fresh frenzy that "the spirits have carried him up there," pointing to the ceiling, and had "put hot irons in his head." (Afterwards it was noted that she had held back her screams long enough for Arnold to make his escape.)

Suspicion of treason grew in the minds of the aides. Arnold's barge had been seen headed down the river. Rumor told of a spy, one John Anderson, taken on the lines. Captain Jeronimus Hoogland arrived from Jameson's post with a packet for General Washington. Hamilton did not open it, but Hoogland must have known and said enough about it to strengthen the shocking thought that Arnold had fled to the enemy.

In mid-afternoon, Washington returned from West Point, where he had found no Arnold, the defenses neglected, and the garrison scattered. The packet Hamilton handed him was all too revealing. The papers that had been taken from the stockings of a southbound traveler were all in Arnold's handwriting: a pass for John Anderson, a plan of the West Point fortifications, a detail on which of them were out of repair and the points from which they could be attacked, a return of the cannon and their placement, the number of men at West Point and its dependencies, and a copy of the minutes of Washington's most recent council of war. If these documents were not enough, André's impulsive letter confessing his errand was conclusive of Arnold's guilt.

Hamilton and McHenry were immediately sent galloping the dozen miles to Verplanck's Point to try to intercept Arnold, who was surely making for safety on the *Vulture*. Hamilton sent back word from Verplanck's that they were too late, as was evident from letters from Arnold, from the vessel, to Washington and to Peggy. Hamilton tarried long enough to alert General Greene, commanding the army at Tappan, on the west shore, to hasten a brigade to King's Ferry: the British, despite discovery of the plot, might attack West Point that night.

At the Robinson house Washington was taken up to see Peggy Arnold. Her mad scene convinced him she was innocent, but his promise that she would not be harmed did not quiet her alarms. A

THE PRICE OF INDEPENDENCE

few days later she was escorted to Philadelphia by Major Franks.

Washington appeared impassive at dinner at four o'clock, though for him and his Generals there was never a meal more melancholy. Arnold, in his letter to Washington, had had the effrontery to declare that "I have ever acted from a principle of love to my country. . . . The same principle of love to my country actuates my present conduct. . . ." Washington delivered, unopened, the traitor's letter to his wife.

The hours of that long evening, until 2:00 a.m., were taken up with Washington's dispositions for the protection of West Point. The next morning, Joshua Hett Smith, whom Arnold, in his missive from the *Vulture,* had sought to exculpate, was brought in from Fishkill for interrogation. Washington found him "to have had a considerable share in this business," indeed "has confessed facts sufficient to establish his guilt." (Afterwards, at his formal trial, he was judged not guilty "of being privy to Arnold's traitorous designs," but he later went to New York and received maintenance from the British).

André, anguished and sleepless, was taken under heavy guard to West Point and thence to army headquarters at Tappan, New York, just above the New Jersey line. On Friday, September 29, on Washington's order, he was tried by a board of fourteen general officers. He straightforwardly admitted that he had been within the American lines, under an assumed name and in disguise, and that he had secured military information for Sir Henry Clinton. Letters from Beverley Robinson, Sir Henry Clinton, and even from Arnold were submitted to the court. They argued that André entered the American posts under a flag, and therefore was under the orders of Arnold, the American Commander, and must be released. The board unanimously found he was a spy from the enemy and should suffer death. Washington approved the sentence.

While imprisoned in the village tavern (which is still standing), André was the object of general pity, while imprecations were called down upon Benedict Arnold. With Washington's approval, informal offers were made to free André if the British would give up Arnold; they met with scornful rejection. Deeply distressed at André's plight, Sir Henry Clinton made every effort to save him, including holding a conference of officers of both armies.

André was hanged at Tappan at noon on Monday, October 2, 1780. Arnold lost no time in pressing the British for maximum payment for his defection.

Mutiny

BRIGADIER GENERAL ANTHONY WAYNE'S COMMAND OF PENNSYLVANIA CONTINENTALS WAS SUFFERING DEEP AND PECULIAR DISTRESSES. THE ELEVEN REGIMENTS AND CORPS OF artillery, 2500 men and officers, had encamped in "Jockey Hollow," adjacent to Morristown, New Jersey, at the end of November 1780. There, they repaired old huts and worked on fortifications. Their issues of rum were discontinued; they washed down their dry bread and beef with cold water. They were literally out at elbows; Wayne planned to have the tails of their coats cut off to make patches, and he could have had their battered hats turned into serviceable caps if only the Pennsylvania Council would send needles and thread. The men's over-alls were tattered, "and what was once a poor substitute for a blanket (now divided among three soldiers), is but very wretched living and shelter against the winter's piercing cold, drifting snow, and chilling sleets."

Wayne warned against threatened rebellion: "Our soldiery are not devoid of reasoning faculties, nor are they callous to the first feelings of nature. They have now served their country for near five years, poorly clothed, badly fed, and worse paid . . . they have

not seen a paper dollar in the way of pay for near twelve months."
(If they had been paid in continental money, the year's wage of a
private, $78, at that time had the purchasing power of slightly
more than $1.00 in silver). "For God's sake," Wayne implored,
"direct every exertion . . . in procuring a complete uniform for the
line, which, with some hard cash towards making up the depreciation, will enable me to prevent, very probably, disagreeable
consequences. . . ."

The depreciation was to be compensated in "new tenor" paper
money of the states, intended, after March 1780, to displace the
worthless continentals. But the reformed issues followed the old
into discredit.

The Pennsylvania regulars longest in service had enlisted "for
three years or during the war." Shivering and hungry, they now
gave this careless wording particular examination. They took it to
mean that they were entitled to release at the end of three years,
whether or not the war was then over. Many were illiterate and
had signed the enlistment paper with their marks; they had never
heard the word "syntax." But their construction was accurate. Otherwise why mention "three years"? If the end of the war came
sooner, there would be no reason for holding them in an army.

When the men complained that their time had expired and they
should be discharged, the officers put them off, arguing that the
point could not be settled without their papers, which were not in
camp. Stretched out enlistments caused envy of recruits of other
states who received large bounties. The Pennsylvanians who had
entered the service before February 1778 received only the Continental bounty of $20, those after that date got an additional $100
from the state, and there were later modest supplements for special
groups. By contrast, recruits in the lines of other states received up
to $750 in bounty, and were enlisted for short terms, at the expira-
tion of which they could sign up again for another bounty. Even so,
money sent to reward new recruits in the Pennsylvania line had not

arrived or had been insufficient, so that some enlistees had had to be released.

The army was to be reorganized on January 1, 1781. The eleven Pennsylvania regiments were to be consolidated and reduced to six, and the rank-and-file soldiers were all to be kept, though surplus officers would be "deranged." This approaching reshuffling was a disquieting element in the camp.

New Year's Day passed without trouble, but around eight o'clock that night, cheering started in one regiment. The officers who repressed the noise thought it was due to liquor, of which every man in the line had been issued half a pint. An hour later the disturbance broke out again, and it was general. Men turned out of their huts with arms and knapsacks. Somebody sent up a rocket, others fired muskets. Some troops were ordered back to the huts, but they piled out again as soon as the officer's back was turned. Half the men were in commotion and could not be quelled. As if by a previous understanding, they began to move in a body toward the cannon parked in Mrs. Wick's orchard. The officers who opposed them were shot. The rioters then broke open the ammunition magazine, pulled into the road four field pieces, and fired them. A soldier who ordered the sentinel away from the magazine was killed by a bullet through his head. Captain Adam Bettin set his short spear against a charging soldier and was mortally wounded.

General Wayne, Colonel Richard Butler, and other officers rode up to the milling men, but haranguing did no good. Wayne, always one for a little drama, even if risky, "bared his breast" to any who held they would be better off by removing him from command. They protested their devotion to him, and they declared that they would fight the enemy under him, but they said that they must settle their grievances elsewhere. Regiments already in revolt compelled others to join them. The few who would not be coerced fled the encampment until the storm had passed.

The mutineers had supplied themselves with the horses, wagons, tents, ammunition, food, and forage they would need for a determined march. They took horses from Wayne's stable, but not one belonging to young Temperance Wick, the farm girl who lived near by, for she hid her mount in her bedroom.

Wayne then stationed himself at the crossroads, to make sure that the marchers turned to the left, toward Princeton, Trenton, and Philadelphia, and did not take the direction toward Elizabethtown and the British at Staten Island. In this he had no trouble. In spite of his fears that the rebels would join the enemy, this was never their intention, as was abundantly clear then and afterwards. Another false assumption about the rising was that unruly "Irishmen" had sparked it and kept it flaming. Many in the Pennsylvania line were Scots-Irish, born in Ulster or descended from that stock; they were essentially Scottish, and Presbyterians in religion; though individualists, they lacked the emotional flair, good or bad, which is associated with the Celtic Irish of the southern part of the island.

Wayne sent a message to overtake the troops who had marched away into the night—more than half the camp. His pose was right; he pretended to maintain his authority, refused to use the word mutiny, promised to redress grievances, and pledged that none should be punished for any action "taken on the occasion." He would be glad to meet with a committee (the men's own idea, he declared) composed of one soldier from each regiment. Anticipating joining them, he hoped soon "to return to camp with all his brother soldiers who took a little tour last evening." He dispatched an aide to Washington, who was at New Windsor, with a frank statement of what had happened and information that he and Colonels Richard Butler and Walter Stewart were following to try to retrieve the runaways.

The position of Wayne and his chosen officers, accompanying the mutineers—for a whole fortnight, as it turned out—was delicate. The men had defied all authority and were led only by their sergeants. It seemed demeaning for their rejected General to tag along in the capacity of mere observer, perhaps persuader, and uninvited at that. On the other hand, no one knew better than Wayne that these regiments had been driven to revolt by the criminal neglect of the Pennsylvania legislature. After all, this was a citizen army, not a body of conscripts whose resentments were to be met with summary force. If Wayne appealed to General Washington to call on two or three thousand continentals and militia to march against the mutineers, would they respond? And if they obeyed, and the rebels resisted, what a scene for America's French allies to witness! Wayne was known for his bold enterprise in battle; actually, he was never more courageous than when he used conciliation with his own mutinous troops. The number of mutineers was increasing, for ardent ones returned to Jockey Hollow to solicit recruits to the walkout. Moreover, a hundred women and children were in the truant march.

Wayne and his two officers posted after the malcontents, bringing up their rear as they pressed toward Philadelphia. The General bound himself to corrections which satisfied the committee, but the marchers would not listen to the plea of their representatives to return to camp. The committee tried again, halting the men in a field, where Wayne addressed them, but they were still for going forward.

On arriving at Princeton, they camped behind Nassau Hall, at the College of New Jersey. The committee, thenceforth known as the board of sergeants, once more addressed their complaints to Wayne, Butler, and Stewart. Their leader appears to have been one John Williams, a Pennsylvanian who had been captured by the British, had gotten out of prison by enlisting in a loyalist regiment, and then had deserted back to the patriot army. A court-martial had condemned him to death, but Washington had accepted the recommendation of mercy since he had returned to his duty. The secretary of the board was one William Bowzar, who had been four years in the Tenth Regiment, most of the time as a sergeant, and who wrote a good letter in a practiced hand.

Wayne urged that a deputation go to Philadelphia to present their case to the state legislature. This would prevent the whole body of mutineers from entering the city. Wayne had advised Congress to leave the capital, lest 1500 rebels should, in spite of him, overawe them. Washington directed Wayne to countermand this proposal; if the mutineers made Philadelphia their object and found that Congress had fled, they might take out their anger on the citizens in riot and looting. Considering force as a last resort, Washington inquired of officers at West Point whether the troops stationed there would be dependable.

Sir Henry Clinton, in New York, fifty miles away, learned of the mutiny before word of it reached Washington, who was at twice the distance; British and American spies were constantly crossing the Hudson. Of course Clinton was alert to the possibility of attracting this large body of disaffected enemy troops within his lines by offering at once to satisfy all of their demands and more. He set his secret agents to work, reporting on the prospect of turning the mutiny to British advantage. The information they furnished was fragmentary and much of it incorrect. Sir Henry awaited further developments. The American agents, on their part, were no more accurate; they told of British transports lying in Raritan Bay ready to receive the mutineers, while British troops would land in New Jersey to protect the embarkation. The breakaway of more than half of the Pennsylvania line, so close to enemy headquarters, sent rumors flying. The mutineers guarded their camp at Princeton against all entrants, so that what was brewing in their midst from hour to hour was guesswork to outsiders. Loyalists seized on the event as a fresh sign that the colonies' cause was collapsing. Georgia and the Carolinas were already in British hands, Virginia would be the next to succumb, and here was Washington's army in the north falling apart. The patriots were as alarmed as the loyalists were expectant.

As a matter of fact, both hopes and fears should have been deflated by the observation that the mutineers, once they had defied their officers, preserved order in their march and encampment. They did not spread over the countryside to terrorize and pillage. And they repeatedly assured Wayne that if the British sent a force into New Jersey they would fight for America under Wayne's command.

The demands of the men, already understood, took crisp written form in a communication of the board of sergeants to General Wayne. Those who had enlisted prior to 1778 must be at once discharged with back pay, depreciation pay, and clothing allowance. Men who had enlisted later were entitled to discharge at the end of three years' service, with full pay and clothing. Recent recruits, when supplied with bounty, wages, and clothing, would return to their regiments. There should be amnesty for all participants in the revolt.

Wayne had to hedge on which men were due their discharges and when: on separation from the army they would receive certificates for pay, but only current recruits could expect wages in hard money. He did promise clothing to everybody, though whether the Pennsylvania Council could furnish it was a question.

Wayne's messengers urged the Council to send one or more of its members to him and empower them to treat with the insurgents. Congress, which was meeting in Independence Hall, was of course involved, because a mutiny was a serious threat and terms given to rebels in the Pennsylvania line might be demanded by other units. Congress appointed a committee representing three parts of the country—General John Sullivan, retired, of New Hampshire; Dr. John Witherspoon of New Jersey; and John Mathews of South Carolina. General Arthur St. Clair, commander of the Pennsylvania line superior to Wayne, and Colonel Thomas

Proctor, of the artillery, started for Princeton, as military duty might have prompted them to do earlier. With them went Lafayette and Lieutenant Colonel John Laurens, who were on their way to Washington's headquarters. All of them reached Trenton on the afternoon of Thursday, January 5.

St. Clair and Lafayette kept on to Maidenhead (Lawrenceville). Their plans for meeting the mutineers next morning at Princeton differed. St. Clair was for restraint in the bargaining. Lafayette, excited by false reports, unwisely wrote his alarms to the French Minister, but he was confident that, whomever else might be murdered by the mutineers (St. Clair and Lord Stirling), he would be welcomed. The patriotic exhortation he intended to deliver to the whole camp would send all, in quickstep and with streaming eyes, back to their duty at Morristown. St. Clair and the Marquis were received by the sergeants, but they were not allowed to harangue the troops. The officers were politely urged to take their departure.

The revolt was four days old when emissaries with overtures began to converge—from the English in New York and the American legislators in Philadelphia. General Clinton led regiments to Staten Island and stationed a couple of warships and a fleet of barges at hand to move several thousand troops to New Jersey. He had drawn a proclamation to the mutineers; they were invited to return to British allegiance, have all their claims paid in cash, and receive protection; they did not have to take service in the King's army unless they chose to. (Incidentally, the proclamation, like most statements issuing from both British and American headquarters, was in language not easy for unlettered men to understand. The Generals could have done with scripts prepared by modern publicity agents).

How could the British get their offer to the Princeton camp? New Jersey militia were patroling all the roads to seal off the rebels from just such an enemy proposition. For a messenger, Clinton chose one John Mason. He was a bitter loyalist who had turned indiscriminate brigand. He had gotten out of jail in New York by confessing his crimes and swearing that in future he would rob and kill American patriots only, and he said he would like to use his talents as a spy. He was landed on the west shore of the Raritan with a guide to take him by back paths to Princeton.

In response to Wayne's plea to the Pennsylvania Council, Joseph Reed, its president, and Brigadier General James Potter, a member, were deputed to negotiate with the mutineers. They set off with an escort of twenty of the Philadelphia Light Horse. Reed was a patriot politician and soldier, a little on the censorious side (he had been critical of Washington), who was not inclined to concede to demands of the rebels in the Pennsylvania line. He stopped at Maidenhead, a safe distance—four miles—from Princeton, to which he preferred not to go because the insurgents had hustled out St. Clair and Lafayette. Learning of his fears, the Princeton sergeants sent assurances that he would be welcomed and treated with respect. The committee from Congress (Sullivan *et al.*) came as far as Trenton, to back Reed up.

Washington dispatched Brigadier General Henry Knox through the New England states, warning of the crisis in the army for want of pay and supplies. The legislatures should furnish at once three months' wages ("in money that will be of some value to them") and a complete suit of clothes for every soldier. Since begging was too often politely heard and promptly forgotten, Knox, on his way back, was to insist on knowing what action had followed his pleas.

New Jersey militia had drawn a distant cordon around the malcontents. The authorities had reports that many people in the state, observing the peaceable posture of the mutineers, sympathized with their complaints. It was doubtful whether the militia would obey orders to attack the camp at Princeton. Also, if force were used, would that not drive the rebels into the arms of the British?

It was probably late Saturday night when John Mason, Clinton's messenger, reached Princeton. He was guided by a young fellow,

James Ogden, about whose life we know less than about his death. The two of them were ushered to the chairman of the board of sergeants. Mason produced a thin, folded sheet of lead in which was enclosed General Clinton's offer to the mutineers. (It has been suggested that the lead wrapping was to fool any captor of Mason, who, not finding Clinton's letter, would not hold Mason as a spy. In fact, the reverse would happen, for the careful casing would prompt any suspicious captor to look inside). The chairman of the sergeants ordered the emissaries to be delivered to General Wayne as prisoners. This was at four o'clock in the morning on Sunday, but Wayne did not begrudge being routed out to receive such proof that the wayward troops would not join the enemy. In a glow of gratitude, he promised fifty guineas each to the two sergeants who had surrendered the spies.

Reed had retreated to Trenton. Not knowing that the mutineers had spurned Clinton's overture, he wrote Wayne, urging him to coax the recalcitrants to come to him. At Trenton they would be farther from British blandishments and closer to Congress, with which they must deal. The rebels should not expect the President of Pennsylvania to come to them. The truth was, Joseph Reed was afraid to go among the mutineers. They might hold him hostage, or kill him. It was only after he had learned that the sergeants had made prisoners of the spies that he became nobly brave; he then told his colleagues of the Pennsylvania Council, "I have but one life, and my country has the first claim for it."

Resolved to die, if need be, with "my country" on his lips, Reed started for Princeton. He had not yet reached Maidenhead when he was met by a guard of sergeants bringing him their trophies, Mason and Ogden. He took them all with him to Maidenhead and put the spies under the guard of two of his horsemen. Then more sergeants came from Princeton with a demand to have the prisoners back in their hands. This was confusing, but Reed complied and followed along to the camp of the insurgents.

President Reed, General Wayne, and his colonels sat late that Sunday night with the board of sergeants. The representatives of the mutineers centered on one demand: the soldiers early enlisted, in 1776 and 1777, were due, and overdue, for discharge, and should be let go at once with back pay and certificates covering depreciation of the paper money, no matter if some had re-enlisted and accepted additional bounties. These actions had been forced on them by the officers, through fraud or physical punishments.

Reed was impressed by the stories of coercion by officers. He wrote out conditions of settlement. Those whose terms had expired and who had not freely entered on new enlistments were to be discharged. The enlistment papers could not be promptly collected and consulted. In their absence every man could swear to what his status was, and no honest soldier would perjure himself. Wayne's promise of forgiveness for acts of mutiny was to stand.

Wayne and his Colonels disliked this solution because Reed was admitting that officers had browbeaten and deceived the men. However, it was then midnight, and the sergeants withdrew, promising to discuss the terms with the body of troops in the morning.

Meantime, those of the officers who had been defied by the mutineers, and who had had no part in the negotiations, urged force to subdue the insurrection. This was the language of St. Clair, Lafayette, and Laurens at Morristown, where only a hundred or so soldiers remained in the huts. The officers cooling their heels in Pennington near Princeton were less restrained in demanding military repression. They thought Wayne, Butler, and Stewart should not have remained with the rebels to try to conciliate them; mutiny deserved instant putting down and punishment. Some of the castoff officers had contributed, by their misguided actions, to drive the soldiers to desperation, but they did not sufficiently blame themselves, or feel enough for their ragged regiments.

On Monday morning Reed's terms of settlement were agreed to by the mutineers as a body, except for the makeup of the committee to pass on disputed enlistments. According to Reed, it would be composed of members of the deputations of Congress and the Pennsylvania Council. The men demanded equal representation. This Reed rejected out of hand, saying it implied distrust of the state, "which has ever been attentive to the wants of the army." This last was a barefaced lie. The mutiny had been caused principally by the state's neglect. It was only because of the mutiny that the Pennsylvania authorities were humping themselves at that moment to find clothing and send auditors to fix on depreciation certificates due the men.

Reed and Wayne insisted that the mutinous regiments should march Tuesday morning from Princeton to Trenton for official approval of the settlement. Reed told the sergeants that at Trenton the men would be nearer to the committee of Congress which had final authority. Also the promised clothing—now reduced to "overalls and some blankets"—would be delivered there. Reed wanted to edge the insurgents farther from the British. He would try to break up the body of some 1750 by dropping off 1000 at Bordentown and Burlington. He wished that Wayne would go away, as the mutineers "take countenance and spirit from having him among them." Reed failed to consider that their attachment to Wayne was balanced by a lack of confidence in himself.

Reed hoped that on the march to Trenton the sergeants would call a halt so that he could address the body. He was disappointed; the regiments went into a tight camp beside the Delaware River and posted extra guards to prevent communication with anyone in the town. Reed's officials had ordered all boats moved to the Pennsylvania shore. He urged that the committee from Congress should withdraw some distance from the mutineers; he himself "would not be within their guards . . . for any time, lest some wicked rascals . . . should suggest mischief." The committee took quarters across the river in Morrisville, Pennsylvania.

On Wednesday morning the sergeants stipulated to Reed that

the men should remain together under arms until all due for discharge were given their papers. Reed summarily rejected this demand; after a time the sergeants consented that those discharged should give up their arms and would then be free to leave the camp.

The messengers from the British, Mason and Ogden, were now given up to the committee of Congress. Lord Stirling, the only Major General in Trenton, ordered a court of inquiry, and it pronounced them spies and sentenced them to be hanged. After the execution at Morrisville their bodies were left dangling. Reed did not want Wayne's promise of a hundred guineas, the reward for turning over the spies, to be left dangling also. He called the two sergeants before him and thriftily wheedled them out of their prize money. He protested to General Washington that the captors were content with doing their patriotic duty, but he confessed to the tightfisted Pennsylvania Council that he had artfully cheated the simple fellows.

General Washington ordered a thousand New England troops at West Point to be held in readiness to march against the mutineers; however, encouraging reports from Trenton suspended the movement.

The Councilmen and Congressmen returned to Philadelphia, leaving the aftermath of the mutiny to the committee on disputed enlistments and to those of the officers who had been accepted by their regiments. Reed had pressed to get the business over with, not waiting for delivery of the enlistment papers from Morristown and elsewhere. It appeared that men had enlisted on a surprising variety of conditions, which, even with the papers in hand, would have required time to puzzle out. As it was, every soldier, except the recent recruits, was at liberty to settle his status by his oath. Some perjured themselves, but a third of the mutineers had their discharges legitimately. Most of these would have been willing, even eager, to re-enlist, and for the duration of the war, if only

Pennsylvania had sent enough of its paper currency to give every man a month's pay. Arrears of pay and depreciation allowances they would wait for, but without something in hand they drifted off or enlisted in New Jersey regiments. Each man who remained in the service was supplied a pair of shoes, woolen over-alls, a shirt, and blanket. They were all furloughed home for two months, and each was given a ration for every twenty miles he had to travel.

The mutiny in the Pennsylvania line was concluded at Trenton about January 25, 1781. Five days before this, two hundred men in a detachment of New Jersey continentals stationed at Pompton refused to obey their officers and struck out for Trenton. Their long service, sufferings, and complaints were the same as those of the Pennsylvanians, whose example had inspired their outbreak. Colonel Israel Shreeve followed them to Chatham, their first stop. There Colonel Elias Dayton commanded another Jersey detachment, some of whom joined the Pompton men in two days of disorder. They disregarded the relief they were to get from acts hastily passed by the New Jersey legislature (depreciation allowance and higher bounty), which were intended to forestall a Pennsylvania-style mutiny. The men demanded that their oaths be accepted in determining which were eligible for immediate discharge.

Colonel Dayton argued the rebels out of this summary method of exit from enlistments, and he assured them that their wants in other respects would be met; the faithful Reverend James Caldwell was already in camp to distribute money from the legislature. Thus mollified, the sergeants begged Dayton to ensure them of a general pardon if they returned to their duty, which he did.

Giving three cheers for their pardon, the Pompton men, with some of those from Chatham, marched for their old huts under Shreeve's command.

Meantime, General Washington, at New Windsor, at once resolved that this new insurrection would be put down by military means. He wrote to Congress, "I thought it indispensable to bring the matter to an issue and risk all extremities. Unless this dangerous spirit can be suppressed by force there is an end to all subordination in the Army, and indeed to the Army itself." From West Point he ordered detachments from Massachusetts, Connecticut, and New Hampshire regiments, with three field pieces, to march to Pompton under General Robert Howe.

This was a toilsome tour of duty, against fellow soldiers, and through two feet of snow in the mountain passes. To reach the troubled scene as quickly as possible, the punitive expedition struggled through the drifts in midnight marches. Howe's orders from Washington were to subdue the mutiny unconditionally and to execute the most active offenders. Washington and his bodyguard, with Lafayette, set out for Ringwood to be at hand if needed. At that place General Howe was met by Lieutenant Colonel Francis Barber, who had been sent by Shreeve to report the state of affairs at Pompton. The men had lapsed from their promises at Chatham, had many times refused to obey orders, and had menaced some of their officers.

General Howe, to make sure of his own detachment, in a predawn speech impressed upon them "the heinousness of the crime of mutiny." He then surrounded the Pompton huts and had field pieces trained on the post. Lieutenant Colonel Barber went in and commanded the men to march without arms to the parade ground. Some were willing to comply, but others refused unless their conditions were met. Howe then gave them five minutes in which to obey. That brought them out.

The Jersey officers gave Howe a list of the worst offenders, from which he had them select three, one from each regiment, to be tried by court-martial on the spot. The sergeants who had led the revolt had behaved well since Chatham, but one of them, Sergeant Major George Grant, was included in the trio for trial. This was because he had been in principal command. Two sergeants, David

Gilmour and John Tuttle, were considered most culpable from first to last.

These three were sentenced to be shot forthwith. Twelve of their companions, men who were thought to be hardly less guilty, were told off as executioners. The condemned were made to kneel in the snow, and Gilmour and Tuttle were dispatched. At the last moment, Grant was pardoned, as it appeared that he had been forced by others to play his part in the mutiny.

After the executions all was submission in the Jersey line.

General Wayne had managed well in the face of a major mutiny. Instead of standing in a humiliating light, he had discharged his responsibility by remaining with the rebels and ending the outbreak by peaceable means. Six months later, however, he was obliged to take a leaf from Washington's book and meet disobedience with stern measures.

At the end of February 1781, Wayne was ordered to lead a detachment of Pennsylvania troops to strengthen Lafayette, who was opposing the British in Virginia. Of his former command, Wayne had lost more than 1300 by discharge, the remaining 1250 were on sixty-day furlough, and the few new recruits were jailbirds who had been willing to be released from behind bars. York, Pennsylvania, was appointed the rendezvous for 800, who were to come from the different regiments in March. The men were slow in assembling because, said Wayne, of the "delay of the auditors who were . . . to settle and pay the proportion of the depreciation due them, which, when received, was not equal to one-seventh part of its nominal value." The cheat came home to the soldiers as soon as they tried to buy with the paper; the people of York told them that it was worthless and that the troops "ought not to march until justice was done them." With the memory of the January mutiny fresh in their minds, they were stimulated "to try it again."

By the last week in May, a decent detachment was equipped and ready to go to the relief of Lafayette. The day before departure, when the troops were paraded, a few of the boldest malcontents called out that they must be paid in real money and "were no longer to be trifled with." These noisy ones were ordered to their tents, refused to obey, and were either knocked down by the officers or confined.

Within a few hours a court-martial had condemned six to death for exciting to mutiny. Two were pardoned, but four were shot in the presence of their comrades. This "liberal dose of niter" restored order in the detachment, though at the cost of distress to Wayne and his officers.

The foregoing is Wayne's account, which varies in particulars from the records of two courts-martial held at York, from hearsay reports that were made soon afterward, and from the recollections, many years later, of a soldier who witnessed the happenings. The farther away, in place and time, from the actual scene, the more gruesome the narrative becomes and, doubtless, the less reliable. The stories of some had the detachment marched past the corpses; the surrounding weeds were spattered with blood and brains.

The effects of the succession of mutinies on the American war effort are conjectural. Congress was stirred once again to exhort the states to provide money for the army; John Laurens, in his successful mission to France, pleaded for more aid, reminding the French of the recent outbreaks; possibly Maryland's consent to bring the Articles of Confederation into force was hastened by disorders among the troops. In any event, the mutinies proved to be the darkness before the dawn. Many of the very men who refused duty in New Jersey and Pennsylvania helped to vanquish Cornwallis in Virginia in October of that same year of 1781.

Congress was menaced in its own capital in June 1783 by mutinous troops of the Pennsylvania line. The involvement of Congress was partly accidental, since it sat in the Statehouse, where also met the Executive Council of Pennsylvania to which the soldiers' protests were principally directed. Failure of the local authorities to furnish protection sent Congress to Princeton, Annapolis, Trenton, New York, and back to Philadelphia. The episode pointed up the need for a federal district over which Congress should have exclusive control, and also for a degree of federal power over the militia of the states.

In mid-June Congress received from sergeants in the Philadelphia barracks a remonstrance against being discharged until they were paid. Congress took no action on this irregular proceeding. A few days later President John Dickinson of the Pennsylvania Council transmitted to Congress letters from Colonel Richard Butler and William Henry, of the Third Pennsylvania Regiment at Lancaster. They wrote that eighty soldiers under arms had rebelled against their officers and were on their way to Philadelphia "to co-operate with those now in the city . . . to procure their pay (or perhaps to possess themselves of money at any rate)." Butler sent officers after the mutineers to try to persuade them back to Lancaster, the only place where they could be paid; there furloughs would be at their option. This was the second time around for Colonel Butler, who more than three years before had argued similarly to mutineers from Morristown.

Congress at once named a committee, with Alexander Hamilton its chairman, which appealed to the Pennsylvania Council to avert the threat. The Council should call out militia to intercept the mutinous marchers before they could join forces with the restless troops in the Philadelphia barracks. The Council refused, explaining that the militia would not respond unless and until the mutineers committed some outrage. Thus balked, the committee of Congress sent Major William Jackson, the Assistant War Secretary, to meet the rebels. He was to assure them of fair treatment when they had returned to their officers and to offer them provisions if they stopped where they were. But the marchers kept on their way and reached the city Friday morning, June 20. They brought the total of troops in the barracks to 500. All seemed quiet; Congress met as usual that day and adjourned till Monday morning. General Arthur St. Clair, commander of the Pennsylvania line, was summoned.

However, around noon on Saturday the committee notified President Elias Boudinot that the soldiers at the barracks had defied their officers and seemed likely to make trouble by evening. Boudinot called the members of Congress into session at one o'clock. They found the Statehouse surrounded by 300 troops with fixed bayonets, some of them pressing close to the windows of the Council chamber. Dickinson, the head of the Pennsylvania Council, announced that the mutineers, commanded by seven sergeants, had confronted the Council with a demand. They wanted authority to choose commissioned officers to redress their grievances. "You will immediately issue such authority and deliver it to us," the mutineers threatened, "or . . . we shall instantly let in . . . injured soldiers upon you. . . . You have only twenty minutes to deliberate on this important matter." Dickinson reported that the Council had unanimously rejected this peremptory message.

Congress ordered General St. Clair to attempt to march the troops to their barracks. At the same time General Washington was asked for a detachment to suppress the insurrection. After sitting uncomfortably for three hours, during which Congress was denounced by drunken soldiers, the members made a peaceful exit from their hall. St. Clair got the disorderly men back to the barracks with the promise that they could name officers to put their case before the Pennsylvania Council. The mutineers held arsenals and several pieces of artillery; it was doubted whether the militia would be any protection. Congress met again that evening in a determined mood. The Pennsylvania Council should be informed that the authority of the United States had been insulted. Unless the city was restored to safety, Congress was prepared to move to Princeton or Trenton.

The committee of Congress met with the Pennsylvania Council

on successive days. The Council regretted the affront to Congress, but reported that the militia could not be depended upon unless the disorders grew worse. Hamilton, for Congress, urged that failure of the state to uphold the dignity of the national body would give an unfavorable impression abroad, and that it might endanger the peace negotiations, which were then in progress. The Council hoped that the mutineers were becoming more submissive.

This trust was dashed by instructions of the sergeants to the commissioned officers who were dealing with the Council. The mutineers would support the officers in "compulsive measures should they be found necessary." If the officers were guilty of any trickery, "Death is inevitably your fate."

President Boudinot issued a proclamation declaring that the danger in which Congress stood required that it quit the capital and remove to Princeton. This finally roused the Pennsylvania Council to muster 500 militiamen to restore order. The detachment sent by Washington from the Northern army was nearing the city. The officers who had helped to foment the revolt deserted the mutineers; other officers who had negotiated for the men were arrested. The rebels laid down their arms, and the Lancaster contingent marched back to their station.

Hirelings

WHAT LATER WAS GERMANY WAS A PATCHWORK OF SOVEREIGNTIES IN THE EIGHTEENTH CENTURY. ASIDE FROM PRUSSIA, A POWERFUL STATE UNDER FREDERICK the Great, most of the others were insignificant in extent and influence. They were principalities or dukedoms no larger than an American county or, in some cases, township. Their rulers, as a group, were pretentious, self-indulgent, lingering in the tradition of feudalism. Their tiny and extravagant courts contrasted with the neglect, indeed, the exploitation, of the people, who made no protest against oppression. It was from these petty potentates that George III of England hired troops to increase his forces against the rebellious colonies in America. He had applied without result to Russia and Holland, but found the German kinglets eager to serve his wishes. They drove hard bargains, not because they had a care for their people, but because England was rich, and in pressing need of soldiers.

These gentry were shipping out their subjects to encounter hardships, danger, perhaps death, in a foreign land, in a quarrel in which they had no concern, but several of them did not neglect personally to keep up their populations. Frederick II, the Landgrave of Hesse-Cassel, was said to have fathered more than a hundred children. His son William, who at the time of the Revolution governed the independent county of Hanau, was a comparative slacker as progenitor, for he begat only seventy-four bastards. Frederick-Augustus, Prince of Anhalt-Zerbst, apparently was less industrious in recruiting his small population of 20,000, for he chose to reign *in absentia,* spending most of his time in Switzerland. He furnished 600 troops to the British in America. The most to be said of him is that he was the brother of Catherine the Great of Russia.

Though furnishing mercenaries was a familiar practice (Hesse had done so ten times in that century), supplying the British for service against rebellious American colonies drew impressive censure from Mirabeau, Schiller, Frederick the Great, and English and other European liberals. Frederick was contemptuous of a Landgrave who "sold his subjects to the English as one sells cattle to be dragged to the shambles."

The "treaties" between the "high contracting parties" were in fact leases of men, or, where the Germans were casualties in the war, bills of sale. The wording of one, dated February 4, 1776, is typical: *"Be it known to those concerned,* that H.M. the King of Great Britain having thought proper to receive a Corps of Infantry from the Troops of H.S.H. [His Serene Highness] the Hereditary Prince of Hesse Cassel, Reigning Count of Hanau, to be employed in the service of Great Britain . . . their respective Ministers . . . after exchanging their full Powers, have agreed upon the following Articles." Chief provisions were that "The said S[erene] Prince grants . . . a corps of 668 Men Infantry who shall be at the entire Disposal of the King of Great Britain." The corps, composed of fit men "in the best possible Condition," would be completely furnished "with Tents, & every kind of Field Equipage," ready to march within six weeks to "be delivered to the Commissary of

H. B. My. [His Britannic Majesty] " at the place of embarkation. The Serene Prince would "furnish the Recruits Annually that are required"—that is, would fill the ranks of those killed or incapacitated by wounds or disease. The British would pay and treat these troops in every respect as they did their own. The "Levy Money for every Foot Soldier," the price going to the Hereditary Prince, was 30 Crowns Banco, equal to £7 4s. 4½d.

"Three Men that are wounded are to be reckoned . . . for one Man killed." If any company should be entirely destroyed, the King must bear the expense of recruiting substitutes. Further, the King of England would grant to the Prince "an annual Subsidy of 25,050 Crowns Banco [£5845] during the time these troops shall be in his Pay." Notice of expiration of the subsidy had to be given a year in advance, unless the troops had already been returned to their country. King George would begin pay of the corps fifteen days before they left their quarters, and he would bear all expenses of their march, transport, and shipment home. The Prince did reserve to his own officers the administration of justice, and stipulated that his troops should not be singled out for especially dangerous service.

The fawning attitude of the Prince of Hesse to King George is evident in his letter, in his best English, to Lord Suffolk, who had directed the negotiations for mercenaries. He speaks of "the luck I have had to be able to show in some manner my utmost respect and gratitude to the best of kings, by offering my troops to his majesty's service." He trusts that the members of his regiment may be animated by his own "attachment and utmost zeal," and "May the end they fight for answer to the king's upper contentment." There was no alliance, no moral commitment to the British cause, only personal—actually, pecuniary—allegiance.

The major contingents were obtained from Brunswick and Hesse-Cassel. The treaty with the Duke of Brunswick was the first one made, on January 9, 1776. The terms were similar to those recited above, except for the numbers of soldiers and the payments involved. The Duke of Brunswick yielded to His Britannic Majesty 3964 infantrymen and 330 unmounted dragoons, completely equipped at expense of the Duke, but no horses for the cavalry. The troops were to march from Brunswick in February and March. The Duke promised to take no rakeoff from the men's wages, but the British made sure of this by paying them directly, in America. The wounded who could not serve further were to be returned to Europe at the King's expense. The Duke would furnish recruits annually to fill the ranks. However, the King had to bear the expense in case of such disasters as shipwreck or deaths in epidemics of disease. The Duke appointed the officers, whom he warranted to be expert, and in whose hands would be discipline of the troops. The Brunswick soldiers were not to be treated as more expendable than the British, nor were they to be called for hazardous service that others did not share.

King George would pay the levy-money of thirty crowns per man, and grant an annual subsidy of £11,517 17s. 1½d. from the day of signature of the treaty as long as the troops were in the King's pay, and double that amount (£23,035 14s. 3d.) for two years after the return of the troops to the Duke's dominions. Further, as a bonus for prompt compliance with the King's need, he would pay two months' wages prior to the march, and bear the expense of the march.

"According to custom, three wounded men shall be reckoned as one killed; a man killed shall be paid for at the rate of levy-money." The King was required to replace a soldier killed, and the Duke had to replace one deserting or dying of ordinary causes. One interpretation of this provision is that the King had to pay levy-money for a Brunswick soldier when he enlisted, plus thirty crowns if he was killed, and that this "blood money" was pocketed by the Duke, nothing going to the family of the dead. In any case, the Duke received some $35 for every one of his soldiers killed, and $11.66 for every one incapacitated by wounds.

The treaty with the Landgrave of Hesse-Cassel, made January

15, 1776, was in some respects more favorable to the German Prince. The King entered a defensive alliance with the Landgrave, who would furnish 12,000 men completely equipped, with artillery if desired. The levy-money per soldier was the same thirty crowns as with others, but the subsidy was proportionately larger, 450,000 crowns, or £108,281 5s., per annum, to be continued, but not doubled, for one year after return of the troops. The Landgrave not only received twice as much per man as the Duke of Brunswick did, but he wangled £41,820 14s. 5d. on a claim against the British dating from the Seven Years' War. For this extra allowance, Lord North's government offered a questionable reasoning. It was a part of the free spending that marked the necessity to secure German mercenaries.

The knowledgeable historian Eelking calculated that the British paid to the German Princes annually £850,000 for their soldiers, plus £70,000 a year for the subsistence of these troops, and, in addition, continuance of the subsidies for one or two years following the war, up to £1,150,000. The largest sum went to Hesse-Cassel, £2,950,800; Brunswick got £750,000, about half as much went to Hesse-Hanau, and smaller amounts were paid to Anspach-Bayreuth, Waldeck, and Anhalt-Zerbst.

Of the total of 30,067 German mercenaries shipped to America from 1776 to 1782, some 18,000 sailed in the first year. Nearly half of all those sent over, 12,562, did not return to Germany; 7750 were lost by death, and 4808 chose to remain in America.

Much of the recruitment had been abrupt and harsh, and many of the men, when they found they were to be sent to a distant, strange land to face unknown perils, deserted on the way to the Dutch port, which was frequently Dortrecht. Some jumped overboard into the Rhine; others eluded the vigilance of the officers when they were landed to be inspected by the British commissary deputed to receive them. In March 1777 Hessian recruits mutinied when the Lieutenant carelessly left the boat in which they were embarked. Captain Kornrumpff, with his officers and "some good Chasseurs" raced to the scene. "7 Recruits leap'd on shore whom we pursued and recovered 4 of them, the other 3 got into a House . . . & upon our threatening to take them by force, the peasants of the village threatened to protect them & I was obliged to retreat my People, for we ran the Risk of being put to Death."

After the first contingents for America were furnished and the news got back of the blood spilt by Waldeckers in the attack on Fort Washington and of the wholesale capture of Hessians at Trenton, recruitment of new units was harder, though the British called for them urgently. Artisans fled the towns; peasants deserted their fields. At Ochsenfurt, troops of the Margrave of Anspach refused to embark. Their officers put up no stern resistance. As soon as the Margrave was notified, he took horse to the place, where he commanded obedience and quelled the rebellion. Others of the princelings, supported by Sir Joseph Yorke, the British ambassador to Holland, took the precaution of shepherding their reluctant subjects aboard ship and watching them sail for England. Dread of the long voyage to America in crowded small transports was a principal cause of resistance of the recruits. One and a half tons of vessel capacity were allowed for each soldier, including six women per company and perhaps a few children, but provisions and equipment had to be accommodated in the same space.

When the troops were mustered and turned over to the British agent at the point of embarkation, they collectively took oath "to be true to his sacred Majesty King George the 3rd . . . for the Service we have taken in the truest & unalterable sense," and then repeated it individually. The sovereigns were not always faithful to George, nor to their men. As the pickings got lean, part of the troops supplied were good physical specimens, but others were too old or too young for their duties. The promised equipment might also be lacking. The Duke of Brunswick dispatched his troops for a chilly voyage without overcoats. Before leaving Portsmouth, their

Commander, Baron Riedesel, had to borrow £5000 from the British to make up the worst deficiencies.

The transports lying at Portsmouth in June 1776 were "being supplied with water and provisions for a quarter of a year. . . . On one of the Brunswick transport ships," which Captain Pausch of the Hesse-Hanau artillery visited, "there were 450 men not counting the women and children. Even after occupying the deck three times, alternately, they cannot inhale the fresh air. The Colonel . . . with sixteen officers and the Ship-Captain, all occupy a cabin not much larger than ours. For the privates, there are three tiers of bunks one on the top of the other. There will be a great deal of sickness among these poor people on account of their great number, and the small space allotted to them. It is said . . . that there is another vessel containing 550 men, nearly an entire battalion." A German Captain was dispatched to London to beg the King to remedy the crowding. Pausch's own vessel, the *Juno,* had been in the slave trade; her human loading then must have made the occupancy by the Hessian troops seem roomy.

Captain Pausch and all of his boys were landsmen; if they had ever been afloat before, it had been only on their passage on the Rhine to the Channel port. Pausch described the storm that struck terror into his company in July 1776: ". . . this gale . . . became so violent, that the Captain, who was generally a most courageous man and a daring mariner, lost his courage. So, also, did the sailors. All the sails which were hoisted were torn by the wind into tatters, and the main mast (the strongest) was broken short off. Each successive wave following the other swept over the deck or rather the ship; and so much water came into the vessel, that those who slept in the lowest bunk under the forward deck with their baggage, were flooded; and this . . . although all the openings and air-holes were covered. Now the ship would lay on one side, and now on the other—her masts touching the waters, which now rose around the ship higher than the masts. At times we seemed to be in a deep abyss between the walls of water. Every one of us, including the Captain himself, expected every moment would be our last; and each one appeared reconciled to the inevitable, giving up all hope of ever seeing America, or his fatherland again."

The German soldiers in America, most of whom had been rudely jerked from their native surroundings, suffered from homesickness, and under trying conditions. Major Carl Maurmeister wrote from Philadelphia in May 1778: "For four and one-half months the Hessian troops have received no news from the Fatherland. Convinced, as we are, that we are . . . warmly remembered, we are at a loss to understand why we have had no assurance of it for so long. We have been sending letters with every packet." He found comfort in writing, even if replies were few and far between. An enlisted man was more despondent at apparent neglect. After writing that all the soldiers from his village were alive and well, he complained, "My dear parents and brothers and sister, I do not know what to do because you do not write. Do you think that I am dead or did you forget me entirely? Or are you glad that I left you?"

Captain Pausch wrote in his journal: "Each of my men who was sent to the Hospital was not only afflicted with dysentery, but, as the hospital doctors told me, talked day and night of fathers, mothers, brothers, sisters, cousins, and aunts—besides, also, talking over and repeating all kinds of German village deviltry—calling now this one and now that one by his baptismal name until they had to stop for actual want of breath! For this disease there is, as is well known, but one remedy in the world, viz: dear peace, and a speedy return; and with this hope I comfort my sick daily. With those still alive and well, I am perfectly satisfied; for they find plenty of solace in the Canadian girls and women."

The evil reputation given the German mercenaries increased their loneliness. "Hessians" became a term of hatred. What reason had they to come and fight and despoil the colonists? Ignorant

Americans were told, and believed in part, stories about their inhuman cruelties. When the prisoners of Trenton and Saratoga were expected at particular places on their march to detention camps, the country people would come in from miles around to view the "monsters." On the other hand, Congress from the first used several means to persuade the German troops to desert. Men who lived in the German-speaking parts of Pennsylvania and Maryland were active in distributing handbills, in the German language, promising free land to those who would embrace the advantages of American settlement and citizenship. A foretaste was the pipeful of tobacco wrapped in the leaflet.

Also, wherever German prisoners of war were held for a time, numbers of them were encouraged to take employment in the vicinity, on farms or in iron works. Those having trades were well paid, and even those who could only serve as laborers in town or country at least enjoyed a measure of freedom. Congress in October 1777 informed the Governor of New York that if laborers were lacking in the lead mines of the state, prisoners of war would be furnished for that service. Not a few of these P.O.W. hirelings married daughters of their employers or of other families in the neighborhood. On the whole, during the war Americans tended to be disabused of the worst reports of the German troops. The British Commanders found that if units of their German allies were stationed long in one place they formed connections in the district, with resulting increase in desertions. At the end of the war a high proportion of German soldiers chose to remain in this country. This was actually encouraged by the Duke of Brunswick, who did not want to have to put supernumeraries on his pension rolls. Particularly he would not have need of returning staff officers, and he urged that chaplains, paymasters, surgeons, and others who could readily find employment in America should remain here. On his return to Brunswick, General Riedesel's division was reduced to an infantry regiment of two battalions and a small dragoon regiment.

The Hessian high command admitted to nearly 3000 deserters in the course of the war, many of them from other parts of Germany who had joined Hessian units for the purpose, it was thought, of securing passage to America. Some who defected came in after a general pardon was proclaimed.

One reason for the high rate of desertion by German troops could have been their observation of the fairer treatment of American enlisted men by American officers. The heavy-handed dealing of Lieutenant Krafft, as told by himself, may not have been typical, but it had the sanction of his superior. Krafft's Hessian groom angered him by some blunder. "Having no stick with me, I took my sword with the sheath and struck him several times. But the sheath unexpectedly slipped off and the groom throwing up his left arm, I dealt him a severe cut below the elbow to the bone. I was in anxiety myself though I had done it unintentionally. I went to Colonel von Gosen, told him the whole story myself and he pardoned me without any reproachful remarks, even in spite of the earnest complaint of the groom."

Though the British depended heavily on their German auxiliaries and were paying correspondingly well for their service, the top Commanders in the first years did not get on together. General Leopold von Heister criticized General Sir William Howe's operations in 1776. Howe influenced the British ministry to secure Heister's recall. Lord Suffolk complained to General von Schlieffen, the Hessian representative in London, that "Heister is worse than useless, and his presence at the head of the German soldiers in the field is a constant source of anxiety and trouble." Suffolk tried to put the blame for the defeat at Trenton on Heister, though the latter could rejoin that the fault was Howe's; he had placed that garrison distant from support. The Elector of Hesse-Cassel reluctantly yielded to the British demand, for Heister was an excellent soldier. The claim was that Heister was relieved on account of his age (he was sixty-two), and that he was needed at home for report and consultation. He was given all honors in his departure from America, which he left in an armed transport with ship-of-war escort, but he died shortly after reaching Cassel in October 1778. He was succeeded by General Wilhelm von Knyphausen, who remained at the head of the German troops until 1782.

Nor were the expensively hired German soldiers valued by all of the British officers. General Haldimand from Quebec in 1779 wrote Sir Henry Clinton that "the Germans were unfit by nature and education for the American service." On their part, the Germans, who had nothing but their professional pride to sustain them, undoubtedly resented the superior airs of their companions in arms. A German officer wrote home of "the confounded pride and arrogant bearing of the English, who treat everyone that was not born on their ragamuffin Island with contempt." However, Lieutenant Anburey was an honorable exception. Describing the battle of Freeman's Farm, he said that when the British line was hard pressed, "General Riedesel exerted himself, brought up the Germans and arrived in time to charge the enemy with great bravery."

It was common to charge the German troops with plundering, doubtless partly because they were a distinguishable group. Of course orders forbade marauding and pillaging; foraging parties were not supposed to drive off cattle without paying for the animals. The punishment for disobedience was "30 or more strokes with a stick on the backside," often many more if the culprit was sentenced to run the gauntlet. On landing at Head of Elk in 1777, after suffering deprivations in the protracted voyage from New York, ten Hessians were so punished. Lawless acts against the inhabitants were often committed by stragglers from the marching columns, or by detached parties. In late September of 1778, Sergeant von Krafft of the von Bose regiment was on a forage above King's Bridge, New York. Heavy rains drove thirty Jaegers and chasseurs to shelter in the local church. His journal records:

"Finally a search was begun and a large potato-field was cleaned out and many other luxuries brought in. Fowls, pigs and beef were slaughtered, although everything had to be done secretly. As usual when on the march we received nothing but salt pork, crackers and rum for rations. In short we led, as the Hessians termed it, a Hussar life. . . . Constant complaints were made to the Yagers and to us that cattle had been slaughtered; but the matter was not very closely investigated by the Staff and other officers." Next day, after a march of some miles, "The foraging commenced again . . . during which some of the soldiers began to plunder. Many of the houses, which I saw afterwards, had been left in a deplorable condition and the soldiers had made a good haul. We were not forbidden to get provisions, but very strictly admonished not to take anything from the people in their houses. However even when they were caught in the act, the punishment was not equal to the prohibition. For a few days we had an abundance of good food and this was my only booty."

Four hundred Hessian and Bayreuth troops raided Hackensack, New Jersey. They found no garrison there, burned the courthouse and principal residences, and plundered at will until a superior force of Americans arrived and drove them back to the Hudson. Musketeer Döhla recorded: "We gathered fine plunder, gold and silver watches, silver forks and spoons, furniture, good clothes, fine English linen, silk stockings, gloves and cravats. My own booty, which I brought safely back, consisted of two silver watches, three necklaces of silver, a pair of women's woolen stockings, a pair of men's summer stockings, two men's and four women's shirts, of fine English linen, two fine table cloths, one silver tablespoon and one teaspoon, five Spanish dollars and six York shillings." It would seem that he was sufficiently loaded down, but he had packed up, and was compelled to throw away on the retreat, eleven yards more of linen, two dozen silk handkerchiefs, six silver spoons, and a silver goblet. Of course pillaging was not confined to the soldiers of any one nationality; Americans, both patriots and loyalists, did their share.

If the German troops distressed the Americans, the American summer climate was an affliction to the Germans. Dr. Johann Schoepff, chief surgeon of the Anspach-Bayreuth soldiers, like so many Europeans, suffered from the heat. The battle of Monmouth "was remarkable," he said, "from one circumstance which has not its parallel in the history of the New World; without receiving a wound, fifty-nine men fell on our side solely from the extraordinary heat and fatigue of the day," and many of the rebels likewise. After giving a harrowing description of sunstroke ("blood gushes from the mouth and nostrils"), he observed that the German troops were especially exposed to this danger, "enveloped as our men are in heavy woolen garments and tight leggings, and carrying the entire weight of a gun, sixty cartridges, knapsack, and rations, they cannot but suffer doubly from all the discomforts of such days." The English provided their troops with lighter clothing for summer.

Dr. Schoepff, still on the subject of dangerous summers in America, blamed attacks of "cholera, with incessant bilious vomiting and purging" on the hot seasons. His cholera could not have been the real thing, for the condition was "generally arrested in one or two days by . . . emetics and cathartics—and quite often without them—as soon as the unusual . . . quantity of bile . . . had been ejected."

His Anspachers were addicted, in America, to spirituous liquors. "A quart of rum is given to a man in seven days, but the majority take twice as much in that time, and the injurious effects of intemperance are often manifested by internal derangements, slow fevers, general loss of strength, with which train of symptoms many depart from this world." Excessive drinking, he thought, was responsible for what he observed in two-thirds of the autopsies he performed in the hospital. "Large or small clots in the cavities of the heart and the large vessels . . . are white and of a thick, viscid consistency, like a febrinous coat on the blood in inflammations, or like the inorganic gelatinous membranes which I have often seen covering the surface of the lungs and other internal organs after inflammations." Perhaps to sustain his ardor in a compulsory service in a foreign land the poor Anspacher had to do violence to his insides.

Hannah Winthrop, of privileged social position, described, uncharitably, the entrance of the Saratoga prisoners, English and German, into Cambridge as "a sorded set of creatures in human form. Poor, dirty, emaciated men, great numbers of women who seemed to be the beasts of burden." Some infants had been born on the road, and they peeped through the gridirons and other utensils on their mothers' backs. "The women were barefoot, clothed in dirty rags. Such effluvia filled the air while they were passing, had they not been smoking all the time, I should have been apprehensive of being contaminated by them. . . . Hessians, Waldeckers, Anspackers, Brunswickers, etc. etc. followed on." If the Cambridge dame had come on that 200-mile tour barefoot she would not have cut much of a figure herself. One of the hardships of the German prisoners of Saratoga was the active hostility with which they were met as they were herded about the country. The consideration shown them by the American officers was not generally repeated as they passed through or camped near towns or villages. Not that all Americans exulted in the captives' humiliation. The hated "Hessians" on occasion found kindness from low and high alike.

Already at Saratoga a German officer had written, "Clothes were not to be thought of, for they were daily torn into shreds in this wilderness." And six months later, at Cambridge: "The soldiers have . . . worn their clothes for three years, and that, too, on ship-board, through woods, and during the winter in the barracks! The officers, who on leaving Canada took nothing with them except their worst clothes . . . are now sighing for new apparel."

Another officer wrote of the barracks on Winter Hill, Cambridge, that it was "built of boards, and the windows are of paper, so that we have had plenty of fresh air this winter. . . . If our furniture were better, and our dress and equipments, now so ragged as scarcely to cover our nakedness, it would not be quite so bad."

When General William Phillips went to take command in Virginia, in March 1781, the Prince Frederick Regiment was among his 2000 troops. The women of the Brunswickers were left behind in New York, "and the husbands of many would never return. There were girls who had been children when the war began and who were now grown; there were some fatherless, some orphaned, who had no means of livelihood except to turn to prostitution. A barracks master named Clarke 'interested himself' in these 'poor girls,' but orphanages were filled to overflowing and nothing could be done about them. Houses where German women established themselves were tolerated until someone complained, whereupon the women were dispersed perhaps to find themselves shelter in some garret or cellar. Jobs were scarce; it was a lucky girl who found someone who would let her work for food and shelter." *

In November 1778, when the German prisoners of war had been about a year in Cambridge, it was determined to march them to Virginia, where the climate was milder and food more plentiful. The route was by Enfield and Simsbury, Connecticut, through the Berkshires to Canaan and Salisbury in the same state; thence to Amenia, Newburgh, and Goshen in New York, through Hackettstown, New Jersey, then by Valley Forge, Lancaster, York, and Hanover in Pennsylvania. In Maryland the road lay east of the hills, through Taneytown and Frederick; then it reached into Virginia by Leesburg, Culpeper, Orange, and so ended at Charlottesville. The larger places—Hartford, New York, Trenton, Phila-

---

* Louise Hall Tharp, *The Baroness and the General*, 357. This spirited, knowledgeable book views the American Revolution through the eyes of the Riedesels.

delphia, Baltimore—were all purposely avoided. The small American guard—sometimes for short stretches there was no guard at all—could not prevent escapes in cities; quartering in barns or camping along the roadsides was safer for discipline. Through the Berkshires the track, not worthy being called a road, scaled heights and plunged down to icy streambeds. A toil for the marchers, it was worse for the poor horses, dragging baggage and supply wagons. Progress was slow, and some days of rest were allowed. Crossing the larger rivers—the Connecticut, Hudson, Susquehanna, Potomac—in flatboats required hours at each stream, and involved a few drownings.

The trek—almost 680 miles—took over three months, and often the weary men, women, and children had to spend their nights bivouacked in the winter woods with no covering. Food was scarce in the thinly populated districts through which they passed. The guards, relays of militia, took little pains to prevent desertion by the Germans along the way. Madame Riedesel and her children had a comfortable vehicle for the journey and a baggage wagon besides; the privations were greater for the footsore marchers. However, the wife of the German General, after a long day of travel, was many times refused food and lodging. "Why have you come out of your land to kill us, and waste our goods and possessions?" was a question which she could not answer. Her only reply was to point to her three small daughters, hungry and wan, and beg aid for them. That brought a response, though usually grudging.

Finally arrived at Charlottesville, and discovering that the English prisoners were to be quartered there, the Germans were taken into the hills a few miles to the west; there barracks were supposed to have been constructed for them and supplies of provisions had been ordered laid in. The weather had been smiling until the last lap of the trudge. Now snow fell. The barracks were found to be roofless, and many of the prisoners preferred what shelter was afforded by the woods. Except for tainted meat, the only food was cornmeal. The cut-up carcasses of cattle and hogs had been rubbed with ashes, because salt could not be procured, and were buried in pits in the earth; the top layers turned putrid, and those below were smelly and wormy. Governor Thomas Jefferson made excuses for the bad reception.

From this depressing beginning, conditions in the prisoners' camp soon improved. The men finished building the barracks, General Riedesel distributed large quantities of vegetable seeds, and gardens and poultry yards furnished fresh supplies. Those who chose to take employment in the surrounding country were allowed to do so; a couple of hundred deserted and established families in that locality.

When General Leslie entered eastern Virginia and Lord Cornwallis was expected up from the Carolinas, it was feared that the English would retake the Saratoga prisoners. In November and December 1780 they were marched farther inland, the English to Frederick, Maryland, and the Germans to Winchester, Virginia. In these places they were later joined by Cornwallis' army, which had surrendered at Yorktown. It was not until May 1783 that the last were released.

Broken Engagement

CONGRESS WELCHED ON THE TERMS OF BURGOYNE'S SUR-
RENDER, TO WHICH GATES HAD AGREED. THIS WAS A
SORRY EPISODE, THOUGH IT TURNED OUT THAT THE BRIT-
ish also intended to break their word. Members of Congress who
joined in the violation of the "convention" of capitulation self-
consciously protested that they did not subject "the Honour of the
House or of its Constituents to any unfavourable imputation from
the world." They did exactly that. The unspoken motive was to re-
claim an advantage which General Gates had forfeited. The convention provided that Burgoyne's troops should be returned to Europe on the promise that they would not fight against the United
States in the present conflict. But nothing prevented them from
being used for garrison duty in England or elsewhere, releasing
forces that might be transported to America in time for the next
campaign.

Judging from the record, this oversight on Gates' part did not
immediately stir Congress to correct it. News of the surrender
came to Congress at York, Pennsylvania, on October 21, 1777—

not from General Gates, but in letters from Washington at White-marsh and Putnam at Fishkill, both of which had enclosed copies of a letter written by Governor George Clinton, at Kingston, on October 15. Clinton wrote that at eight o'clock the previous evening "a capitulation was signed, whereby General Burgoyne and [his] whole army surrendered themselves prisoners of war." It was not until ten days later, on October 31, that Colonel James Wilkinson, Gates' Adjutant, arrived with official notice from Gates with a copy of the convention. After copies were dispatched to Washington by express, these papers were referred to the board of war. The committee of intelligence was to publish the convention. The states were recommended to set apart a day of thanksgiving for the signal success over the country's enemies.

From York, Eliphalet Dyer wrote to Gates on November 5, giving thanks for "the glorious Success with which the Almighty have Crowned your most faithful Endeavours," and assuring him that Congress are "entirely satisfied in your Closing the Convention, at the time, and in the manner you did." Three weeks later, when Congress gave evidence of wanting to wriggle out of Gates' engagement, Lovell of Massachusetts wrote to the General: "the drift of the Proceedings was by no means intended to throw any slur on your acceptance of the Convention."

The laggard Wilkinson explained that he had sundry papers to lay before Congress, "as soon as he could have time to digest and arrange them." Also, he had answers to questions about the situation of the American army and that of the enemy "before, at the time of, and since the capitulation of Gen. Burgoyne."

Congress gave Wilkinson until November 3 to get his information in order. Evidently in the interval he had become aware of criticism of Gates for yielding too much to the vanquished Burgoyne, and he mustered excuses. He had it in charge from General Gates to represent to the Congress "that Lieutenant General Burgoyne, at the time he capitulated, was strongly entrenched on a formidable post, with twelve days' provision." The reduction of

Fort Montgomery and progress of the enemy up the Hudson endangered the arsenal at Albany, "a reflection which left General Gates no time to contest the capitulation with Lieutenant General Burgoyne, but induced the necessity of immediately closing with his proposals, hazarding a disadvantageous attack, or retiring from his position for the security of our magazine; this delicate situation abridged our conquests, and procured for Lieutenant General Burgoyne the terms he enjoys." If Burgoyne had been attacked, "the dismemberment of our army must necessarily been such as would have incapacitated it from further action." Having chosen as he did, General Gates, "With an army in healthy vigour, and spirits, now awaits the commands of the hon^ble Congress." Wilkinson then tendered numerous papers, communications between Gates and Burgoyne, and a report of men and material surrendered.

The next day the elated Congress passed over the apologies for Gates, and formally thanked him, Lincoln, Arnold, and the other officers and troops for the victories at Bennington, Fort Schuyler, and Saratoga. Particularizing the crowning success, Congress reversed the excuses Wilkinson had offered. The main enemy army of 6000, under Burgoyne, "after being beaten in different actions and driven from a formidable post and strong entrenchments, [was] reduced to the necessity of surrendering themselves upon terms honourable and advantageous to these states [and] to Major General Gates." The board of war was ordered to have a gold medal struck and presented to Gates.

Two days afterwards, Congress, still in the mood of high satisfaction, approved a proposal of the board of war that Colonel Wilkinson receive the brevet of Brigadier General. This was "in consideration of his services in [the Northern] department, being strongly recommended by General Gates as a gallant officer, and a promising military genius, and having brought the dispatches to Congress, giving an account of the surrender of Lieutenant General Burgoyne and his army, on the 17th day of October last."

A fortnight later, Congress had second thoughts about the com-

plete conquest at Saratoga. The committee to which the return of
ordnance and stores surrendered had been referred reported that
there was astonishingly less than had been expected. There were
no standards, military chest, medicines, or tents. The quantity of
powder was minimal, only seventeen barrels; fixed ammunition
was inconsiderable; the 4647 muskets did not equal the number of
prisoners, "and all these muskets are unfit for service." The number
of bayonets was "greatly inferior" to the muskets, and bayonets and
cutlasses were without scabbards or belts. Most unaccountably,
there were only 638 cartouch boxes. An express went to Gates de-
siring answers to questions such as "What is become of the standards belonging to . . . General Burgoyne's army?" "Where is the
military chest and medicines?" "What is become of the cartouch
boxes?" "How comes the quantity of powder and cartridges to be
so small?" "Was there any destruction, waste, removal or concealment of the arms, tents, colours, treasure, or other military stores
belonging to General Burgoyne's army from the time the first proposal was made, on the 13 October, to the time of surrender?"

Congress was not prepared, on mere report of deficiencies in surrendered goods, to recede from the convention. It was *"Resolved,
that it is not to be understood that the embarkation of the troops
under Lieutenant General Burgoyne is in any wise to be delayed
on account of the foregoing queries if transports arrive before the
answers are returned and the enquiry directed is finished."* In this
temper of trust and forbearance, motions that a committee should
repair to Albany, and that General Heath should determine the
state of Burgoyne's supplies prior to surrender, were defeated.

Despite the feared shortages, and the permission given Burgoyne
to return his army to Europe, General Gates was much in the as-
cendant. Thomas Mifflin promoted his friend's glory and thereby
shook off criticisms of his own performance as Quartermaster General. Congress allowed Mifflin to resign that office on the plea of
ill health, but continued his rank as Major General (without pay)

and named him to the board of war. Mifflin accepted, and so did Adjutant General Timothy Pickering, but Robert H. Harrison, Washington's secretary, declined. Thereat Congress was informed "that General Mifflin has expressed a warm Sollicitude that Major General Gates should be appointed President of the Board." Mifflin's esteem for Gates implied a lack of confidence in Washington as Commander in Chief. Mifflin urged the preferment of Gates "from a conviction that his Military Skill would suggest Reformations in the different Departments of the Army essential to good Discipline, Order and Oeconomy, and that his Character and Popularity in the Army would facilitate the execution of such Reformations . . . a Task . . . more arduous and important than the formation of any new Establishment, however wise it may be in Theory."

Congress lost no time in adding Gates, Joseph Trumbull, and Richard Peters to the war board. Gates was informed he should be president of it in view of "the high sense Congress entertain of the general's . . . peculiar fitness to discharge the duties of that important office, upon the right execution of which the success of the American cause does eminently depend." Gates was "to officiate at the board, or in the field, as occasion may require." This appointment placed Gates above Washington in conduct of the war.

At the same time, Congress, in a whirl, attempted to prod Washington. A committee of three was named to repair to the army and consider with Washington "the best . . . means for carrying a winter's campaign with vigour and success, an object which Congress have much at heart."

This was one of the most untimely proposals, to give it no harsher name, that Congress ever made. Whether the success at Saratoga was the mad excitant, or Congress was simply incapable of realizing the desperate condition of the army, fortunately Washington answered with a stinging reproof. Also the committee deputed for the outlandish errand—Robert Morris, Elbridge Gerry, and Joseph Jones—did not share the delirium of their fellows. The departments of Quartermaster and Commissary of Purchases were in collapse, the surplus of paper money was hastening to its ruin, the loan offices were drained, taxes did not exist, and the neglected troops were starving and freezing on the eve of worse suffering at Valley Forge. Rather than sell for worthless currency, the farmers kept their grain in the sheaf; Congress was directing Washington, after giving due notice, to impress the wheat within seventy miles of his camp, assign 150 soldiers to thresh it, and compel the mills to grind.

Congress now began to suspect Burgoyne's good faith, which led to unworthy means of retracting what Gates, and Congress itself, had at first accepted. Information was received that General Howe, or General Burgoyne by Howe's direction, was about to apply for leave to embark the surrendered troops from Rhode Island or some part of Long Island Sound. Since such a request, if complied with, "may be attended with consequences highly injurious to the interest of these United States," therefore Congress resolved it "be utterly rejected." The troops in question, "when they do embark, must be shipped from the port stipulated by the convention [Boston] and no other." The idea was that, as the enemy held both Rhode Island and New York, it could be the British design to liberate many of the surrendered soldiers. Generals Gates, Heath, and the Council of Massachusetts were to be alerted against the possible ruse.

Congress was not deterred from finding grounds for quarrel with Burgoyne when Gates reported that the enemy was not at fault in the surrender of arms and supplies. Gates accepted Burgoyne's word that the military chest and standards had been left in Canada; "the other suspicious Appearances"—James Lovell quoting Gates—"sprang from the Conduct of our own People and certain Necessities, but not from any Breach of the Convention by the Will of Genl. Burgoyne or his Officers." Another delegate said Gates accounted for the arms being unfit for service, and the want of cartouch boxes and scabbards for the bayonets; on the whole "things have been conducted tolerably well."

Congress prepared to search the best writers on international law, in the determination of catching Burgoyne in error in one respect or another. Daniel Roberdeau of Pennsylvania wrote to Governor Wharton, at his temporary capital at Lancaster, hoping that copies of Pufendorf, Vattel, and Grotius had been brought there from Philadelphia. Wharton was able to oblige, and the legislators fortified themselves from high authority. An early question was whether those missing cartouch boxes did not fall in the category of "arms" that were to be yielded up.

Burgoyne objected to instructions of Congress to General Heath that the noncommissioned officers and privates of the convention troops be individually described, as to birthplace, age, physical measurements, and complexion, so that anyone breaking his parole could be identified. Burgoyne claimed that General Carleton had paroled his American prisoners at Ticonderoga without any such requirement. However, Elias Boudinot, the American Commissary of Prisoners, exhibited proof to the contrary.

Also, Congress questioned whether the transports proposed to be furnished to take the convention troops to Europe were of sufficient tonnage to accommodate them along with the necessary provisions and fuel. General Heath, who had charge of the prisoners, should satisfy himself on this head. Also, any balance due from the British to the United States for maintenance of the prisoners must be paid in gold or silver at the rate of 4s. 6d. to the continental paper dollar. This was far more in hard money than the equivalent in continental paper currency, but Congress offered the excuse that the British had depressed the latter by their industry in counterfeiting.

Henry Laurens, President of Congress, wrote to General Heath that these conditions, insisted on before embarkation could take place, "will employ some days and gain so much time" without impugning the honor of the United States.

Omissions by the surrendered enemy were marginal and

disputable—"mere bagatelle" Henry Laurens called them—
and would not have stood in the way of faithful execution of the
convention had Congress been so disposed. Then Burgoyne impetu-
ously furnished a better handle for the United States to refuse compliance. He complained in a letter to Gates that the quarters provided for his officers at Cambridge were inferior to what the
capitulation called for, and that, therefore, "the public faith is
broke" by the victor. It was explained in reply that there were
problems in finding room in an already crowded town, and it was
felt that the accusation was "highly wrought." But this justification
did not keep Congress from making the most of Burgoyne's hasty
words.

Late in December, Congress spent two long days in committee
of the whole, assembling its indictment that would permit it to
sidestep the Saratoga agreement. President Laurens had been driven
to his bed by gout in both feet and for three days and nights had
not slept, he declared, as many hours. He offered to resign his office, but his determination to prevent Burgoyne's troops from returning to Europe was stronger than his sufferings. Laurens permitted himself to be carried to his presidential chair, where he was
swathed in blankets. The grave Dr. John Witherspoon congratulated himself that he had arrived at York "just in time to help on"
the blocking of Burgoyne's departure. So far as can be told from
the scantily recorded votes, only four delegates constantly opposed
the shabby conduct of Congress: Dana, Ellery, and Dyer from New
England, and Harvie from Virginia; the excellent Abraham Clark
from New Jersey stood with them until the very last, then voted
with the great majority.

On December 27, 1777, the committee of the whole reported its
escape resolutions. The first in effect called Burgoyne a liar. His
charge of a breach of faith by the United States, Congress recited,
"betrays a disposition of availing himself of such declaration in
order to disengage himself and the army under him of the obliga-

tions they are under . . . and . . . the security which these states have hitherto had in his personal honor is hereby destroyed." Next, Burgoyne had not ordered the cartouch boxes and some other accoutrements to be delivered up as required by the convention, and Congress doubted Burgoyne's word that his army standards had been left in Canada. Nevertheless, Congress would overlook the noncompliance by Burgoyne, solemnly ratify the convention, and release the prisoners "whenever the King of Great Britain shall . . . cause his ratification of the . . . agreement to be properly notified to these states," not alleging any falsity on the part of Congress. Until then the embarkation would be "suspended."

Of course the royal assent, if given at all, could not reach the United States for several months, and then more time must elapse before the convention troops could be landed in Europe. That is to say, the loophole that Gates had allowed in the terms of surrender was closed. The prisoners of war would be kept in America past the time that the enemy could place them on guard duty and release other troops to be shipped over for the coming campaign. Within a few days Congress approved, with verbal changes, the conclusions of the committee of the whole.

Congress had no business interfering in the terms of surrender agreed upon by the military Commanders, Gates and Burgoyne. Congress did not demand the right to ratify General Lincoln's surrender of Charleston to General Sir Henry Clinton. Certainly Congress did not, later on, expect that King George would approve the articles of capitulation of Lord Cornwallis at Yorktown. Nevertheless, the Americans yielded to the temptation to break the engagement and keep the surrendered troops prisoners on this side of the water. Nothing was said of the remissness of the American hero, though Horatio Gates as much as admitted his fault in his effort to explain it away. The blame, with whatever straining, had to be put on Burgoyne. The Continental Congress, in the conduct of the Revolutionary War, was often unwise and more often neglectful of its duty to its fighting men and to the whole people, but it usually managed to avoid hypocrisy, or worse, dishonesty. In refusing to carry out the conditions given Burgoyne in the Saratoga surrender, several members of Congress too much protested their virtue. The President of the body dismissed the few opponents of the disingenuous measure as "timorous dunces." "The Justice and good Policy of the Act," he declared, "will be acknowledged by every disinterested court in Europe." Baron de Kalb, the European, doubtless saw the conflict between integrity and expediency, but Henry Laurens assured him that "Mr. Burgoyne's duplicity will be quoted as a precedent by future Writers, while the resentment of Congress will be recorded as an example of sound policy." Witherspoon pronounced the obstruction by Congress "both just, and necessary."

General Burgoyne remonstrated against the suspended embarkation of his army, and asked permission for himself, with some of his officers, to sail for England on account of his health. Congress refused to recede from its action, but allowed Burgoyne to embark immediately on parole, with promise to return if required. Months later Sir Henry Clinton protested the continued detention of the convention troops, but Congress declined to answer the "insolent" demand.

The foregoing is what was known to Americans. More than 150 years later it transpired that all the while the British high command had intended the falsity which Congress had suspected. When the papers of Sir Henry Clinton became available, they disclosed a letter from General Howe to General Burgoyne, dated November 16, 1777. Burgoyne was instructed to "give your secret Directions to the Commanding Officer of the Navy, convoying the Transports, who is instructed to follow your Orders for the Destination of the Troops, that, when they are embarked he is to proceed with the British Artillery Men and Infantry to New York, my design being to exchange the Officers for those of the Rebels I sent in last winter, in full Confidence of receiving an equal Number in Return, which, notwithstanding my repeated Applications has been pointedly refused under the most frivolous Pretences." Howe added, "I conceive it is necessary to use every possible Precaution to keep the Enemy ignorant of my Intentions, as on the least suspicion the Troops wd. be infallibly stopt."

General Washington refused to release prisoners in his hands equal in number to those liberated by Howe on the ground that he would not exchange soldiers who had been well treated and were in excellent physical condition for the unserviceable wrecks that Howe was returning.

Howe was willing that the German troops in Burgoyne's surrendered army be returned to Europe, for he had a low opinion of their performance.

So the two sides, the American Congress and the British Commanders, were alike willing, on one excuse or another, to break a solemn engagement. The only difference was that the Americans held the whip hand and were able to prevent the embarkation of the prisoners onto British vessels which would transfer them to the power of the enemy.

The convention troops, though they loudly complained that they were badly quartered and fed in Cambridge, were star boarders, so long as the British paid in gold for their keep. The hard money was most welcome to the New England economy. When it became evident that the prisoners were not to be given up on any terms, the British refused further payments, and the United States determined to march them to Virginia, where they could be most cheaply maintained.

Flaming Frontiers

THE WARFARE SPONSORED BY THE BRITISH AGAINST INTE-
RIOR SETTLEMENTS DURING THE AMERICAN REVOLUTION
WAS IRRESPONSIBLE ON THREE MAIN COUNTS: IT INVOLVED
the killing of unarmed inhabitants, including women and children,
the indiscriminate destruction of homes and plunder of belongings,
and the employment of Indians whose savagery was not prevented.
Typically, the raiding parties have been called "vultures . . . glut-
ting their appetites in the Mohawk and Schoharie settlements."
The principal Indian leader was "the monster Brant," and the
Tory officers, Colonel John Butler and his son, Captain Walter
Butler, were no less villainous. The recital of particular cruelties in
place after place, including chance individual murders and tortures,
has documented the picture and deepened its bloody coloring.

On the other hand, the conflict on the frontier, while directed by
military authorities from Canada, was part of the civil war between the loyalists and the patriots. The loyalists, it is explained,
were in arms seeking redress of grievances or revenge for expropriation of their property and expulsion from their communities. They

were meeting violence with violence. Some were in uniform, as Sir John Johnson's Royal Greens or Colonel John Butler's Rangers, but others joined the retaliatory bands as volunteers.

Excuse for participation of five of the Six Nations of Iroquois —the Oneidas were neutral—is harder. True, they were traditional allies of the British, and they affected hostility to colonists who broke from duty to their King. Also certain Indian villages were destroyed in military expeditions and Indians were massacred by parties of patriots in years prior to the massive punitive expedition of Sullivan's army in 1779. Thereafter, when the Indians were able to continue their attacks they were plainly giving tit for tat. The red men had seen their hunting grounds taken over by westward-moving white settlers. The Indians' best hope of preserving their way of life in familiar places was by defending British rule. At the same time, the tribes were attached to their "White Father across the Waters" because his agents gave them brass kettles, blankets, muskets and ammunition, and rum, while treaties with the colonists were less rewarding.

Faults were not all on one side. American military officers courted Indian allies, utilized warriors in joint operations, and encouraged friendly bands to attack villages of the "hostiles." However, the patriots' success in attracting Indians' help in the border warfare was on a smaller scale and, if only for that reason, was less reprehensible than the practice of the British and loyalists.

Sullivan's scouring of the Iroquois country was provoked. The British, loyalists, and Indians were the first offenders. The Indians were sharers in, if not perpetrators of, the most revolting crimes against the frontier settlers. The villages of the tribes were the only possible objects of attack; the desolation of their towns was complete. If left anything to come back to, the red men would have promptly resumed their ravages. To a great extent their lives as well as their habitations were the forfeit, for many perished in the exile with the British in Canada, to which they were driven. However one views it, and comprehending all of the sufferers, the fighting on the frontiers was a melancholy chapter of the American Revolution.

Thayendenagea (Joseph Brant), the Mohawk, war chief of the Iroquois, was the villain of the piece, even more in story than in fact. His career was a bundle of contradictions. He became the principal man in a matriarchal society, but the identity of his mother is unknown. He smeared paint on his face to terrify his enemies, but his portrait was painted by a famous artist to please his friends. A Christian, he translated Scripture into a savage tongue and built a church, but he was blamed for the murder of women and children, and his knife caused the death of his own son. He went from smoky lodges in the forest to be entertained in the drawingrooms of London. He gallantly kissed the hand of Queen Charlotte, but refused to bow dutifully before King George. A Baroness praised his "polished manners," but he doctored himself with boiled rattlesnake. He failed to prevent the expulsion of his people from their lands and living, then re-established them in exile. He displayed the extremes of tenderness and cruelty, but was esteemed for balanced judgment.

Brant was born in 1742, in the wilderness on the banks of the Ohio, and he died in 1807, waited on by slaves on his estate in Canada. He was the protégé and brother-in-law of Sir William Johnson, Royal Indian Superintendent. He was in Sir William's campaigns in the French and Indian War, first as a stripling follower at the battle of Lake George, later as a warrior in the capture of Niagara. Sir William sent him to Moor's Indian Charity School in Connecticut. Here he arrived in 1761, "considerably clothed, Indian fashion, and could speak a few words of English." After less than two years with his books, he returned to the Indian country on a missionary errand, but promptly enlisted to defend English claims against Pontiac's rebellious Western tribes.

When Pontiac's rising was quelled, Brant built himself a good house at Canajoharie, married the daughter of an Oneida chief, and settled down to one of his few intervals of peace and domesticity. He became widely known in all the tribes as Sir William Johnson's agent in councils. When Sir William died in 1774, he left his empire of influence with the Six Nations of Indians to his son, Sir John Johnson, his son-in-law, Colonel Guy Johnson, and Joseph Brant. This was the eve of the American Revolution, in which historic epoch the work of the old, wise superintendent was to be destroyed forever. His successors held the tribes, except for the Oneidas, loyal to the British, but that proved the Indians' undoing.*

Of Sir William's heirs, Joseph Brant is rightly the best remembered. His bloody struggles in the frontier warfare were fervently aided by his sister Molly, Sir William's long-time mistress and wife. After the peace Brant did more than others to salvage his people's losses. Only he was the champion who triumphed over defeat.

The battle of Lexington gave Guy Johnson and Brant the signal for action. They summoned the tribes to councils and took principal chiefs in their escort to Montreal, where they pledged to Sir Guy Carleton, Governor of Canada, their eagerness to fight for the King. Brant was commissioned a Captain in the British army and sent to repeat to Their Majesties the Indians' allegiance in the conflict. Brant talked about leading 3000 tribesmen against the rebellious colonists, though he never commanded more than a third of that number in an engagement.

Brant's first powerful stroke, August 6, 1777, was his ambush of General Nicholas Herkimer's 800 militia, who were marching to the relief of Fort Stanwix (now Rome, New York). Colonel Barry St. Leger was besieging Stanwix in his march from Lake Ontario to join Burgoyne's thrust into the Hudson valley. Learning of Her-

* See James Thomas Flexner's moving account, *Mohawk Baronet, Sir William Johnson of New York.*

kimer's near approach, St. Leger detached Tories (Royal Greens and Butler's Rangers) and Brant's Indians to destroy the reinforcement. Brant chose the ravine of Oriskany creek for the ambush.

Herkimer had sent forward messengers to the fort to arrange for a sortie by the garrison the moment the militia appeared. St. Leger's force would be beset front and rear. The signal was to be three cannon fired in rapid succession. Long past the hour expected, no guns were heard. Herkimer was for waiting, but his officers goaded him to press ahead. Actually his prudence could not have saved his men from the death trap. They had to descend the steep slope, cross the boggy bottom, and struggle up the other side. Their encircling enemies were posted to spring when Herkimer's column was negotiating the deep gully.

Herkimer, on his white horse, was a target. His mount was killed, and he was badly wounded in the leg. The musketballs poured in from unseen assailants. Amidst the confusion of surprise, the General was carried to high ground; there, propped against a tree, he directed the rally of his militia. The Indians, before a man could reload, pounced with tomahawk and knife. Herkimer countered this by posting his soldiers in pairs, one to fire while the other recharged his piece. The fighting, however, became hand-to-hand, bayonets and hatchets against gunstocks. Some of the goriest fighting of the war took place in and bordering that gorge of Oriskany. The rear guard of 200, protecting the wagons, had not entered the sink, and they escaped the Indians' pursuit. The surrounded 600, though rapidly falling, took such a toll that Brant's warriors sounded their cry of retreat, "Oonah! Oonah!" The Tories dispersed with them into the forest. How murderous the in-fighting was speaks in the casualties: the killed outnumbered the wounded probably by three or four to one. The count of the fallen is uncertain; Herkimer's militia lost 200 to 250, the attackers perhaps a hundred fewer. That the Rangers and red men withdrew made the carnage technically a victory for the Tryon provincials, but they were too exhausted to follow up their desperate resistance.

Their better success was in the aftereffect on the Indians. Back at Stanwix, furious at their punishment and fearful of Benedict Arnold, who was nearing to rescue the fort, they rioted, broke open the stores of liquor, and menaced their British Commander. As often after a fight, whether they won or lost, neither Brant nor anyone else could control them. St. Leger's invasion stopped at Stanwix. Instead of reinforcing Burgoyne, he retraced his march to Oswego and Canada.

With proper care, the worthy General Herkimer would have survived the amputation of his leg. As it was, gangrene ended his weeks of suffering.

A mid-nineteenth-century chronicler wrote of the Wyoming valley in northeastern Pennsylvania, "The scenery around is wild and picturesque, while the valley itself might be chosen for another paradise." The earliest settlers were led by the benevolent Moravian Count Zinzendorf, apostle of good will and peace with the Indians. Loveliness of nature and harmony of life were reversed in the sequel. From the time the first permanent community was established, in 1769, there were thirty years of bitter dissension between rival claimants of Pennsylvania and Connecticut (the "Pennamite-Yankee wars"). As if a punishment for internal violence came the horror of massacre and desolation by Tories and Indians in 1778. A generation later, in 1808, a tavern keeper, Jesse Fell, demonstrated that "stone coal" (anthracite) could be burned in an open grate. Thenceforth the future of the valley lay underground. The richest crop was not corn, but coal. Farming yielded to furnaces and factories, and to the latest desecration, strip-mining.

The modern city of Wilkes-Barre is about at the center of the Wyoming valley, which reaches twenty-five miles along the north branch of the Susquehanna River. High hills enclose a level some three miles wide. In 1778, in spite of occasional Indian forays and the settlers' own disruptions, the valley contained about 5000 people. With the outbreak of the Revolution, many Tories had left, but many of loyalist sympathies remained among the predominantly patriot population. The valley had furnished three companies to the continental army and retained 700 soldiers in the militia. The fertile fields were the source of large quantities of grain for Washington's troops. The peril of Indian attacks was evident in "forts" on both sides of the river, seven of them in a stretch of ten miles. Most were flimsy affairs, stockaded houses garrisoned by a dozen men, in which families of the immediate vicinity huddled in alarms. Fort Wyoming, at what is now Wilkes-Barre, Fort Durkee below, and Forty Fort above were stronger. Colonel Zebulon Butler was in command in the valley, with a garrison of sixty in Forty Fort.

In June 1778, Guy Johnson and Colonel John Butler, with 400 Royal Greens and Rangers, assorted loyalists, and 500 Indians, set out from Niagara to invade the Wyoming precincts. Though Joseph Brant was afterwards blamed for the atrocities of the Indians —give a dog a bad name—he was not present at Wyoming. The tribesmen, chiefly Senecas, were commanded by Chief Giengwatah, whose name means, appropriately, "He who Goes in the Smoke." At Tioga, the expedition descended the Susquehanna to within twenty miles of the Wyoming, then left their canoes and rafts to march into the valley.

The first act told what was to come. Half of a party of eight men working in a field were killed, the others were captured. They belonged to little Fort Jenkins, which, thus weakened, was easily taken. Near-by Fort Exeter, which was garrisoned by Tories, surrendered. July 1 the invaders were welcomed by the Tory family of Philip Wintermoot, whose log buildings were defended by a stockade. There Johnson and Butler made their headquarters.

Colonel Zebulon Butler immediately called the militia of the valley to Forty Fort, three and a half miles toward the enemy from Fort Wyoming in Wilkes-Barre village. Only 300 responded; others refused to quit the scattered stockades where they were protecting their women and children. With his small force Butler started against the enemy, but he then returned to Forty Fort to await reinforcement. The messengers could not bring speedy help for a reason unknown to Wyoming. Washington's army had just fought the fierce battle of Monmouth and was catching its breath at New Brunswick, New Jersey, more than a hundred miles from the invaded valley. Colonel Butler's patience was overruled, the militia were again mustered July 3, and they marched in the hope of taking Fort Wintermoot by surprise. It is hard to credit this optimism, for an enemy force of more than a thousand had spilled over the area. An Indian gave the alarm, and the approaching patriots found the Tories and Senecas drawn up in line of battle. The patriots also formed, with the militia on the left, faced by Indians.

It was on the left flank that trouble first developed for the valley men. Seeing that Indians were getting around the end of his line, Colonel Nathan Denison ordered a company to turn to prevent being enveloped. If the movement could have been swiftly executed, the red men might have been forced back. Instead, in the stress of the fight, the militia company thought they had been commanded to retreat. The whole of the patriot line followed their example. The shrieking Indians closed in with tomahawks. As many in the militia were oldsters and boys, it is remarkable that they resisted in the personal combat before becoming demoralized. Some fled toward the mountains, others were shot as they tried to swim the river. Valley Tories joined the enemy in the slaughter.

Only sixty of the patriot force escaped. Almost all of the officers were killed—a Colonel, a Lieutenant Colonel, a Major, ten Captains, six Lieutenants, two Ensigns. The Tory Ranger Colonel reported 227 scalps taken, "and only 5 prisoners. . . . The Indians were so exasperated with their loss last year, near Fort Stanwix (at the battle of Oriskany) that it was with the greatest difficulty I could save the lives of those few." The raiders lost only three killed and eight wounded.

Through the night after the battle prisoners were tortured, then slain. It is said that "Queen Esther" (also called Catherine) Montour, "the witch of Wyoming," directed this fiendish cruelty. She was one of the third generation of women, part French, part Indian, living with the Iroquois. That night at Wyoming, the tradition is, she commanded braves to hold sixteen prisoners on a rock while she knifed them to death.

Two officers, Colonels Butler and Denison, had collected a remnant of their garrison at Fort Wyoming. The loyalist leader demanded their surrender. Butler was opposed, and when the soldiers insisted that they could not hold out, he made off, leaving the command to Denison, who capitulated. The agreement was that the settlers were to be disarmed, public stores should be handed over, and the property of Tories must be restored. In return, the invaders promised they would respect the lives and property of the people.

The promise that there would be no destruction was completely violated. Colonel Butler, the Tory commander, reported to his superior: "In this incursion we have taken and destroyed eight palisaded forts, and burned about one thousand dwelling houses, all their mills, etc. We have also killed and drove off about 1000 head of horned cattle, and sheep and swine in great numbers. But what gives me the sincerest satisfaction is that . . . in the destruction of this settlement, not a single person has been hurt of the inhabitants but such as were in arms. To those, indeed, the Indians gave no quarter."

While there was no massacre of the general population, the utter devastation of the valley drove the settlers into precipitate flight. The way through passes in the mountains (Water Gap and

Wind Gap) entailed dreadful hardships: babies were born on the trails, children perished. One mother, unable to bury her dead infant, and warned of the visit of wolves, carried the little corpse twenty miles to a settlement. Some families were captured by Indians. Many of the fugitives who, in their dismay, wandered into a great swamp in the Poconos gave the place its name, "Shades of Death."

⌐

In the morning mist, Tory Rangers and Indians pounced upon the settlement of Cherry Valley, New York, in the cruelest raid of Revolutionary border warfare. The day was November 11, 1778. The 200 Tories were led by young Captain Walter Butler, the 500 Seneca and Cayuga Indians by Captain Joseph Brant. Butler had made a loop from the southwest down the Chemung River to the Susquehanna, up to the foot of Otsego Lake and on a dozen miles northeast to Cherry Valley; substituting present place names, the route was by Elmira, Binghamton, and Cooperstown. Brant was on his way from the Susquehanna back to Niagara. It is not known whether the parties joined forces by prearrangement, probably at Oquago (Windsor, near Binghamton), or crossed paths by chance. The excuse has been offered for the Mohawk chief that the meeting was accidental, that he was reluctant to take his Indians on the detour to Cherry Valley, and that Butler was in chief command. On the other hand, a rendezvous seems likely, since Butler's Rangers alone were fewer than the garrison of 250 Massachusetts continentals in the fort of the settlement.

Lafayette, in that area earlier in the year, incident to his abortive "irruption" into Canada, had ordered the village meetinghouse to be surrounded by a strong stockade. Unwisely, the offer of the valiant Colonel Peter Gansevoort to assume command of the important post was refused in favor of Colonel Ichabod Alden, who, like his men, was unfamiliar with frontier fighting. Alden was incompetent besides. In spite of several warnings of impending attack, most pointedly from Fort Schuyler only three days in advance of the tragedy, his only precaution was to send out scouts, and they missed the assailants' approach. Alden did not gather the people and their belongings into the fort, and he and his officers lodged outside of it in dwellings in the village.

The first and bloodiest stroke was by the Indians, and perhaps some Tories, against the home of Robert Wells, ex-judge of the county. The house was packed to the roof with victims. Besides Wells' large family, Colonel Alden, Lieutenant Colonel William Stacey and some sixteen soldiers had quarters there. Dashing for the fort, Alden was shot, tomahawked, and scalped. Stacey was captured. Wells, his mother, wife, brother and sister, daughter, and three sons were murdered. All in the guard of soldiers were killed or captured. Besides those here slain, eighteen or nineteen inhabitants, mostly women and children, in six other homes, met the same fate.

Hugh Mitchell was working in the field when he saw the Indians coming. He hid in the woods until he thought the attack was over. On returning to the burning house he found his wife and three of the children killed and a daughter of ten left for dead. He had got the girl through the door in the effort to save her when she was hatcheted. (The following year General James Clinton tried and hanged a Tory sergeant, one Newberry, for this crime). Every one of the forty homes in the village, and their outbuildings, was burned to the ground.

Meantime, Butler's Rangers surrounded and for several hours kept up musket fire against the fort, whose garrison, though lacking the principal officers, bravely held out. The attackers had no artillery, and did not attempt a storm in the face of grapeshot from the fort. The Indians liked slaughtering helpless villagers better than the peril of dislodging palisaded troops. The garrison was too weak to risk a sortie.

In mid-afternoon, Butler and Brant gathered their Tories and tribesmen and withdrew with sixty prisoners and all the livestock they could collect. The first night's camp was only a couple of miles south of the destroyed village. There the plunder was divided. The prisoners, griefstricken from what they had witnessed, had only the clothes they stood in when yanked from their burning homes, and they suffered in the November chill. Next day, Captain Butler released all of the women and children except for two families. These were held as hostages for the liberation of Butler's mother and her younger children, who were prisoners of the patriots at Albany. Mrs. Samuel Campbell and four children, her mother, Mrs. Cannon, and Mrs. James Moore and her three daughters were kept because their men had been active in the border conflicts. On the second day of the march the Indians tomahawked Mrs. Cannon because she could not keep up. Farther along they murdered the Buxton family on Butternut Creek and burned the buildings. Mrs. Campbell, besides mothering her three children who could walk, carried her youngest, who was eighteen months old. The distress of the hostages was capped when the Senecas reached their castle of Kanadaseago. There the captives were obliged to witness the dance of triumph; the many scalps were paraded to accompaniment of the "death-halloo, the most terrific note which an Indian can raise."

Captain Walter Butler, in his letter to General Schuyler, seeking the exchange of his prisoners for the members of his father's family and others, was profuse in exculpating himself for the murders at Cherry Valley. "I have done every thing in my power," he protested, "to restrain the fury of the Indians from hurting women and children, or killing the prisoners who fell into our hands, and would have more effectually prevented them, but that they were much incensed by the late destruction of their village of Anguaga [Unadilla] by your people." He added the threat that unless his relatives at Albany were released he would "no longer take the same pains to restrain the Indians." General James Clinton promptly agreed to the exchange of prisoners, but with stern blame for the Rangers' and Indians' crimes at Cherry Valley and Wyoming.

Joseph Brant, whose Indians were accused by Butler of the slaughter of the innocents at Cherry Valley, was equally quick to disclaim personal responsibility. An apologist reported that Brant, fearing what would happen when his braves entered the village, meant to reach the Wells house ahead of them. "On his way it was necessary to cross a ploughed field, the yielding of the earth in which, beneath his tread, so retarded his progress, that he arrived too late." This celebrated Mohawk chief, whose step was supposed to be so light that a twig would not snap under his moccasin, was bogged down in the frosty furrows!

The next raid was similarly ravaging and bloody. Count Pulaski, after shifting his cavalry from one post to another, was assigned by Washington to the Indian frontier of New York. Pulaski, in the winter of 1778–79, found his position at Minisink in the Shawangunk mountains, ten miles west of Goshen the worst of all. His horsemen could not operate in the dense forests, nor could they intercept attacks in time to save the occupants of lonely cabins. The Count begged Congress to employ him "near the enemy's lines" and not "in a wilderness where there is nothing but bears to fight." In February 1779 he was ordered to join General Benjamin Lincoln in South Carolina. Had he remained at Minisink a few months longer, the destruction of that village and the tragedy that fell on the local militia in the sequel would not have occurred.

Joseph Brant in July 1779 had a considerable body of Indians and Tories, the latter dressed, or undressed, and painted like red men, at Grassy Brook, on the Delaware. He knew that Generals John Sullivan and James Clinton were preparing to unite their forces to invade the Iroquois country. Brant determined to create a diversion that he hoped would at least delay the start of the expedition. The unguarded settlement of Minisink invited his attack.

On July 19 he led a detachment of sixty Indians and twenty-seven loyalists to surprise the village, and they set the buildings ablaze before most of the people knew they were threatened. Everything was burned—ten homes, more barns, two mills, the empty fort. Several helpless villagers were killed, others were made prisoner. Brant reported that he would have taken more scalps except for "the many forts about the place into which they were always ready to run like ground hogs." Driving the cattle, the band of raiders returned to their companions in the camp at Grassy Brook.

As quickly as news of Minisink reached Goshen, Dr. Benjamin Tusten, commanding the local militia, ordered his men to meet him next day at the scene of the outrage. As only 150 collected, Tusten wanted to delay pursuit until more militia came in. A rash Major, Samuel Meeker, mounted his horse and called on brave neighbors to follow him, while cowards could stay behind. All accepted his challenge. They marched seventeen miles and next morning were joined by a small reinforcement under Colonel John Hathorn, who took command. They stopped where Brant's band had lain the previous night. Counting the number of campfires, Hathorn believed the enemy were of superior strength. He counseled further recruitment before following, but most were determined to press ahead. They were not deterred when Captain Tyler, scouting in advance, was killed from ambush.

Soon the pursuers, standing on a hilltop, could see the Indians preparing to ford the Delaware River. That would be the place to take them at a disadvantage. But Colonel Hathorn did not allow for the cunning of Joseph Brant. While the militia were descending blindly through the forest, the Mohawk leader suddenly turned and got his force into concealment close behind them. To the astonishment of the would-be attackers, Brant himself boldly appeared. He called on the militiamen to surrender and be unharmed, or his larger band would destroy them. A shot that clipped his belt was the only answer.

Brant dove back into the bushes, raised his war whoop, and the fight was on. The Indians and Tories cut off fifty of the militia and surrounded the others. Hathorn formed his men in a square enclosing an acre of ground. The firing kept up from near noon until sundown. Dr. Tusten, in a safer ravine, was caring for seventeen of the wounded when he and all of his charges were discovered and tomahawked. The ammunition of the militia ran low. With horrid yells the Indians and Tories burst through an undefended corner of the square. Hatchets and knives left only thirty of Hathorn's men alive to escape back to the settlements.

Passing over the acre of slaughter, Brant found Captain Gabriel Wisner so fearfully wounded that he could not survive. Rather than leave the man to be the living prey of wolves, Brant said afterwards, he dispatched the poor fellow with his tomahawk. The bones of the battle-dead whitened on the field in the forest for forty years before they were collected and given burial. The defeat of the militia made thirty-three widows in the Presbyterian congregation of Goshen.

New England militia, in an expedition against the Indians in the spring of 1782, captured peltry; in the bundle were eight packages intended to go to Governor Sir Frederick Haldimand of Canada. The accompanying letter, from James Craufurd, "Tioga, Jan'y 3, 1782," transmitted "eight packs of scalps, cured, dried, hooped, and painted with all the Indian triumphal marks." He enclosed a speech of the Seneca chiefs: "Father! We wish you to send these scalps over the water to the Great King, that he may regard them and be refreshed; and that he may see our faithfulness in destroying his enemies, and be convinced that his presents have not been made to ungrateful people. A blue and white belt with red tassels."

Craufurd's "invoice and explanation" covered, among others, package No. 14, "Containing 97 [scalps] of farmers; hoops green to show they were killed in their fields; a large white circle with a little round mark on it, for the sun, to show that it was in the day time; black bullet mark on some, hatchet on others." Scalps in pack No. 4 were painted with "a little yellow flame to denote their being of prisoners burnt alive, after being scalped. . . ." No. 5 was "88 scalps of women; hair long, braided . . . to show they were mothers. Skin yellow ground, with little red tadpoles, to represent . . . tears of grief [of] their relatives." No. 8 was a mixture of 122 scalps "with a box of birch bark, containing 29 infants' scalps of various sizes; small white hoops; white ground." It was said this was the harvest of three years on the frontiers of New York, New Jersey, Pennsylvania, and Virginia. The account, in William W. Campbell's *Annals of Tryon County* (1831), taxes credulity.

These murderous assaults under British auspices on the frontiers of Pennsylvania and New York could no longer be endured. Early in 1779, plans were laid for two bodies of troops, nearly 4000 in all, to join to punish the raiders. The larger force collected at Easton, Pennsylvania, and moved northward. The smaller army went from Canajoharie, New York, by Otsego Lake and the east branch of the Susquehanna to meet the first body at Tioga (now Athens, Pennsylvania). The invasion of the Indian country was to start May 15. Both divisions were delayed far beyond that date. Major General John Sullivan took charge at Easton the last week in May, a month later moved his headquarters to Wyoming (Wilkes-Barre), and did not march until the last day of July. Brigadier General James Clinton took command at Canajoharie the middle of June and got his 200 bateaux, by a twenty-mile land carriage, into Lake Otsego by the end of that month. The east branch of the Susquehanna flows from the foot of the lake, at what is now Cooperstown, New York. To secure a sufficient depth of water in the stream, Clinton dammed the lake, raising its level two feet. He broke the dam the second week in August, and the bateaux, carried on this artificial freshet, reached Tioga and Sullivan's division in a fortnight.

General Washington's orders to Sullivan stressed two requirements. The Indian villages should be not *"merely overrun,* but *destroyed,"* should meet with *"total* devastation." The command was several times repeated. This aim would be best achieved if the troops moved "as light and as little encumbered as possible. . . . If much time should be lost in transporting stores up the river, the provisions for the expedition will be consumed, and . . . the whole enterprise will be defeated." For this purpose they were to reject every article of baggage that could possibly be dispensed with. Washington remonstrated because Clinton burdened his division with excessive supplies, but this turned out to be fortunate because Pennsylvania had been stingy with Sullivan and had charged Congress high prices for the flour furnished him.

The summer was waning when, on August 26, 3600 fit men set out up the Susquehanna. The provisions and needed materials were divided between 150 boats and 1400 packhorses. The four brigades were commanded by Generals Clinton (New York troops), Enoch Poor (New Englanders), Edward Hand (Pennsylvanians), and William Maxwell (New Jersey regiments). Colonel Thomas Proctor's artillery consisted of four 3-pounders, two howitzers, and a small mortar. All were under the orders of General Sullivan. The route of this massive penetration of the interior lay north along the east bank of Seneca Lake to its outlet, where lay the principal Seneca "castle," Kanadesaga (variously spelled). The march then turned southwesterly to the farthest point reached, the Genesee River at Little Beard's Town, where Cuylerville now stands. The distance from Easton was 280 miles; the return march began September 15, following much the same way.

The hardships of the march were due more to swamps and mountains than to Senecas and Mohawks. The country of the Iroquois tribes (the Finger Lakes region of central New York) at that time had no white settlements and was traced only by Indian paths. Sullivan's marching formation called for skirmishers and light troops in advance with flanking parties, then the main body

[268]

with packhorses, artillery, and cattle in the center, followed by a rear guard. However, this order was seldom used because of the broken terrain. The force was strung out for five or six miles on narrow trails beside rivers and lakes or skirting densely forested hills. At some places axemen had to open the way for the artillery; corduroy roads had to be laid through marshes that were otherwise impassable by wheel.

The defeat of Indians and their British allies in a battle at Newtown (five miles south of present Elmira, New York) early in the campaign discouraged further resistance, except for a single ambush and occasional exchange of shots. What an emotional chaplain called "a march into the very jaws of the savages" was not that. Instead, the troops stealthily surrounded the villages, only to find them deserted. The Indians captured could be counted on the fingers of one hand. The real business of the expedition was the thorough destruction of the Indian towns, houses, crops, and orchards, which compelled the 20,000 tribesmen to resort to the British at Niagara for bare sustenance.

In the one real fight, at Newtown, 800 Indians, 300 British regulars, and a few Tory rangers were captained by leaders notorious for their ravages of frontier settlements. They were Colonel John Butler, his son Captain Walter Butler, Sir John Johnson, Guy Johnson, Captain John McDonnell, and, commanding the Indians, the Mohawk chief Joseph Brant. They had protected an advantageous position with a concealed fort, a rampart of logs disguised by small leafy trees cut and stuck in front.

On the morning of August 29, Sullivan's scouts detected the breastwork in time to alert the oncoming troops. The fight lasted six hours. The artillery blasted the log defenses and threw shells that burst in the rear. General Poor's men with difficulty ascended a rough steep hillside and gained the enemy's left flank. Here the contest was hottest. The troops used their bayonets to dislodge Indians from behind rocks and trees. All of Brant's encouragement of his warriors did not prevent their flight when they saw themselves about to be surrounded. They made off with such speed that, contrary to habit, they left two score of their dead on the field. Sullivan's troops pursued for two miles, killed and scalped eight Indians, and took two prisoners. Bloody, abandoned canoes were evidence of wounded that had been carried in the retreat. The Americans lost an officer and three privates killed, three officers and thirty-three privates wounded.

In the further progress of the march, every Indian village come upon was left in ashes. A small settlement might have only four or five huts, while larger "castles," especially to the westward, contained twenty-five or thirty, and in one case, more than a hundred houses. Generally these were of logs, but now and then a house was framed, painted, and supplied with a chimney, and contained conveniences for cooking and sleeping. The well-tended fields, 200 acres in one instance, were at the peak of their yield of "corn, beans, peas, squashes, potatoes, onions, turnips, cabbages, cucumbers, watermelons, carrots, and parsnips." There were also tobacco fields and large orchards of apples and peaches. The fruit trees were old, indicating long occupation of the site. Little Beard's Town on the Genesee seemed to have been prepared as the main supply depot of the Iroquois, who were said to have had the help of British troops and Tories in planting the crops.

The Indians clung to their villages until the army was almost upon them, then fled, leaving belongings that could not be carried and their fires still burning. The troops immediately began their work of ruin. The uprooted crops were stuffed in houses, which were then set ablaze, or the houses were pulled to pieces for fuel to consume the crops piled in the fields. Fifty or more men to the acre made short work of the devastation. Fruit trees were cut down or girdled. The regular army ration had been reduced to half, but now there was a surfeit of vegetables and fruit. The packhorses and cattle were abundantly fed without being turned loose in the woods. Smashing pumpkins and pulling bean vines did not call for a soldier's courage, but admirers of the expedition maintained its martial character. On the return march, detachments of a couple of hundred each scoured parts of the area that had been missed earlier.

When yet some miles from the supposed location of Little Beard's Town, General Sullivan detailed Lieutenant Thomas Boyd of the rifle corps to take two or three with him on a reconnaissance. Boyd made the mistake of enlarging his party to twenty-six, which was too many for secrecy and too few for defense. Instead of returning that night, Boyd and his companions slept in the vicinity of the village they sought. Early next morning they foolishly gave notice of their presence. Tim Murphy, the famous marksman, shot and scalped one of two Indians whom they spied. The other escaped and gave the alarm to the band of several hundred under Brant and Butler, who were spoiling for revenge on the invaders.

Boyd's party hastened back toward camp. They had covered five of the seven miles when Indians and Tory rangers rose in the woods all around them. Seventeen of the troops were promptly shot down. Boyd, Murphy, the Oneida guide Hanyerry, and the others tried to dash through the cordon of warriors. Murphy and three more made it, but Boyd and a man named Parker were captured. They were taken to Little Beard's Town and put to the torture. Lieutenant Boyd was stripped naked, tied to a tree, and beaten; his nails were pulled out, an eye was gouged, his ears and nose were cut off and the nose was thrust into his mouth from which the tongue had been sliced. In reporting this horror, Sullivan referred to "other tortures which decency will not permit me to mention." If accounts may be believed these included an incision in the abdomen from which an intestine was drawn and fastened to the tree. The victim was driven around the trunk, around which his bowels were wrapped. If that is true Boyd must have been dead before the final act of cutting off his head. Parker also was beheaded.

As soon as Murphy reached the camp, the light troops were sent to the relief of the ambushed party. They arrived only in time to bury the dead. Next day, on entering the deserted Beard's Town, the mangled bodies of Boyd and Parker were found and buried with military honors.

General Sullivan, in his report to Congress, claimed that his army had destroyed forty towns, scattered houses, and at least 160,000 bushels of corn, together with a vast quantity of vegetables. He believed that, except for one town near the Allegheny River, fifty miles from the main castle on the Genesee, not a single settlement remained in the country of the Five Nations. He declared "there [is not] even the appearance of an Indian on this side of Niagara." Washington had suggested to Sullivan that the Indians, when chastised, might be induced, as a condition of peace, to attack the British at Niagara. It would be highly desirable to have that post in American hands. Sullivan explained to Congress that he was not commanded to capture Niagara, but he might have attempted it if his provisions had been enough for fifteen days more of the campaign. Those on the expedition who were killed or died numbered forty, half of them members of Lieutenant Boyd's scouting party.

In addition to Sullivan's invasion of the Iroquois country, there was a 180-mile march, by Colonel Daniel Brodhead, commanding at Fort Pitt, against the Seneca and Muncy towns on the Allegheny River. His force of 600, including eight Delaware Indians, left Fort Pitt on August 11 and was gone a month. A dozen towns, abandoned on approach of the troops, and 500 acres of corn were destroyed. Packs of deerskins seized, estimated to be worth $30,000, were to be auctioned at Fort Pitt for the benefit of the officers and men. Aside from one skirmish with thirty or forty warriors on the Allegheny, no Indians were encountered. In that exchange of shots the braves were worsted and scampered off, leaving their canoes, gear, and five dead; two of Brodhead's men were slightly wounded.

On the return to Fort Pitt, Brodhead found chiefs of the Delawares, Hurons, and Shawanese offering their services. Thirty Delaware warriors were anxious to go against tribes hostile to the Americans, but Brodhead could not send them out because he had no means of paying them. Some Indian goods, including paint and trinkets, would enable him "to engage the Delawares to harass the enemy frequently." However, a detachment from Fort Pitt was building blockhouses to protect the Delawares' women and children while the warriors were "out against the English and Mingoes."

In spite of the assiduous efforts of Sullivan and Brodhead, a few Iroquois towns with their standing crops escaped discovery and destruction. For the most part, however, the Indians were bereft of homes and food for the year following. The friendly Oneidas applied to be allowed to hunt in the invaded country, to which, they declared, the subdued Five Nations would never return. That winter the expelled tribes crowded the fort at Niagara, refusing to occupy temporary barracks the British offered to erect for them. Many of the Indians, who were not accustomed to salt provisions, died of scurvy.

Nevertheless, Indian raids on the frontier American settlements were resumed betimes, and their menace was not ended until General Anthony Wayne decisively defeated the western Indians in 1794. Late in 1781 General Riedesel presented to Sir Frederick Haldimand, then Military Governor of Canada, a plan concerted with Generals Phillips and Henry Clinton for use of Indians against the western settlements. Niagara, Detroit, and other posts on the Great Lakes would be reinforced with 2000 troops. Detachments would include "Savages, to whom must be given carte blanche to do whatever they will without restriction while striking at the back of the colonies. . . . [T]he Savages . . . should spring out wherever forces assemble against them and fall back on the regular troops posted in their rear. The Savages will love this kind of fighting. Their natural cruelty will be satisfied and they will enrich themselves with booty and be satisfied with the flowing of blood." The proposal ended with the admission that "such excess seems extremely cruel but one must sacrifice something to bring about peace and the common good."

Governor Haldimand disapproved the project for several reasons. The British were already furnishing the Indians with "4000 rations per day at Niagara alone" and could not bring in supplies for an army besides. The frontiersmen would fight to protect their settlements. Lastly, the Indians had proved capricious, and after receiving presents had dispersed and deserted the troops.

Fire and Sword on the Connecticut Coast

B ENEDICT ARNOLD'S RAID ON THE COAST TOWNS ON CON-
NECTICUT WAS AMONG THE MOST WANTON CRUELTIES OF
THE WAR. HE HAD JUST COME FROM HIS DESTRUCTIVE FORAYS
in Virginia, the first assignment the British gave him following his
treason. In Virginia he had the opposition of continental troops
and militia, while in Connecticut he laid waste to New London,
an open town, and burned much of neighboring Groton, which
was defended by a small force. Arnold had early sprung to the patriot cause. He had led Connecticut soldiers in the surprise capture
of Ticonderoga, and he had swept with Connecticut companies to
the victory of Saratoga. With famous spirit he had chastised
Tryon's troops when they withdrew after their attack on Danbury.
He now compounded his treason by visiting ruin on communities of
his home state.

In September 1781, Arnold became the despoiler of his people.
Of course, it was Sir Henry Clinton, the British Commander in
Chief, who dispatched the traitor on his brutal errand. Clinton ex-
plained afterward that his motive in ordering the expedition

against the Connecticut coast was twofold. He would create a diversion from Washington's march against Cornwallis in Virginia, and compensate for his own frustrated design of attacking Rhode Island before the French fleet and army arrived at Newport. He intended that Arnold should bring off or destroy prize vessels, privateers, and valuable naval and other stores collected at New London.

In both purposes the British Commander miscalculated. He was optimistic that he could reinforce Cornwallis at Yorktown in time to prevent Washington from compelling his lordship to surrender. Actually, he had missed his chance to save Cornwallis when he had let Washington and Rochambeau slip by New York on their southward course, and he launched his relief force weeks too late. Clinton's "diversion" against the Connecticut shore in no way changed Washington's well-matured plan to surround and capture Cornwallis' whole army. Clinton also had to express regret, he said, for the unforeseen burning of New London and the high British casualties in the attack on the fort at Groton.

As things turned out, Clinton was completely disappointed and discredited. In a masterful military stroke, Washington was in fact putting an end to the war and assuring America's independence. Clinton, by contrast, dealt a blow, barbarous though it was, against a single locality. Washington was giving a new direction to history, while Clinton and the turncoat Arnold were bloodying their hands amidst the cries of helpless civilians.

General William Tryon had made descents on Connecticut towns earlier, turning the people's dislike of him into detestation. At least his Danbury strike in 1777 was against a patriot war supply depot; he destroyed nearly 1800 tents, 700 barrels of flour, 1800 barrels of pork and beef, and 2000 bushels of grain. For good measure he burned nineteen homes and twenty stores and shops. In July 1779, Tryon, from a fleet of fifty vessels, landed 2600 troops at Fairfield. Some were Germans under Brigadier General Garth.

They put the torch to three churches, two schoolhouses, a court-house and jail, ninety-seven homes, and more than a hundred other buildings. Green Farms suffered a like fate before the incendiaries sailed back across Long Island Sound to Huntington Bay.

Three days later this outfit, joined on Long Island by the King's American Regiment, was back on the Connecticut shore, this time at Norwalk. Breaking camp at three o'clock Sunday morning, July 10, they were briefly opposed by 400 patriots, a third of whom were continentals, and the rest militia and volunteers. Tryon posted himself on a height with chair and table, like a movie direc-tor on location. At six o'clock he ordered Norwalk to be burned. He said he had no such mischief in mind until the people, who re-fused his offer of amnesty, shot at his guards, whom he had sta-tioned to protect the homes. The sacrifice of Fairfield was repeated, with the addition of some mills, vessels, and salt pans. The attack-ers withdrew in the afternoon, but not until they had lost twenty killed and ninety-six wounded in a sharp fight with a small patriot force under General Samuel Holton Parsons, whom Washington had sent to the aid of the place. Parsons had six cannon at "The Rocks"; the enemy, who outnumbered his men three to one, took two hours to dislodge him.

The town of Norwalk in 1781 branded twenty-four persons "In-imical and Dangerous to the Liberties and Independence of the United States of America." They had all been given hearings to show cause why their names should not be enrolled in the town clerk's office, in accordance with the act of the General Assembly "more effectually to prevent robberies, and plunders of our open and secret enemies." All were men, all had English names. One supposes that the officially stigmatized twenty-four were embraced in the question voted on in 1783, "whether those persons who have gone off and joined themselves with the enemy, should return back and inhabit in this town. Past [*sic*] in the negative."

After the outrages committed on neighboring places, the people of New London knew what to expect when it came their turn.

Arnold's expedition of thirty-two transports with 1500 troops —British regulars, loyalist units, and German *Jaegers*—sailed from New York on September 4 and anchored off Long Island, opposite New London, at two o'clock the next afternoon. Arnold's plan was to cross the Sound at night and surprise New London and Groton, on opposite sides of the Thames River, before any resistance could be mustered. At first the wind was from the south; then it shifted to the north. Dawn found the attacking vessels still trying to beat into the harbor. Colonel William Ledyard, commanding the militia of the district, saw the flotilla plainly from the near-by heights; he had a few hours in which to prepare what defense he could make. Earlier, rumors of the hostile intent had been disregarded, for others had proved unfounded.

Ledyard now alerted the small garrisons of Fort Trumbull on the New London side, which had twenty-three militiamen, and Fort Griswold on the Groton side, which had thirty. Trumbull was an earthwork fronting the water, entirely open on the land side. It mounted a dozen 19-pounders, some 9-pounders, and a few lighter pieces. Fort Griswold, on the high bank above Groton, was stronger, a rectangle of stone walls, with bastions at the corners facing the river. It was surrounded by a ditch, above which the embankment was thickly set with sharpened stakes projecting a dozen feet. Colonel Ledyard fired alarm guns, the signal being two reports in rapid succession. The enemy knew of this in advance from loyalists of the place, and they followed the two discharges from the fort with a third from one of the ships. By custom, three guns meant not danger, but good news, as of the capture of a prize by a New London privateer. Consequently, response to Ledyard's alarm was slowed. He dispatched messengers to the surrounding country to bring in the militia, and appealed to the Governor for more distant help.

The British fleet did not get into the harbor until nine o'clock on the morning of September 6. Long before that both towns, New London, which had some 5600 people, and Groton, two-thirds the size, were in consternation. Women and children, on horse or cart if the family had such, or afoot and bearing what precious possessions they could snatch, were hustled to safety some miles away. A few remained to guard invalids or aged persons who could not be moved, hoping to persuade the enemy to spare them. In some cases those who fled wandered that day in the woods and hills before finding shelter for the night, and they did not make their way back until next morning.

In New London a knot of townsmen, resolved to defy the attackers, collected on a piece of high ground. They had no officer among them, no organization, and no plan. They would have been a sacrifice to their hasty courage had not a ship captain in their number urged them, instead of standing in the open, to divide into two parties and shoot from behind stone walls that lined the roads over which the enemy had to advance. About 130 men made all speed to join the little garrison in Fort Griswold. They were chiefly volunteers—farmers, tradesmen, and a few sailors. They came with muskets, fowling-pieces, pitchforks, whatever weapons they could lay hands on.

The American vessels in the harbor were struggling against the wind to get up the river beyond the towns. More than a dozen finally succeeded; the others were left a prey to the marauders, along with unrigged craft at the shipyards. The ship *Hannah* had recently been brought in as a rich prize, her cargo said to be worth $400,000. She could not be moved; most of her lading had been stored ashore, but only a small portion of it was got away.

On landing, Brigadier General Arnold divided his force into two parties of about equal numbers on opposite sides of the harbor. Advancing on New London, on the west shore, with Arnold, were some regulars, but mostly Tories—the American Legion and the Loyal Americans, the latter under command of Colonel Beverley

Robinson, who had figured in Arnold's treason. The Groton contingent, under Lieutenant Colonel Edmund Eyre, was composed of two regiments of regulars, the German *Jaegers,* a few artillerymen, and the New Jersey Volunteers, loyalists.

Arnold had his troops enter New London from both south and north. They quickly overpowered a few guns on Town Hill and a single piece that had been kept simply for public ceremonies. Fort Trumbull was even less of a problem to the attackers. Captain Adam Shapley's orders from Colonel Ledyard were, if directly assailed, to abandon his post and get his score of men across the river to Fort Griswold. The enemy approached Fort Trumbull from the unenclosed rear, which was not defensible. Shapley's gunners spiked their cannon and escaped to three boats, but in rowing to the Groton shore seven of his men were wounded and all in one boat were captured. The survivors, few as they were, made a welcome addition to the Griswold garrison.

Arnold had been told by "friends to government in the town" that Fort Griswold would fall an easy prey, as it was in an unfinished state and feebly held. He made no doubt that his order to Eyre would be quickly executed. However, when Arnold, standing in Fort Trumbull, turned his glass on Fort Griswold, he saw that his loyalist informants were mistaken. Griswold was in good shape for resistance. Also, American vessels that he had expected would be prevented from ascending the river when the guns of Griswold were turned on them had already passed up beyond the fort. Arnold therefore dispatched an officer to countermand his order to attack Griswold. Tragically, his reversal came too late.

Already Colonel Eyre had sent a flag with a demand for Fort Griswold to surrender. Colonel Ledyard, after hasty council with his officers, refused. The British Commander sent a second message, promising that if he was obliged to take the place by storm the captured garrison would be given no quarter. This caused another anxious conference in the fort. Ledyard believed that his small complement of defenders would be reinforced by the militia that he had summoned from the surrounding country, some of whom could already be seen approaching. He therefore repeated his reply that he would resist to the last extremity.

The enemy, some 800, had lain protected behind rocky ridges. They now advanced in two parties in solid ranks. The first column was led by Colonel Eyre. Ledyard had ordered the fort to reserve its fire until the attackers were within close range. A cannon with a double load of grapeshot was placed in charge of a skillful gunner from one of the New London privateers. At the discharge, a gap was opened in the front line of the British. Twenty men fell, among them Colonel Eyre. The enemy command was then taken by Major Montgomery of the second division. He had his men scatter and work forward, crouching and using every cover in the terrain. The British artillery could not be brought up because of the rough ground.

Under furious fire of cannon and musketry, Montgomery's troops converged and joined their companions of the first group in the ditch. Now came the crisis of the fight. The bank was steep and high; the sharp stakes of the fraise stood too thick and stout to be wrenched out. Redcoats were hoisted on the shoulders of their fellows below to claw their way to the parapet. Muskets from the fort found certain targets in the struggling mass of attackers. The cannon were useless, but the solid shot hurled from the top killed some and wounded more. One defender of giant strength loosed the heaviest balls from two hands at once.

When the assailants reached the embrasures they met thrusts of "spears," actually boarding pikes, brought in from the privateers. Major Montgomery, rushing at a narrow opening, was skewered and killed on the instant, it was said, by Jordan Freeman, a black man. A chance musket ball cut the halyard of the fort's flag. As

soon as the flag dropped it was replaced on a pike, but the attackers took its fall as a sign of surrender, and pressed in with renewed
ardor.

The militia had failed to come to the assistance of the garrison
of volunteers, and the enemy, in increasing numbers, were inside
the walls. Major Stephen Bromfield, or another British officer who
succeeded the dead Major Montgomery (there was a dispute about
his identity), demanded in the din, "Who commands here?" Colonel Ledyard saw that further resistance was hopeless, and answered, "I did, Sir, but you do now." He advanced, offering his
sword, hilt first. Thereat the enemy officer ran Ledyard through
with the tendered blade. As Ledyard fell from the death wound
several Americans who stood near sprang to attack his assailant,
but they were cut down. This was the testimony of American
eyewitnesses of the deed, and it was not disputed by the enemy.

At the moment of Colonel Ledyard's surrender of the fort, only
five or six of the defenders had been killed, and eighteen wounded,
but now began an indiscriminate slaughter. A few of the garrison
at a distant point had not understood that they were to lay down
their arms. Briefly they kept up the fight, a circumstance later cited
by the British as excuse for their determined slaughter in the surrendered fort.

The Americans rushed for safety, some into the barracks, but
more huddled in the magazine. The British fired by platoons into
the latter until an officer, with anguished cries, stopped the sys-
tematic murder. The victims who survived said he did it to prevent
exploding the fort, since much powder was strewn about, ready to
ignite the main supply. This would have been a good motive, but
probably he was actuated by mercy. Many of the living and dead
of the garrison had multiple bayonet wounds, as though inflicted in
senseless passion on the helpless.

The Fort Griswold fight lasted forty minutes. After the massacre, the fallen were stripped nearly naked by their foes. Arnold, in

his report to Sir Henry Clinton, said that when the attackers entered the works they "found" eighty-five Americans dead and some sixty wounded, most of them mortally. Sir Henry, in general orders describing the action, used the same words, in effect denying that there had been any killing after the garrison had surrendered. No dependence could be put in the word of Benedict Arnold, and General Clinton, having deputed him to command the expedition, probably felt himself precluded from any correction. Making all allowance for angry partisan charges by the defeated, the evidence of pitiless mass slaying of the disarmed garrison is not to be doubted.

Arnold reported that of his attacking troops, forty-five were killed and 145 were wounded. The wounded who died on the return voyage were buried on the Long Island shore or at sea. Sir Henry Clinton, who regretted such heavy casualties, did administer an oblique rebuke to Arnold.

The British evacuated the fort, and orders were given to an artillery officer to blow it up. Thirty or more of the worst wounded Americans were thrown pell-mell on a heavy artillery wagon. In starting this load of misery down the slopes toward the shore, the handlers lost control of the unwieldy vehicle. It gathered speed in the descent until, near the bottom, it struck a large tree, which stopped it. The wounded gave voice to their agony in the abrupt collision and recoil. They were put in a near-by house, paroled, and left without attendance. Thirty prisoners who were unhurt were rowed out to the British shipping and, on arriving at New York, were stowed in the notorious sugarhouse.

The enemy from the river watched to see the fort explode. The artilleryman had laid his train of powder to the magazine, ignited it, and fled. But at some point the fuse went out—perhaps, some thought, because it was wet with blood.

Before and during the attack on Fort Griswold, the British masters of New London burned and otherwise destroyed most of that town. The count afterward listed sixty-five dwellings of ninety-seven families, thirty-one stores and warehouses, eighteen mechanics' shops, twenty barns, a church, the courthouse and jail, wharves, and all of the shipping except sixteen vessels that had escaped upstream. Fifty iron cannon were disabled, some by having their supporting trunnions knocked off. Benedict Arnold, explaining the holocaust to General Clinton, claimed that he had intended no such devastation of dwellings; they had unexpectedly caught fire when gunpowder in various warehouses had exploded and a change of wind had spread the conflagration. Clinton thought the ruin of homes was unfortunate. The fact was that isolated houses, to which the flames could not have leaped, were consumed, showing that they were deliberately set ablaze. In a few cases citizens reached their dwellings in time to put out fires that had been started in several rooms. At Groton, a half-mile or more across the river from New London, twelve dwellings, four barns, two shops, two stores, and a schoolhouse were reduced to ashes. American narrators, though not inclined to exculpate the enemy troops, were sure that British sympathizers in the towns, such as those who had told Arnold where to strike, had had a hand in the work of destruction.

The losses to individuals also deprived the patriots' war effort. New London may not have been, as Rivington's *Royal Gazette* vengefully exulted, "the magazine of America," but it did contain large quantities of West Indian and European goods, brought in by the active privateers, and the shipping facilities of the place were severely crippled. The most recent prize, the *Hannah,* was set afire; it drifted across the harbor and burned to the water's edge. Most of the people were rendered homeless. A committee of the Connecticut legislature reported, in surprising detail, that as a result of the British ravages, the New Londoners were poorer by £53,696 9s. 8d., citizens of Groton by £7712 14s. 10d., or a grand total of £61,400 4s. 6d. The British *Annual Register* for 1782 said, in summary, "Every thing on the town [New London] side of the river was destroyed by fire. Nothing was carried off except such small articles of spoil as afforded no trouble to the conveyance" (read plunder).

Sir Henry Clinton, in general orders, expressed "his obligation to Brig. Gen. Arnold for his very spirited conduct on the occasion; and he assures that general officer that he took every precaution in his power to prevent the destruction of the town, which is a misfortune that gives him [Arnold, presumably] much concern."

Rivington was more gleeful. He ended his account of the raid: "The breast of every honest loyalist can not help emotions of joy on finding that the most detestable nest of pirates on the continent has at last (the measure of their iniquity being full) attracted the notice of his Excellency the commander-in-chief. . . . [T]he blow now given [to New London] will affect the sensitive nerves of every staunch rebel on the continent."

The other side of the coin was abominable. A committee of the legislature to inquire into the disabilities of New London and Groton people caused by the raid reported in January 1783. Fifty-two were left widows with minor children. A sampling reveals that Mary Allen, widow of Captain Samuel Allen, had six children under twenty-one, "and a small real and personal estate." The widow of William Bolton "was left with seven children under the age of sixteen years, and no estate." "Theod[or]a Williams, widow of Captain John Williams, Jr., was left with eight children under ye age of seventeen years, and about £70 of real and personal estate." "Bridget Ledyard, widow of Let [Lieut.] Younge Ledyard, was left with four children under the age of nine years, no estate, but a small house lot; the house burnt, and what was in it." Thankful Stanton, widow of Captain Amos Stanton, was one of few who had any personal estate, but her £200 were in soldier's notes and state securities, subject to discount; she had seven children under the age of twelve years.

Nicholas Starr was killed in Fort Griswold; his widow, Hannah, died soon after of a fever, leaving four children between the ages of two and eight, and about enough property to pay the debts of her soldier husband. "Jerusha Leeds, widow of Captain Cary Leeds, was left with six children under the age of eight years, and no estate. Captain Leeds was wounded in the foot, of which he never recovered, took cold and flung him into a fever of which he died." "Mary (Harris) Shapley, widow of Adam Shapley, left with four children; Mary, Joseph, Abigail, and Benjamin. The eldest, Daniel, died on the prison ship in New York in November."

It is not surprising that the widows with young children had little or no income, for their husbands had been artisans who depended on their earnings to support their families. Where occupations were given, the men were described as weaver, clothier, blacksmith, shoemaker, house carpenter, ship carpenter, cooper, ship joiner, "cloather." The widow of the last, Elizabeth Adams, had four children under eleven years, "a small house and a small piece of rocky land under no improvement nor worth improving." Her husband had lived "wholly by his trade."

Among those who were wounded in the attack, and remained disabled, was John Starr, a volunteer, who was struck in the foot and right elbow by musket balls. Fifteen months later, "Ulcers continue forming to this time . . . and pieces of bone issuing out of the sores. he is a man in low circumstances though of good character, has a wife & children which before he supported by his industry & which he is now rendered wholly incapable of doing." Captain Solomon Perkins, a volunteer in the fort, was determined to work insofar as he could in spite of remarkable hurts. He received "a musket ball through the neck and arm another through the side, and sundry thrusts of the bayonet through the Stomach . . . which had caused nervous irritations, spasams &c and rendered him unable to perform hard labour." "Lieut Park Avery a volunteer [was] wounded in the fort by a bayonet taking off part of the cranium and totally extirpating his right eye." Another Lieutenant

Avery was singularly tough, if one believes the account of the damage he suffered. He lost an eye, his skull was broken, "some of the brains [were] shot out," he was bayoneted in his side, but for all that he survived for forty years.

A supplemental report described Daniel Stanton, Jr., of Stonington. He heard firing at New London, mounted his horse and sped to Fort Griswold "& entered & made himself a volunteer in defense of the fort. In the action he received twenty-one wounds in the head, body, & limbs with ball & bayonet of all which he is fully recovered," except for a wound in the "ancle," which disabled him. He was given £6 a year from the day of his injuries until he should be fit again. Others received pensions ranging from £3 to £20. Most of the unhealed wounds were fractures of the joints.

When the "larum" guns were heard, both old and young volunteered to defend Fort Griswold. One of those killed was only fifteen; another lad, sixteen, escaped unhurt. A son of Captain William Latham, variously described as fourteen, twelve, or ten, was taken along by his father to help fetch powder from the magazine. A man of sixty was known for always responding to calls. Few in the fort had ever been under fire before.

On the other hand, John Hempstead, wounded in the fort, recorded, "I had the command of a company of militia of forty od men, & I never Saw but Seven of them that day, as they lived upon the shore, and ther famely ware exposed to the ravagis of the Enemy." Companies of militia from the surrounding country, some of whom could be seen in the distance from the fort, did not come in until after the fight. A Lieutenant Colonel of militia was found by court-martial to be guilty of neglect of duty in not attacking the enemy. He was described as an admirable citizen, but "not suitably qualified for military service." He was cashiered. A Captain and a Lieutenant of the Eighth Regiment, also cashiered, did worse; they were found guilty of "plundering in a wanton and shameful manner the goods of the inhabitants of Groton on the day of the

battle." Several officers, tried for failure to respond with their militiamen, were exculpated. Colonel Ledyard had fired on American
vessels to prevent them from running up the river with seamen that
he needed in Fort Griswold. Two or three hundred seamen "deserted from Privateers & shipping in order to plunder."

These examples of bad behavior inspired a memorial the next
year of fourteen citizens to the Commandant of the ports of New
London and Groton. They declared, "From the late attack . . . it
was . . . evident that the militia were not, and could not be here
in time to be of any service." Therefore the forts should be regularly garrisoned, Griswold with 150 men, Trumbull with a smaller
number. The legislature approved the plea.

In 1793 the state legislature assigned 500,000 acres ("the fire-
lands") in the Connecticut Western Reserve in Ohio for relief of
the sufferers in enemy raids on Greenwich, Norwalk, Danbury,
New Haven, East Haven, Ridgefield, New London, and Groton.
Comparatively few got benefit from this provision. It was already
twelve to fifteen years since the losses had been incurred, the wild
lands were at an uninviting distance, and many of the owners finally allowed their allotments to be sold for taxes.

Burden of Command

GENERAL WASHINGTON'S BURDENS OF COMMAND DUR-
ING EIGHT YEARS OF WAR WERE UNCEASING. THEY WERE
HEAVIER BECAUSE HE REFUSED TO ENCROACH UPON CIVIL
authority belonging to, but often not exerted by, Congress and the
states. The deficiencies of others compelled him to act with one
hand tied behind him in army administration, in planning campaigns, and in actual clash of battle. The wonder is that, though he
learned as he went along, his own mistakes, which were at times
serious, were comparatively few and were triumphantly overcome.

Washington's initial embarrassments flowed from importunate
foreign officers. Europe had recently been at peace. When the nations reduced their armies the conscript common soldiers were
grateful, but surplus officers, turned loose on half pay or none, had
lost their occupation. From France and from French possessions in
the West Indies, but from elsewhere also, many came to America
seeking military employment. Generally they had the promise of
commissions, given them by Silas Deane, the American agent in
Paris, or at least their passage and a favorable introduction to Congress. In presenting themselves they did not understate their pre-

tensions; their sponsors, whom Deane wished to please, were similarly glowing in their behalf. Besides, Deane believed that the rebellious colonies stood in need of military talent, though he far exceeded his authority and was incautious in his willingness to supply it.

Arriving at Philadelphia in the early months of the war, the boasting foreigners found Congress compliant in granting them commissions, pay, perhaps their expenses in coming over, and referring them to Washington's camp for assignment. Qualified military engineers, rare in this country, the Commander in Chief eagerly accepted, though in limited number. As the influx continued, others, who sought line positions, could not be placed. Most knew no English, could not understand orders given them, and could not transmit directions to troops. They became worse than useless where they demanded rank superior to that of American officers who were serving faithfully at personal sacrifice. An individual foreigner who appeared with high claims might be problem enough, but likely he brought with him an entourage of junior attendants whom he insisted should be gratified with appropriate stations.

Of all the foreign officers who adventured upon America, the Frenchman Philippe Charles Tronson du Coudray stirred the most contention. Mercifully, after a short stay, he removed himself. He arrived in May 1777, attended by eighteen officers and ten sergeants, and paid a flying visit to Washington's headquarters at Morristown on his way to Philadelphia. He did not disclose to the Commander in Chief the terms of his contract with Deane, dated September 1776, but talked airily of his accomplishments and left the impression that he was destined to head the American artillery. Washington at once warned Congress that Brigadier General Henry Knox, who had built the artillery arm to high proficiency, should not be outranked or he would surely resign. Further, it was desirable that the artillery be commanded by an American. If the French artillerists were to be received, perhaps they could be assigned to a distinct but subordinate corps.

When du Coudray exhibited his agreement with Deane, Congress was surprised that he had been promised a commission as Major General and was to have "the direction of whatever relates to the Artillery and Corps of Engineers." Immediately Duportail and his associates of the French engineers showed their hostility to the presumptuous newcomer. More importantly, Knox and two others of Washington's most dependable Generals, Greene and Sullivan, notified Congress that if du Coudray was to outrank them they begged leave to resign. Congress knew that Deane had no power to give du Coudray such extravagant assurances, but the delegates, in a quandary what to do, resented the interference of the trio of American officers and answered that they were free to quit.

Here was a pretty mess for Washington, who was threatened with disruption in two critical and connected services at just the wrong moment—wrong because General Burgoyne, pushing his army down from Canada, had compelled American evacuation of Ticonderoga, the main fortress blocking his march to the Hudson. Fortunately, Congress worked out a compromise with du Coudray; he was assigned to staff duty as Inspector of Ordnance and Military Manufactories and compensated for his large expense in bringing his party to America, and his accompanying officers were commissioned at modest ranks. The Americans, who had been rebellious at the prospect of du Coudray *et al.* taking over their bailiwicks, were mollified.

This arrangement for the thrusting French Major General was required to stand only briefly. Du Coudray was bound to be the man on horseback. Instead of leading his mount onto the Schuylkill ferry, he insisted on remaining in the saddle. The horse shied, plunged overboard, and his rider was drowned. Doubtless there was sorrow in France at the loss.

⌐

The whole story, for the Americans, for three months (August–November 1776) had been one of retreat before the enemy. The battle of Long Island had been a massive defeat. The disgraceful scamper at Kip's Bay had been retrieved next day by the repulse of the British at Harlem Heights, but then the patriots had been driven from White Plains to huddle in the higher hills just to the north. Here, in the cold days of early November, Washington's depleted force was in sorry state. Tents had been lost; men slept on the icy ground or shivered on sentry duty coatless, in the tatters of summer clothing. Some had no cooking pots. The sick filled the "hospitals," the homesick deserted at will, those of the heartsick militia who had been engaged for no specified term melted away. Commissioners from the states did not come to the camp to choose new officers of their contingents; consequently, there were no officers to re-enlist troops. Washington exhorted the soldiers whose terms would expire within the month to remain in the service of their country, but in vain.

The enemy army withdrew from White Plains to Manhattan Island. Washington and his officers wearily guessed that General Howe would attack Fort Washington, the only stronghold on Manhattan in patriot hands, then move into New Jersey and strike for Philadelphia. Washington felt obliged, against the wisdom of warfare, to divide his slender force. Heath with 4000 must guard the Highlands; Charles Lee with 7000 should defend against a northward thrust; Stirling had 1000 in the vicinity of Elizabeth, New Jersey, to check a crossing from Staten Island. Washington himself would take post above, at Hackensack, with a few more than 2000 Maryland and Virginia continentals. He called on Governor Livingston for New Jersey militia, but they did not come.

The immediate question was whether to defend Fort Washington. Two hundred feet above the Hudson on the east bank, it was slightly upstream of Fort Lee, which stood atop the palisades on the west shore. Fort Washington's precipitate cliff was unassailable from the river side and was defended elsewhere by indifferent outworks. The earth embankments mounted thirty-six cannon. The garrison of more than 1200 was commanded by Colonel Robert Magaw, who was confident he could hold out against assault until

BURDEN OF COMMAND

the end of the year. General Nathanael Greene, commanding the companion Fort Lee, was equally insistent that Fort Washington could and should be defended. He argued that it fastened many enemy troops to upper Manhattan; if the place was in danger of falling, the garrison could be evacuated across the river under the guns of Fort Lee. Another defeat would further dispirit the country. Lastly, the twin fortresses were essential to prevent British warships and tenders from passing upstream.

On the other hand, except for Fort Washington, the Americans had been ousted from Manhattan Island; the Commander in Chief was moving to the west side of the river, which was probably to be the area of the enemy's offensive. British vessels had broken through the obstructions placed in the channel and had not been deterred by gunfire from the forts. If Fort Washington were not evacuated in time and were compelled to surrender, loss of its garrison, armament, and stores would be a severe blow. If Fort Washington fell, Fort Lee would become useless.

General Washington, in fatigue of mind, could not decide between the pros of abandonment and the cons of defense. He conferred with Greene and Putnam at Fort Lee on November 14. Greene had prejudged the case by reinforcing Magaw, and he had not removed surplus stores from Fort Washington, as the Commander in Chief had intended he should do. Washington did not interfere. The next day, back at Hackensack, he had word from Greene and Magaw that the British had sent in a demand for surrender of Fort Washington, or the garrison could expect no mercy. Magaw replied that he would defend the place to the death. The Commander in Chief hastened to Fort Lee for further consultation, but he still could not decide.

Before dawn on November 16, Washington and his companion Generals visited the fort, but it was now too late to evacuate it. Attack on the outer defenses had already commenced. Washington and the others left Magaw to his fight.

In the assault, General Howe used 8000 men, led by Lord

[293]

Percy, Lord Cornwallis, and General Knyphausen. They attacked from every quarter except the western cliff, which could not be scaled. The Americans resisted bitterly, but were driven from the outer redoubts until they overcrowded the fort itself. The decisive push up rocky steeps was made by Hessians under Colonel Johann Rall, the same who, six weeks later, was to be mortally wounded in Washington's surprise descent on Trenton. It was to Knyphausen that Magaw surrendered his sword.

General Washington, in anxiety at Fort Lee across the river, received messages that foretold the disaster. At four o'clock on the afternoon of November 16, 1776, a total of 2818 officers and men laid down their arms and were marched out of the fort, prisoners of war. In a despairing gesture the great guns of Fort Lee were turned on the position the enemy had captured, but to no effect. Having some protection from their fortifications, the Americans' casualties, except for prisoners, were less than those of the enemy, though, in proportion to numbers engaged, the defenders' loss was heavier. Of Americans fifty-nine were killed, and ninety-six wounded; of their foes, seventy-six were killed and 374 wounded, the Germans suffering most in each category.

General Washington wrote Congress that he hoped to hold Fort Lee. Three days persuaded him to evacuate it as useless, since the neighboring stronghold was lost. Again his hesitant delay was costly. On a rainy night, Cornwallis with 4000 men crossed the Hudson, six miles to the north, to ascend the palisades and march on Fort Lee. Notified by Greene of the peril, Washington took horse from Hackensack. He galloped in just ahead of the British, in time to lead the garrison of 2000 across the Hackensack. So hurried was the departure that breakfast kettles were left boiling. The ammunition in the fort had been removed, but 300 tents, 1000 barrels of flour, all entrenching tools, and most of the baggage fell to the captors. In the surrender of Fort Washington and the abandonment of Fort Lee the Americans lost 146 cannon, some as large as 32-pounders, 12,000 shot and shell, 2800 muskets, and 4000 cartridges. The forfeit of men, food, and equipment was severely felt in the retreat across New Jersey.

The blame belonged to Greene for his overoptimism, but more to Washington for his indecision. If the Commander in Chief had made up his mind promptly and differently, his subordinates would have executed his orders and salvaged what was sacrificed by delay. However, it was easier for Washington's critics to be wise after the event than for the wearied leader, in pressing emergencies, to judge correctly and instantly. Washington did not allow fault on the Hudson to discourage him from brilliant achievement on the Delaware.

⌐

Benedict Arnold, after his treason, became a Brigadier General in the British army. In December 1780 he was sent to Virginia with a small fleet and 1600 men. After ravaging the valley of the James River, he fortified himself at Portsmouth, a short distance up the Elizabeth River from Chesapeake Bay. He imperiled supplies from Virginia and the middle states that were going to General Nathanael Greene's weak force, then opposing Lord Cornwallis in North Carolina. Further, Arnold might be reinforced and detach troops to press Greene from the north as Cornwallis was pursuing him from the south. Washington's intensified anxiety for the fortunes of Greene did not permit him to send men from the depleted army guarding the Hudson. Nor did the Southern states Greene was struggling to defend furnish him militia and supplies. The Southern campaign, from the bad start of the surrender of Charleston and the defeat at Camden, had been obliged to fend for itself.

The French army of 4000 was idle at Newport, Rhode Island. Washington inquired of Rochambeau whether he would move to Virginia. The French General replied that, by direction of his government, his troops could operate only in conjunction with the

French fleet. The fleet could not leave Newport harbor while a superior British squadron was on watch off Gardiner's Island.

That seemed to be that, so far as help from the French was concerned, until, unexpectedly, in early February 1781, Washington learned from Rochambeau that a storm had damaged the enemy ships in their exposed anchorage. One great man-of-war had been driven ashore, others had been dismasted, another had been blown nobody knew where. Snug at Newport, the French vessels had not suffered.

Here was Washington's opportunity, and Rochambeau almost asked him to take advantage of it. If Admiral Destouches now had a superior force, could he take his entire fleet and 1000 of Rochambeau's troops to scotch Benedict Arnold in the Chesapeake? Those battered British ships would be repaired or others would appear in their place, but in the few weeks intervening Arnold's force could be routed and the traitor himself be executed. Lest the French should think the Americans were shirking, Washington would stretch a point and send down Lafayette with 1200 light troops to cooperate in the project.

Rochambeau was cordially agreeable and wrote that he was consulting Destouches. After some delay the Admiral came to a decision. It was a letdown for Washington. Maryland and Virginia had requested a small flotilla to chastise enemy "pirates" raiding Chesapeake shores. Destouches had dispatched a sixty-four and two frigates, which he judged sufficient to chase out the marauders, but this detachment would also be more than a match for Arnold's forty-gun ship and some smaller vessels.

Again Washington faced the separate demands of states which did not consult the over-all plans of the Commander in Chief! It was depressing to have the states do so little on their own account, but maddening when they diverted the French fleet, which should be at Washington's disposal, to an inferior purpose. As matters stood, the small detachment under deTilly included no troops, and without them Arnold could not be destroyed. It later transpired that Destouches did not send a larger warship because it drew too much water to enter the Elizabeth River, and of the sixty-fours only the one assigned was coppered and thus fast enough to keep up with the frigates. DeTilly took no troops because slow-sailing transports would delay the expedition. But this explanation, reasonable enough in itself, was after the disconcerting fact.

All Washington could do while he awaited news from Hampton Roads was to caution General Greene to avoid a battle with Cornwallis' disciplined regulars, for defeat of the feeble Southern army would "complete our misfortunes." Rochambeau had to give the American Commander a report on "what might have been." Had Washington's bolder proposal been broached earlier, he and Admiral Destouches would have embraced it, but Destouches had acted in good faith on the limited requisition of Maryland and Virginia for a skeleton squadron. Now it was too late, for the British ships, less injured by the storm than had been believed, had come back to block up the French fleet in the Newport harbor.

Late in February came word that deTilly had been unable to attack Arnold's post, but had not been idle otherwise. No pilot would venture to take his big warship up the Elizabeth River, so Arnold's defenses were not pounded. But deTilly had captured the British frigate *Romulus,* four transports, and a privateer; he had burned four more transports and taken 500 prisoners. He was returning to Rhode Island, but hoped Destouches would order him back to have a go at Arnold with the captured *Romulus.* Washington directed Lafayette to hold his troops at the head of the Chesapeake until he knew that the French controlled those waters.

A few days later, Rochambeau sent an officer posthaste to Washington. DeTilly had done better than he knew. On the vessels he captured were letters that persuaded the French at Newport to follow the American Commander's original proposal. Destouches was going to the Chesapeake with his whole fleet, bearing more than a thousand of Rochambeau's troops under Baron Vioménil. As a just punishment for Arnold, the British *Romulus* would ascend the Elizabeth River with French frigates and blast the traitor. Washington at once empowered Lafayette to join the game and, if the French approved, continue the expedition into North Carolina to the relief of General Greene.

This called for a personal meeting with the French officers at Newport, and Washington and his staff rode the distance in less than four days. The American Commander was received with a celebration in his honor. He could not understand the delay in sailing of Destouches' fleet, but saw it go to sea on the afternoon of March 8. This was only a day and a half ahead of pursuit by Admiral Marriott Arbuthnot from Gardiner's Bay.

Washington learned from Lafayette that he awaited French mastery of the Chesapeake to bring down the troops from Annapolis. Von Steuben was optimistic in his recruiting and training of Virginia militia to join the planned combined attack on Arnold at Portsmouth. In Washington's worry over whether Destouches would arrive in the mouth of the Chesapeake before Arbuthnot, he tortured himself with the reflection that if only deTilly, who was unopposed, had taken the full squadron and a detachment of troops, he would have succeeded. Washington incautiously included this blame of the French in letters to a number of friends, marked the passage "private," and thought no more of communications.

Then came news that the French and British fleets had met and battled off the Virginia Capes. Though Destouches' ships were less damaged than Arbuthnot's, the French Admiral calculated that his foe could get into the Chesapeake first. Destouches therefore sailed back to Newport, leaving Arnold safe as ever to pursue his mischief. It was a dark hour for Washington. His hope that the French would give him naval control of the coast was dashed, certainly for the time being. Greene had suffered a defeat at Guilford

Court House. Recruiting lagged. The continental money would not buy food and forage, and when these were impressed they could not be brought in unless teams and teamsters were also impressed. The most Washington could do to prevent complete disaster in the South was to direct Lafayette—Destouches or no Destouches —to go to Greene's aid.

This was the wrong time for an embarrassing accident. Some of Washington's letters were captured by enemy partisans lurking in Smith's Clove, that dismal defile in the Hudson Highlands. His letter to his kinsman, Lund Washington, promptly appeared in Rivington's *Gazette,* the New York loyalist newspaper, on April 4, 1781. Its publication was what would today be called a score in psychological warfare. Most of Washington's missive was innocent enough, about affairs at Mount Vernon, but then came the indiscreet comment: "It was unfortunate . . . that the French fleet and detachment did not undertake the enterprise . . . when I first proposed it to them. The destruction of Arnold's corps would then have been inevitable before the British fleet could have . . . put to sea. Instead of this the small squadron . . . was sent, and could not, as I foretold, do anything without a land force at Portsmouth."

Washington's pang at the exposure was the keener because Lafayette, especially solicitous for close cooperation with the French, was upset by the publication and notified him that it had set Philadelphia buzzing.

Rochambeau was too good an ally to find quarrel in lapse of language. In a letter to Washington he took note of Rivington's disclosure because Washington, in the captured letter, had implied that the French had had the choice of sending the full fleet or a small detachment, and had shirked by offering only deTilly's few ships. Actually, he reminded Washington, the mini-squadron was all that Virginia, Maryland, and Congress had requested. Rochambeau referred to his files, and invited Washington to consult his own, to show that the American Commander's proposal for the whole fleet and troops reached Newport only after deTilly had departed. As soon as Rochambeau had learned of Washington's wishes he had eagerly responded. Destouches would explain why he had been delayed in loading supplies on the ships. Rochambeau closed with a pledge of instant compliance with Washington's orders.

Of course Washington had to acknowledge this considerate remonstrance. His trusted aide Alexander Hamilton had left the staff, but the Commander in Chief called him back to compose the proper answer. It was that the offensive letter to Lund might have been tampered with by the British, but the import of it was not to be denied. High diplomacy required frank admission and sincere apology. Washington explained that he had not uttered such criticism to any public body; the passage in question was to a friend, a private citizen. With slight revision of Hamilton's draft, he concluded with assurance of his "entire . . . esteem and attachment." Rochambeau responded in kind. Thus an awkward incident that might have impeded imperative cooperation of the French allies was erased.

French assistance to the rebellious colonies, though prompt in munitions and money, was slower in combatant forces. The French commanders—Rochambeau with 5000 troops and Ternay with ten warships—arrived at Newport in July 1780. These forces were, substantially, idle for a full year; their only contribution during that time lay in drawing off a superior British squadron to blockade the Newport harbor. The second division of French soldiers and ships was bottled up at Brest and remained an object of disappointed desire. Washington was so occupied with the problems of the enfeebled American army that he was unable to visit and personally welcome the allied Commanders until they had been on this shore for more than two months. The delay in making use of the foreign comrades in arms was, ironically, caused by the fact that the Americans were too weak to be helped. The postponement of collaboration could not be laid to the former lack of aggression of the enemy, for British campaigning in the South was furious beginning with the capture of Charleston in May 1780; Cornwallis trampled over the Carolinas and Virginia, checked only by the defensive strategy of General Nathanael Greene.

It is not too much to say that the American cause depended upon the resolution of George Washington. No collapse of support, no adversity in the field could swerve him from fortitude and fidelity. Americans celebrating the triumph of independence forget the culpability of Congress and the indifference of many of the states, both of which spelled governmental breakdown. Inferior in character of delegates, and frequently with as many as five states unrepresented, Congress made little of its acknowledged powers, nor did it have the courage to exercise others which the plight of the country demanded. Congress was, in fact, perversely obstructionist. The committee that had been sent to headquarters, which had learned of and was capable of interpreting the dire needs of the army, was dismissed. When Greene protested the conditions against which he had struggled as Quartermaster General, Congress welcomed his resignation and was for severing him completely from military service. Washington succeeded in having Greene continue for a time. Then the Commander in Chief had to become his own Quartermaster. Pickering, when appointed as Greene's successor, postponed reporting for duty.

The continental currency would buy nothing. Food and forage, reluctantly impressed, could not be moved to camp because teams were unprocurable. The winter at Valley Forge had been a crisis endured, but the near-starvation continued into summer months, when the country abounded in food. Who, not on the spot, Washington exclaimed in July 1780, would "believe that our Army, weakened as it is by the expiration of . . . enlistments, should at times be five or six days together without meat; then as many without bread, and once or twice, two or three together without either." Many of his men had "scarcely as much clothing as would cover their nakedness, and at least a fourth of the whole . . . not even the shadow of a blanket, severe as the winter had been." As transport was so deficient, the expedient was to march the army to a new district, eat that out, then repair to another location.

Congress cried to the thirteen states; they did not answer, not even to the Commander in Chief's personal entreaties. The states were supposed to fill their battalions to 24,000 men by June 20, 1780; two weeks later, on the eve of the appearance of the French allies, the whole number of American recruits that had reported to camp was thirty! A week after that, Washington had to admit, "not a thousand men that I have heard of, have yet joined the Army." When stopgap bodies of militia came in, they had to be sent home for lack of means to feed them. Brigadier General Ebenezer Huntington wrote: "I despise my countrymen. I wish I could say I was not born in America. . . . The insults and neglects which the Army have met with from the country beggars all description. . . I am in rags, have lain in the rain on the ground for forty hours past, and only a junk of fresh beef and that without salt to dine on this day, received no pay since last December . . . and all this for my cowardly countrymen who flinch at the very time when their exertions are wanted." Connecticut regiments that had had no meat for ten days mutinied, and with bayonets they prevented officers from seizing their leader, a private. Fortunatley this revolt was short-lived and did not spread, but it showed that even the best troops would set a limit to their sufferings.

General Washington was grieved that, at the moment of French assistance, the American army presented a distressing spectacle. Moreover, the low morale of his shifting camp reflected the mean spirit of the country. Here were strangers, come 3000 miles to help vindicate the colonies' cause, while the Americans themselves were woefully slack in their own behalf. Ragged uniforms and flat bellies were badges of honor in men who would fight for their freedom, but a dejected country, careless of its fate, was a disgrace. Not the least of the thanks owed to the French was their forbearance over the melancholy situation that greeted them. They did not hold Washington responsible for the sorry state of his country's effort. On the contrary, they sincerely praised the nobility of his purpose under all his discouragements. At the same time, as Commander in Chief, he could not escape embarrassment bordering on humiliation. The French, restless for action, could not be expected to understand the doings, or non-doings, of Congress, much less the lapses of the states. The French were soldiers and sailors, not politicians. In their eyes, Washington was the chief man in America, which was the fact. Like it or not, he had to accept responsibility for faults that were not his own.

Out of these depths, Washington rose to his supreme military achievement. It was to be Trenton over again, triumph over near-despair, but now on a vastly greater scale; not a sudden stroke in a single night, but an anxiously executed campaign, embracing divers forces, through months of marching and voyaging.

Washington conferred with Generals Rochambeau and Chastellux at Wethersfield, Connecticut, in late May of 1781; unfortunately, Admiral Barras, now in command, was unavoidably detained at Newport. It was agreed that the effort of the combined French and American armies should be against the British at New York. It was judged impracticable to transport the troops 450 miles from the Hudson to Virginia, where Lord Cornwallis was disregarding the weak opposition of Lafayette and Wayne. These officers, and of course Greene in the Carolinas, would be best helped if General Clinton, threatened in his main base at New York, was compelled to order up troops from the Southern states.

However, there is reason to believe that Washington had already resolved to make the campaign in the South. His determination was strengthened by the inspiring news, three weeks later, that a large French fleet, under Admiral de Grasse, would visit the American coast in mid-July. If the warships of de Grasse and Barras together could give superiority over British sea power, the blow against the enemy by combined naval and land forces might be struck in the Chesapeake.

In any event, pending the arrival of de Grasse, the French army marched down from Rhode Island for a joint attack with the Americans against the outer defenses of New York on the night of July 2, 1781. The allied plan of surprise was discovered by the British, and it was a failure. Washington and Rochambeau withdrew their troops to camp at Dobbs Ferry, twenty miles up the Hudson. They made a second demonstration against New York which did not impress Sir Henry Clinton and served only to convince the allies that the enemy was too strongly entrenched to be dislodged. Washington had slightly more than 5800 troops, rank and file, only about half the number he had promised Rochambeau he could bring to the French army of 5500.

Then on March 14, news came from Admiral Barras that shifted the whole situation and decided the next moves. Admiral de Grasse was coming to the Chesapeake with twenty-nine warships and an army of 3000. Washington bent every energy, in his appeals to the states for men and supplies and to the Public Financier for money, to enable the allies to destroy the enemy in the South.

Lord Cornwallis, obligingly, was digging in a Yorktown, Virginia, a few miles above the entrance of the York River into Chesapeake Bay. Lafayette was admonished to prevent the escape of his lordship until a total concentration of French and American forces could surround and capture him. De Grasse and Barras, their combined fleets superior to any the British could bring to Cornwallis' relief, would block the mouth of the York. American and French armies, somehow conveyed to the distant place, would crush the enemy in his fortified camp.

This ambitious plan, the most far-reaching projected by Washington, depended for success on many problematical factors. The movements of fleets, allied and enemy, were dependent on wind and wave, not to speak of the caprices of Admirals who discovered unexpected foes afloat. Would Northern soldiers endure Southern summer heats, which were not only sweltering, but believed to be pestilential? How could supply wagons and artillery be hauled through rutted roads by teams that were few and weak? Would Cornwallis, pray heaven, stay fixed to be caught, or would he, on approach of the hunters, drop down into North Carolina? He might employ his many vessels at Yorktown to sift through a blockading fleet, or march his forces northward to safety. Most of all, could the chancy concentration be accomplished and victory be achieved within the two months, before de Grasse, as he warned, had to quit the enterprise and sail for his destined station in West Indian waters?

The first deviation from design threatened promptly. Admiral Barras was to convoy French heavy artillery and 1500 barrels of salted meat from Newport to the Chesapeake, where he would unite his squadron to the larger one of de Grasse. But Barras preferred an expedition to harry the enemy off Newfoundland. That extraneous errand would have killed Washington's undertaking before it was commenced. Fortunately, Washington and Rochambeau were able to persuade Barras to fall in with the composite scheme.

The American commander had to leave half of his troops with General William Heath at West Point, to guard the Highlands against enemy ascent of the Hudson. The remaining Americans marched August 19, and they were across the river by King's Ferry two days later; the French followed by August 25. Then came a hazardous attempt at deception. The allies, on their course through New Jersey, would skirt New York City at a sufficient distance to avoid attack, but near enough to make the British fear their base was to be assaulted via Staten Island. Unless New York was the object, Clinton's spies would argue, why were extensive bakeovens being constructed at Chatham, New Jersey, for the French? Above all, why did Washington, heavily encumbered, trundle along flatboats mounted on carriages, unless these were for the river crossing? To prolong British uncertainty the Commanders kept the destination of the allied armies a profound secret.

The cautious Sir Henry Clinton did not come out from his fortress of Manhattan. When the march of the allies reached Princeton, their intention to move southward was unmistakable, but by then Sir Henry had lost his chance to nip in the bud the campaign against his subordinate, Lord Cornwallis.

As much of the heavy baggage as could be put on boats at Trenton went by water to Philadelphia, where the troops of both nations paraded through the streets. The Americans, in shabby clothes compared to the elegant uniforms of the French (white with piping in pastel shades), yet made a soldierly appearance. Those members of Congress who were in the capital looked on. John Adams, always ready with a comment, thought his countrymen in the marching ranks did not all turn out their toes properly. He and his colleagues in Congress would have done well to prevail on the people of the states to turn out their pockets in support of the forces bound for what was destined to be the last mass encounter of the Revolution. Incredible as it now seems, Washington made this arduous campaign with an empty war chest.

From Philadelphia, Rochambeau and his staff went by boat to Chester, to view the remains of the forts on the Delaware river. Washington and his aides had ridden three miles farther on when a courier brought him a dispatch announcing that de Grasse was actually in the Chesapeake with twenty-eight warships and an army of 3000. His tension relieved, Washington hastened back to Chester to give the joyful tidings to Rochambeau. Several Frenchmen described the meeting. Though themselves demonstrative, they were astonished at the exuberance of the American Commander. Washington abandoned all reserve, flung his arms about his colleague, and bubbled over with his long-awaited news.

The armies marched across the dozen miles of the Delaware peninsula to the head of the Chesapeake (at Elkton, Maryland). The vessels that had been collected there for passage down the bay were too few to take more than the artillery and the smaller part of the troops, so Rochambeau generously left the shipping to the Americans and marched his men to Baltimore. At Elkton, Washington announced to the armies the arrival of de Grasse in the lower bay and hinted that a month's pay might be forthcoming for the Americans. Robert Morris made this festive suggestion a reality. He had chased after Rochambeau to Chester and borrowed $20,000 from the French war chest. This loan supplied the first wages that the continentals had ever received in hard money.

At Baltimore the motley vessels were not more or better than those at Elkton, but now it was expected that de Grasse would send vessels and protecting frigates up the Chesapeake to help fetch down the armies. Actually, the winds were lazy; Washington deplored the slow progress southward of the crowded flotilla.

Relieved as he was by the promptness of de Grasse, Washington was worried for the safety of Admiral Barras, who was sailing to the Chesapeake from Newport with the siege guns and provisions for the combined armies. No word of his whereabouts had been received. Had he met a larger enemy squadron and been defeated?

Great as his hurry was, Washington could not pass Mount Vernon without a flying visit, the first to his beloved home in more than four years of warfare. There he entertained his French guests. He had hardly taken to the road again when he received an alarming message. De Grasse had sailed from his station in the Chesapeake to fight a British fleet, and after the battle he had disappeared. Now the York River was open for Cornwallis' escape. Had de Grasse been worsted, and was a victorious enemy already sending transports to rescue Cornwallis' threatened army? It was bad enough to have Barras wandering Washington knew not where, but the departure of de Grasse for a sea fight might mean the undoing of all that had been planned. The American Commander at once ordered the boats bearing troops down the Chesapeake to put into harbors for fear of British intrusion. For the remainder of his ride southward he had to live with tortured thoughts.

Washington and his companion officers reached Williamsburg, Virginia, on September 14, less than four weeks after the start from the Hudson. He was welcomed by Lafayette and by General Saint-Simon, who was commanding the 3000 French troops brought by de Grasse. The salutes and a dinner tendered by Saint-Simon were gratifying, but not the headshakes that greeted Washington's prompt inquiries about de Grasse and Barras. Nobody knew anything of the naval Commanders and their fleets except that the mouth of the York was empty of vessels. In spite of his opportunity, Cornwallis had remained at Yorktown, a dozen miles down the peninsula; indeed, he was diligently continuing to fortify himself on his cliff.

An immediate problem was provisions for the allied army, which would be swelled when the main forces arrived from the Chesapeake. Virginia and Maryland had abundant food, and the Governors of the two states were alerted to start supplies toward the scene of action and keep them coming.

Washington's anxiety over the fortunes of Barras and de Grasse was soon happily ended. Within twenty-four hours of his arrival at Williamsburg, he received a dispatch from de Grasse; the Admiral had had the better of an engagement with the British fleet off the Virginia Capes, had captured two frigates, and was back in the Chesapeake. Moreover, Barras had joined him unharmed, and even undetected, by the enemy's warships. DeGrasse promptly sent in a vessel to fetch Washington and his companion officers to the flagship, the *Ville de Paris,* for the conference for which the American commander was most eager.

His questions of the Admiral were predetermined, and brought welcome answers for the most part. Could de Grasse remain beyond October 15 if victory had not been achieved by then? Yes, he would stay, if necessary, through that month, and Saint-Simon's troops would not leave before him. Would de Grasse send a few frigates up the river beyond Yorktown to prevent escape by Cornwallis northward? No, the Admiral was afraid of destruction by the shore batteries or by fireboats. However, he would supply a contingent of 2000 marines, if needed, to add to the allied armies. Also he would land heavy cannon and some powder.

Washington chafed at the frustrating delay in his return trip to Williamsburg. Contrary winds in Chesapeake Bay and the James River kept him absent and idle four precious days, when every hour could contribute to success or failure. He did have the satisfaction, as he entered the James, to see the troops arriving from the upper bay.

Word came that British Rear Admiral Robert Digby was on the coast with transports and a small squadron of warships. In Washington's eyes Digby presented no threat, as the French fleets of de Grasse and Barras together numbered thirty-six vessels. De Grasse did not agree. When an aide of Rochambeau took the Admiral news of the cruising enemy, he found that volatile man already informed and excited. De Grasse wrote his army colleagues that he had to get to the open sea to find and attack Digby. He himself was vulnerable within the Capes, as he could not maneuver if the foe came against him. He would sail as soon as the wind was favorable. He would leave a token of vessels on guard, but the main fleet might not be able to return. He did ask the advice of Washington and Rochambeau, but that seemed *pro forma.*

This proposed ruin of the whole enterprise to corner Cornwallis stirred headquarters at Williamsburg to instant action. Washington and Rochambeau wrote letters of remonstrance which they confided to Lafayette to deliver. They argued that de Grasse's role in the siege was anything but passive, for the moment he withdrew his ships a British fleet would enter and bear away the last soldier from Yorktown.

Washington was on tenterhooks for a reply. Would de Grasse repent of his mad impulse to forfeit the success that lay within the allied grasp? Actually, the Admiral's retraction came as suddenly as his wild threat. Without the benefit of the generals' pleas or Lafayette's persuasion, the sea dog decided, on the advice of his own officers, to remain on watch, and he gave every assurance of close cooperation. Joy itself can be wearing, and Washington in this campaign had experienced more than his share of swift alternation of grave concern and blessed release. No matter what the crisis of apprehension, he never relaxed his preparations for destroying the enemy, and was probably grateful for busy duties that distracted from besetting fears.

The Commander in Chief's reconnaissance of Cornwallis' position convinced him that the Yorktown defenses were too strong to be taken by open attack. A siege was necessary, with gradual approaches by means of trenches interspersed with an array of batteries. The armies marched from Williamsburg on September 28 and camped in a great semicircle a mile from the enemy's works, the French on the left, the Americans on the right. Yorktown lies on a bluff, some sixty feet high, which bulges into the river. At that time, streams a half-mile apart flowed through marshes before dropping, in deep ravines, to the York. The level space between them offered the only corridor for attack. Cornwallis' garrisons, mainly in Yorktown, though there were a few at Gloucester Point, directly across the river, numbered about 7500 men. The allies, embracing the Virginia militia, a French contingent brought down by Barras, and marines from de Grasse's fleet, exceeded 16,000, the largest force Washington had ever commanded. The sailors of the French fleets also swelled the strength of the besiegers.

The American officers, except for von Steuben, who had had experience in Europe, were pupils of the French in laying out the trenches and placing the batteries. All troops not otherwise assigned were ordered to cut saplings and fashion them to reinforce the sandy earthworks. Ten days sufficed for opening the first "parallel" (a long trench with forts at intervals). The heavy guns were dragged from the nearest James River landing across the peninsula and mounted. Soon half a hundred cannon were blasting British embrasures and throwing shells within the works. There were American and French casualties, but the Yorktown garrison took far worse punishment. Cornwallis held on because he kept hoping that Sir Henry Clinton would keep his promise to send a rescuing fleet from New York. The fusillade from a second, nearer parallel brought Cornwallis' innder defenses to ruin.

His Lordship did not wait for the last act of the attackers, which would have been a storm of his crumbled works. His ammunition was exhausted and his camp a dreadful spectacle of destruction, death, and disease (smallpox). On October 17, 1781, the British commander asked Washington for the terms on which he would accept surrender. The formal ceremony took place two days later. Lord Cornwallis, unworthily, pleaded illness and did not lead out his beaten garrison. As he laid the duty on his second in command, General Charles O'Hara, Washington directed O'Hara to take orders from the American second in command, General Benjamin Lincoln. Similar ceremonies at Gloucester Point closed the scene, except for the officers' dinners, tendered by victors to vanquished. Exclusive of sailors, the captured British and Germans numbered 7241. Also surrendered were the military chest, all war materials, and the vessels in the harbor.

Lieutenant Colonel Tench Tilghman, Washington's long-time aide, was honored with the victory dispatch to Congress. His news was appropriately greeted, and he was congratulated. One item of business remained. Tilghman required cash to pay for his relays of horses from Yorktown to Philadelphia. But lo, the Continental treasury was empty. The members of Congress passed the hat and each contributed a dollar to discharge the debt.

The capture of Cornwallis' entire army was practically the end of the fighting war, but vexations continued during the two years in which hostilities lasted.

Restless Camp

T HE VICTORY OF THE AMERICANS AND FRENCH OVER CORN-
WALLIS AT YORKTOWN IN OCTOBER 1781 ENDED THE SERI-
OUS FIGHTING IN THE REVOLUTION. WASHINGTON'S ARMY
lay idle at New Windsor, New York, adjacent to Newburgh.

In December 1782, the officers, long out of pocket in the camp
on the Hudson, sent a petition to Congress. It was entirely submissive to the civil authority. Congress was addressed "with all proper
deference and respect" as "the supreme power of the United States
. . . our head and sovereign." The plea was signed by Major General Henry Knox and twelve officers of lesser rank, on behalf of all
officers of the army "and our brethren the soldiers."

"We find our embarrassment thicken so fast," they asserted,
"that many of us are unable to go on further. . . . We complain
that shadows have been offered to us while the substance has been
gleaned by others. . . . Our distresses are now brought to a point.
We have borne all that men can bear—our property is
expended—our private resources are at an end . . . We, therefore, most . . . earnestly beg, that a supply of money may be for-

warded to the army as soon as possible. The uneasiness of the soldiers, for want of pay, is great and dangerous; any further
experiments on their patience may have fatal effects."

Large sums were due for deficiencies in rations and clothing.
The officers were willing, on retirement, to accept full pay for a
term of years in place of half pay for life. But they felt that it
would be criminal to conceal their dissatisfaction at injuries which
in the course of seven long years had "made their condition in
many instances wretched." Major General Alexander McDougall
and Colonels Robert Brooks and Mathias Ogden were named a deputation to present the petition to Congress.

The distresses of Congress, like those of the unpaid army, were
"now brought to a point." While the fighting war lasted, Congress
had managed to rub along by one expedient and another, including generous aids from France. Now that peace loomed, accumu-
lated debts could no longer be supported by patriotism and postponement. The suffering army, which must still be kept intact, was
the worthiest and most insistent creditor. Not only the honor but
the safety of the country hung on finding pay for the troops—
back pay, present pay, future (retirement) pay. The treasury was
woefully inadequate. Congress was more to be pitied than censured, for, by the faulty existing constitution, it bore responsibility
without corresponding authority. Congress could command no
funds of its own, and it could only beg contributions from the wayward, reluctant states, some of which, indeed, were wartorn.

Congress named a grand committee—one member from each
state—to respond to the army's petition.

The financial embarrassment of Congress, to give it no harsher
name, was summarized in a report on the public debt. At the end
of October 1781, Congress had requested of the states $8 million
for the service of the ensuing year. Of this only $420,031 was re-
ceived during 1782 and January 1783. The sum in the treasury
—mostly from France—available to Congress to carry on the

public business in 1782 was $1,545,818. However, pay, rations, and clothing for the army amounted to $5,713,610, without taking account of camp equipment, fuel, horses and forage, hospital expense, and other large items. In conclusion, "the whole sum which Congress could command was not sufficient to pay the interest due on the public debt."

The exact size of the public debt, or how it was divided between classes of creditors, was not known, and, in fact, would not be ascertained for another ten years. Three weeks after Congress exhibited its poverty—not for the first time—the Superintendent of Finance was asked to estimate the principal of the public debt to January 1, 1783, specifying foreign debt, debt due the army, debt due on loan office certificates, and amounts owing on liquidated and unliquidated debt. If it were possible to secure steady income, pledged to payment of interest on the debt, that was the most that Congress could expect and it might serve in the emergency. For if the debt had sure value because the interest was regularly paid, the certificates would be confidently bought and sold, and they would serve as the basis of loans. Then the army could be paid, except for immediate needs, not in cash, but in evidences of public debt which the soldiers could sell or borrow upon.

A week after its appointment, the grand committee on the plaint of the impoverished officers showed the straits to which they had come. James Madison and Richard Peters proposed that the Superintendent of Finance be consulted on the propriety of applying to France for yet another loan. Sponsors of this expedient did not want to appear unreasonable, but "the crisis of our affairs demanded the experiment; . . . money must if possible be procured for the army." Desperation inspired far-fetched arguments. If France refused, she would not like to see Great Britain extend the needed help. (But who would expect the enemy to succor the departing colonies?). If France squeezed out still more money to pay American troops, she could rejoice as her praises were sung in every state by the men who were disbanded. Others objected "as honest men ag[ain]st levying contributions on the friendship of France . . . whilst the unwillingness of the States to invest Congress with permanent funds rendered a repayment so precarious." In spite of these scruples, three members were told off to sound out Robert Morris.

That evening, January 13, 1783, the grand committee gave audience to the deputies from the army. General McDougall repeated the requests in the petition: some pay immediately, adequate provision for the remainder, and half pay for officers on retirement. He spoke for both officers and soldiers, "painted their sufferings & services, their successive hopes and disappointments throughout the whole war"; he foresaw serious consequences from worse neglect "when the necessity of their services shd be over." One part of McDougall's speech revealed the underlying problem, as his hearers well knew. The most intelligent in the army, he testified, "were deeply affected at the debility and defects in the federal Govt., and the unwillingness of the States to cement & invigorate it." He had an eye to the future as well as the present. If the Confederation fell apart, the benefits expected from the Revolution would be lessened; the states might fight each other, and the officers would be embroiled in civil war.

The Congressmen wanted to know the worst: what steps might the army take if no pay could be immediately furnished? The deputies from camp answered that no plan had been formed, but that "there was . . . reason to dread that at least a mutiny would ensue." If the soldiers broke faith with the public it would be hard for the officers to control them, because the public had flagrantly broken faith with the soldiers. McDougall asserted that the army was "verging on that state which . . . will make a wise man mad." Colonel Brooks feared that another refusal of the soldiers' plea would "throw them blindly into extremities." Colonel Ogden wished not to return to the army if he had to be "the bearer of bad news."

Three from the grand committee—Hamilton, Madison, and Rutledge—were deputed to propose a reply. Their task was the harder because signs multiplied that the unpaid troops were soon to be disbanded. General Greene notified Congress that the enemy had evacuated Charleston. Plans were afoot to auction off military equipment no longer needed, especially horses, which were expensive to maintain. At the same time, means of recruiting funds faded. The Superintendent of Finance convinced Congress not to importune France until debts already contracted were provided for. A week later, on January 24, notice came from the valiant Robert Morris that "made a deep and solemn impression on Congress." Danger from the enemy was disappearing, and he saw little prospect of the country doing justice to its creditors. "He wod. never be the Minister" of such a wrong. Therefore he proposed not to serve longer than the coming May unless the debt was put on a proper footing.

After conferring with the Financier, Hamilton's trio ticked off answers to the various demands of the army, though they amounted to nothing more than empty promises. As to present pay, the Financier should "be ordered . . . as soon as the state of public finances will permit to make such payment and in such manner as he shall think proper." As to arrearages of pay, "the states [should] be called upon to complete, without delay, the settlements [determine what was owing] with their respective lines, up to the first day of August, 1780, and that the Superintendent of Finance be directed to take such measures as shall appear to him most proper for effecting the settlements, from that period."

It was declared that the troops had an undoubted right to expect security for the amounts found due, but the fulfillment of that expectation was much in the future. The words were: "Congress will make every effort in their power to obtain from the respective states substantial funds, adequate to the object of funding the whole debt of the United States, and will enter upon an immediate and full consideration of the nature of such funds, and the most likely mode of obtaining them."

As to the officers' retirement compensation, they could have half pay for life or elect to receive full pay for (blank) years, to be paid starting one year after the war's end, in money, or placed upon good, funded security at annual interest of 6 per cent.

Concerning settlement of accounts covering deficiencies of rations, clothing, and the like, the committee postponed report until more precise information was at hand.

The problem of pay for the army, especially back pay and the officers' pensions, involved the larger problem of establishing public credit, and that in turn hinged on the willingness of the states to become members in a competent national government. During the war, improvisation had barely sufficed to win victory, but now military effort had to be succeeded by a political campaign. Experience was to prove that the internal struggle for unity was as arduous and required as many years as defense against the external foe had. Congress might squeeze out cash for a month or two of wages for the soldiers to permit them, when disbanded, to reach their homes. They could be given certificates for the remaining sums due them. But how could the certificates be made into more than words and figures on paper? If they were to be worthless promises, the veterans who held them would be cheated. Naturally, they would distrust the Congress that deceived them; they would look to their separate states for relief, and postpone the day of reform of the government.

Robert Morris, the war Financier, had observed that the Articles of Confederation gave Congress "the privilege of asking everything," but secured to each state "the prerogative of granting nothing." When—or whether—the supplications of Congress for money from the states would be answered was "known only to Him who knoweth all things." Therefore, if Congress was to have any credit at home or abroad, it must be able to command a revenue independent of the shameful negligence of the states. As early as February 1781, Congress had begged the right of collecting a 5 per cent import duty. In spite of special entreaties, the states dragged in giving their consent. Finally, after nearly two years, when all others except Georgia had approved, Rhode Island refused the grant. A deputation from Congress was dispatched to beg the recalcitrant littlest state to conform. The emissaries had not ridden far when they learned that Virginia had withdrawn her agreement, so they turned their horses back to Philadelphia.

Congress had not long to wait (January 27, 1783) for official confirmation of Virginia's repeal. But the central government, no matter how its necessities were mocked, could not abdicate or despair. Day after day was devoted to the problem of obtaining money to pay the interest on the public debt. A committee to reply to clamorous creditors was forced to explain that, after two patient years, hope of a sure revenue for the central government had been dashed. "Congress have the mortification to find that one state entirely refuses its concurrence, that another has withdrawn its assent once given, and that a third has given no answer."

The states had hung back with their contributions "in every period of the war." Now they sought to deny Congress funds from another source, import duties. Nevertheless, federal income was "indispensably *necessary towards* . . . restoring public credit and . . . providing for the future exigencies of the war." Congress had no choice but to revive its rejected proposal, urging it now "in a more extensive view." More days of searching discussion produced the resolve to establish "permanent and adequate funds, *on taxes or duties which shall operate generally, and . . . in just proportions* throughout the U.S."

Working out the specifics of a feasible fiscal system was to be an agonizing process. The admirable Hugh Williamson, a member of both Congress and the North Carolina legislature, voiced his lament to another of national views, James Iredell: "We borrow money, and have not the means of paying sixpence. There is no measure, however wise or necessary, that may not be defeated by any single State, however small or wrong-headed. The cloud of public creditors, including the army, are gathering about us; the prospect thickens. Believe me, that I would rather take the field in the hardest military service I ever saw, than face the difficulties that await us in Congress within a few months." Joseph Jones of Virginia reported to Washington that "difficulties apparently insurmountable presented themselves . . . owing to the different circumstances of the several States," and the problem of devising taxes that would operate "generally and equally." "Promises," the North Carolina delegates reported, "even those which are specious, are found to be very light food. Our army and all other public Creditors wish for something more substantial." Hamilton, in the midst of the daily debates, regretted that "the centrifugal is much stronger than the centripetal force in these states," and was grieved by the "fatal opposition to Continental views."

Two riddles, intimately connected, had to be solved. First, what was an equitable basis of the states' quotas of contribution? Second, what forms of federal revenue should be stipulated?

The quotas on which the states paid—or did not pay—the requisitions of Congress were informally determined approximations of the supposed capacity of each. It was now urged that the rule in the Articles of Confederation for fixing quotas be complied with. This was the value of lands granted or surveyed and the improvements (the buildings). If the values were assessed by the states, they would be grossly unequal in the standards employed, and the states would maneuver to minimize the value of their lands. Assessment by appointees of Congress was bitterly opposed. After much wrangling, the proposal was made that the states should report the mere quantity of lands, buildings, and population, subject to review by Congress. This plan, equally imperfect, was finally abandoned for the recommendation that population be the basis of state quotas of contribution. The sop thrown to the Southern states was to count only three-fifths of their slaves.

General Washington knew in advance that some in the camp were in rebellion against the vague reply of Congress to the petition of the officers. Joseph Jones, in Congress, informed him in February of reports in Philadelphia "that there are dangerous combinations in the Army, and within a few days past it has been said, that they are about to declare, they will not disband until their demands are complied with." Alexander Hamilton went further, suggesting that if the unpaid army coerced Congress, this threat would powerfully reinforce the claims of all other creditors. Fear might produce funds where reason and the sense of justice defaulted. Hamilton recognized the peril of his proposal. What if pressure from the military became an actual march on Philadelphia? If swords and bayonets pricked the legislature into compliance, who could know where that would lead? He saw that "the difficulty will be to keep a *complaining* and *suffering army* within bounds." Washington could act through "confidential and prudent persons" to countenance compulsion by the soldiers and at the same time moderate their demands. General Knox, Hamilton suggested, had the confidence of the army, was a man of sense, and "he may safely be made use of."

Washington in reply rejected any such provocative role for the army. He himself would never be the director of military menace to secure payment. If the army were exposed to dissolution without subsistence, the result would be "Civil commotions . . . [that would] end in blood. . . . God forbid we should be involved in it." He was not without hope that Congress and the states would provide for the troops and avoid evil forebodings. He thought it might be advisable for Congress to adjourn for a few months, so the members could convince the people of "the great defects of their Constitution." Such a step would promote the public weal, "for it is clearly my opinion, unless Congress have powers competent to all *general* purposes, that the distresses we have encountered, the expence we have incurred, and the blood we have spilt in the course of an Eight years war, will avail us nothing."

Speaking to Hamilton, his intimate and his former aide, Washington was tender of his own standing and resentful of conniving criticism. He had not forgotten the machinations of the cabal five years earlier, favoring Horatio Gates to replace him as Commander in Chief, in which he believed Gates had participated. The source of the unrest propagated in the army "may be easily traced to the old leaven, *it is said,* for I have no proof of it, is again, beginning to work, under the mask of the most perfect dissimulation, and apparent cordiality."

Those in the army who wanted to bring physical pressure on Congress, to which Washington would not agree, exerted themselves to make him unpopular so they could displace him with a Commander in Chief who would do their bidding. This was the report of members of Congress who knew the temper of the camp. Hamilton said that Washington's extreme reserve and occasional asperity had increased, reducing the favor in which he was held. However, "his firmness would . . . never yield to any dishonorable or disloyal plans into which he might be called; . . . he would sooner suffer him to be cut into pieces."

While Congress groped toward an over-all financial solution that would not furnish the instant cash the army begged, the camp was outwardly quiet. Then suddenly, the rousing challenge of unsigned circulars exploded a bombshell.

The first anonymous communication was brief; it was a call for commissioned officers to meet on the next day, March 11, to consider the recent report of the representatives who waited on Congress. It contained a half-threat, for the conference was to discuss "what measures (if any) should be adopted, to obtain that redress of grievances which they seem to have solicited in vain." General Washington learned of this notice at once, and he disapproved of the irregular proceeding. The next day he saw "with inexpressible concern" an anonymous address to the officers, "handed about in a clandestine manner."

This paper, of some 1200 words, had bite. As Washington several times said, its manner was as skillful as its intent was vicious. The author began by establishing his bond with his suffering fellow soldiers; he trusted that his comparative youth and modest rank would not discredit his advice. Is your country, he asked, "willing to redress your wrongs," or is it one that "tramples upon your rights, disdains your cries and insults your distresses?" The letter from the emissaries to Congress showed how "meek language of entreating memorials" had been answered.

"If this, then, be your treatment, while the swords you wear are necessary for the defence of America, what have you to expect from peace, when your voices shall sink, and your strength dissipate by division? . . . Can you consent to wade through the vile mire of dependence, and owe the miserable remnant of that life to charity, which hitherto has been spent in honor? If you can— GO—and carry with you . . . the pity of the world. Go, starve, and be forgotten!" But, he urged, if resolve for remedy was equal to wrongs suffered, a last remonstrance to Congress should not be "sueing, soft," but "assume a bolder tone. . . . Tell them that the army has its alternative. If peace, that nothing shall separate you from your arms but death: if war, that . . . inviting the direction of your illustrious leader, you will retire to some unsettled country . . . and 'mock when their fear cometh on.'" After this menace, in his closing lines the author pictured the grateful result of an army justly rewarded, "an army victorious over its enemies, victorious over itself."

The supposition of the anonymous writer that Washington

might head the army in dire designs was instantly disappointed. The Commander in Chief, in general orders posted on Tuesday, March 11, disallowed the meeting called for that morning and postponed it four days, until Saturday. This, he told Congress, was "To prevent any precipitate and dangerous resolutions from being taken at this perilous moment, while the passions were all inflamed." "After mature deliberation," the order said, the officers "will devise what further measures ought to be adopted as most rational and best calculated to attain the just . . . object in view." The senior officer in rank would preside and report the result of the deliberations to the Commander in Chief.

The anonymous author was not silenced. In a second letter he pointed out that Washington's order for a postponed meeting sanctioned the need for independent discussion by the officers of the unsatisfactory response of Congress to their complaint. He defended his aspersed anonymity with "it matters very little who is the author of sentiments which grow out of your feelings." If anyone was held up to resentment for the letters he promised to declare himself.

Washington did not wait for the issue of the meeting to beg friends in Congress to promote relief of the anxieties that were rife in the army. He told Joseph Jones, his fellow Virginian, that the alarms had originated in Philadelphia. The camp had been quiet until an officer arrived from the capital city—it was Colonel Walter Stewart—who propagated a dangerous idea. This was that the public creditors looked to the army to compel Congress to make provision for the country's debts. The civilian creditors, it was promised, would join the military in the field if necessary. Washington declared that if the officers, excited to despair, had responded to this summons, they would have plunged the country into "the abyss of misery." As he had arrested such impetuous action, calm remedy could be devised.

The General wisely outlined what was needed. "There is not a man in [the army]," he asserted, "who will not acknowledge that Congress have not the means of payment, but why not, say they one and all, liquidate the Accts. and certifie our dues? are we to be disbanded and sent home without this?" Once dispersed, the soldiers must make their individual applications in innumerable different places that were inconvenient and costly to reach. If accounts were not stated previous to separation, it could never be done. In fact, the army suspected that the bookkeeping had been postponed in order "that individual loss . . . becomes a public gain."Congress could easily and swiftly content the army with certificates of exactly what was owing to each soldier. If there were delegates who were really opposed to doing justice to the army, "tell them, if matters shd come to extremity, that they must be answerable for all the ineffable horrors which may be occasioned thereby." Washington wrote similarly to Alexander Hamilton, with the addition that "the plight of the officers is distressing, beyond description . . . a large part of them have no other prospect before them than a Goal [jail], if they are turned loose without a liquidation of Accts. and an assurance of the justice to which they are so worthily entitled." In a postscript he noted that, since the second anonymous letter had appeared so promptly, the author was in or near camp, and not a member of a cabal in Philadelphia.

The exact correspondence of tremors in the army and the expectaton of impending disbandment was plain in the announcement of Elias Boudinot, the President of Congress, to the Commander in Chief on March 12, 1783, that the preliminary treaty of peace had been signed by the British and American commissioners at Paris on November 30, 1782.

On the eve of the meeting of the officers, Washington wrote that the "Storm [which] suddenly arose with unfavorable prognosticks . . . tho' diverted for a moment, is not yet blown over," and he could not forecast the issue. He reversed his earlier intention not to be present at the gathering, and resolved to deliver his feeling address in person. He rode that morning the two miles from New-burgh to the encampment at New Windsor. He took some re-freshment, it is said, with General Greene and General Knox at Knox's headquarters before going with them to the "new building," or "Temple" (social hall), where the officers assembled.

If his audience needed any winning, his opening words did it. He started to read his manuscript, then fumbled for his glasses, re-marking, "You see that I have grown not only grey but blind in your service."

Most of Washington's spirited appeal was devoted to refuting the anonymous letter that was the occasion of the meeting and that might have determined its tone. The unsigned circular, he de-clared, was "addressed more to the . . . passions than to the reason and judgment of the army. The author," he continued, "is entitled to much credit for the goodness of his pen; and I could wish he has as much credit for the rectitude of his heart. . . ." Instead, the paper insinuated "the darkest suspicion to effect the blackest de-sign" and was "drawn with great art . . . to answer the most insid-ious purposes." It sought to convince the officers of "premeditated injustice in the sovereign power of the United States. . . ."

In a touching recital, the Commander in Chief trusted that at this late day he need not prove himself "a faithful friend to the army." The false champion of the army opened a "dreadful alternative"—if peace ensued, turn swords on Congress; if war, then abandon the country. "My God! what can this writer have in view, by recommending such measures." He must be a provocateur from the British. Since the choice had been posed, Washington was at pains to demonstrate that either course was equally revolting and self-defeating.

The General exhorted the officers to "give one more distin-guished proof of unexampled patriotism and patient virtue . . . and you will, by the dignity of your conduct afford occasion for posterity to say, when speaking of the glorious example you have exhibited to mankind—'had this day been wanting, the world had never seen the last stage of perfection to which human nature is capable of attaining.' "

Washington then withdrew. The "Temple" was really such, for his hearers were left in a devotional state. Knox and Rufus Putnam moved resolves thanking the Commander in Chief and assuring him that the officers returned his affection. The pertinent papers were read to the gathering—the petition of the army to Congress, the report of the committee that had been sent to Philadelphia, and Congress' measures in response to the officers' distress. A committee of several ranks, with General Knox as chairman, in a short half-hour brought in resolves that concluded the business of the meeting. (Knox must have known the contents of Washington's speech beforehand; he was ready with wording of the officers' approval.)

The crisis was over. "The army," said the resolves, "continue to have an unshaken confidence in the justice of Congress and their country, and are fully convinced that the representatives of America will not disband . . . the army until their accounts are liquidated . . . and adequate funds established for payment and . . . the half pay, or a commutation of it." Further, the officers "view with abhorrence, and reject with disdain, the infamous propositions contained in a late anonymous address. . . ." The motives of the officers for entering the service at the commencement of the struggle—purest attachment to the rights and liberties of human nature—"still exist in the highest degree, and . . . no circumstances of distress or danger shall induce a conduct that may tend to sully the reputation and glory which they have acquired at the price of their blood."

It was not known until long afterward that young Major John Armstrong, in the camp as aide to General Gates, was the author of the addresses to the officers that had threatened to touch the match to the tinder. Circumstantial evidence points to Gates as the instigator who guided the pernicious pen of his junior associate. Though Washington sharply condemned the anonymous letters for the fatal mischief they promised to bring on the camp and the country, fourteen years later he retracted, to Armstrong, his harshest censures. This may have been because Washington held Gates to be primarily to blame. Not until 1823, late in his varied career, did Armstrong admit the authorship of the celebrated missives.

Washington was asked by the officers to entreat Congress to take early and satisfactory action on the subject of the army's application. Meantime, some members of the committee from the army were waiting on Congress for the result of the legislators' deliberation.

General Gates signed the minutes of the meeting, which General Washington enclosed with his own letter to Congress. The proceedings, he wrote, terminated "with perfect unanimity, and in a manner entirely consonant to my wishes." The officers gave "the last glorious proof of patriotism which . . . will not only confirm their claim to the justice, but will encrease their title to the gratitude of their country." He begged the earliest compliance with the army's petition, and reminded the representatives, by extracts from his previous letters to Congress, that he had always pressed for proper rewards. He "mingled warmth" with his observations. If faithful officers were to be the only sufferers by the Revolution, "then shall I have learned what ingratitude is, then shall I have realized a tale which will embitter every moment of my future life."

Washington was at concert pitch, but Congress remained in a lower register. The reply of a sympathetic committee thanked the Commander in Chief and officers for their patriotic conduct; the troops were entitled to the gratitude of the country. More substantial was the resolve of Congress that officers, if those of the different states so chose, might elect to commute half pay for life to full pay for five years. Three weeks later the Secretary of War, on his return from camp, reported Washington's wishes concerning measures to be adopted before disbanding the army. It would be chimerical to wait until permanent funds were established. Rather, the accounts should be liquidated; it should be stated to every soldier what was due him. Three months' pay should be given the troops in hand, or at least one month's pay to enable them to go to their homes. Washington was persuaded "that the moment peace is announced to the army, it will be impossible to retain the men who are engaged to serve during the war." When peace was declared, the soldiers should be allowed either to remain in camp until their accounts were settled or to leave immediately. A plenary committee, with the Secretary of War and the Superintendent of Finance, should go to camp to facilitate disbandment. These recommendations were pressing, for the very next day, April 15, Congress ratified the preliminary peace treaty.

Though Washington, in the ferment of the camp, urged his stopgap measure to permit the troops to be discharged, Congress, in the more contented capital, would not be diverted from its comprehensive aim of serving all of the public creditors. As to the form of revenue, numerous taxes were considered but found ineligible —poll tax, land tax, house tax, window tax, salt tax. In the end, on April 18, 1783, Congress asked the states to approve a combination measure to permit payment of interest on the debt and, finally, discharge of the principal. The central tax feature was import duties, specific on listed commodities (mainly imported liquors, coffee, and tea), and 5 per cent *ad valorem* on all other goods. Collectors were to be appointed by the states, but they were to be under the jurisdiction of Congress. The proceeds of these duties, which were to be limited to a duration of twenty-five years, were to be applied exclusively to the public debt. The states were to meet requisitions totaling $1,500,000 annually. Quotas were to be based on population, a census to be taken every three years. States were urged to complete their cessions of Western lands.

Though Congress pleaded with the states to accept this temporary funding scheme, the response was even slower than it had been to the earlier plan of 1781, and no more satisfactory. Pennsylvania and Delaware agreed to give their approval when all other states had done so, but New York, in the spring of 1786, attached to its acceptance conditions which Congress found defeating. Governor George Clinton at first balked at the request to call the New York legislature in special session to reconsider its unfavorable action. When he complied with the renewed appeal of Congress, the legislature refused to withdraw its reservations. So Congress was thrown back on the old discredited method of requisitions, and the public finances remained in disarray until the national government was established under the new Constitution.

The aborted second attempt of the Continental Congress to put itself in funds, even had it been swiftly embraced, would not have yielded money in time to pay the army on discharge of the troops. The Bank of North America could not lend the necessary sum—more than half a million cash. Except for the patriotic willingness of Robert Morris, the Financier, to extend his personal credit for the purpose, the soldiers would have been disbanded empty-handed. Morris would issue his own notes, payable in six months. The difficulty was that he had determined to leave office at the end of May 1783, and he absolutely declined to put his reputation in the hands of a successor who would be responsible for redeeming the notes. Congress thereupon asked him to remain in his post, which he did until November 1, 1784. Morris immediately (June 1783) set about signing his thousands of notes, but they did not arrive in the camps until most of the troops had been furloughed home. It is uncertain at what discount the soldiers' notes were exchanged for cash. They circulated on a par with specie in Philadelphia, but holders elsewhere, especially to the southward, suffered losses when they sold their pay warrants. Reports were that some, hard pressed for daily living, accepted as little as fifteen or twenty cents on the dollar from speculators. Robert Morris, when he left office, declared that all of the army pay notes had been redeemed.

Vexation at Paris

AFTER SIX AND A HALF YEARS OF MAKING WAR, TWO YEARS MORE WERE NECESSARY TO MAKE PEACE. THE ENEMY VIRTUALLY CEASED MILITARY AND NAVAL OPERATIONS against the United States following the surrender of Lord Cornwallis; then, for the Americans, the contest became one of negotiation in Europe. This involved more than a settlement with the foe. Ironically, more problems arose from the designs of the ally, France, than from the obstinacy of England, the antagonist. When the terms of peace were to be fixed; it became increasingly clear that France hated England rather than loving the rebellious colonies.

"His Most Christian Majesty, our generous ally," had entered the struggle to get revenge on England for defeat in the Seven Years' War, which had ended fifteen years earlier. True, France

The material in this chapter is drawn, with grateful acknowledgment, from Professor Richard B. Morris' comprehensive treatment, *The Peacemakers* (New York, Harper & Row, 1965).

was pledged to securing the independence of the American rebels, but this was to deprive Britain of her most valuable possessions. That done, France determined to limit the power and prospects of the young nation she had helped to free. The American peacemakers promptly discovered that the dominant figure with whom they must contend was not George III, nor Louis XVI, but Louis' Minister of Foreign Affairs, Count Vergennes. That cunning servant of Versailles wished to control the present and future of Europe, America, and even of European penetration of the Far East. He jockeyed with all of the sovereigns, or, more accurately, with their spokesmen in the circle of contentious diplomats. Of the rulers themselves, the most aggressive was Catherine the Great of Russia, and next to her, of more humane stripe, Frederick the Great of Prussia, and then Joseph II of Austria. The Ministers of these three were of varying importance, Prince von Kaunitz of Austria being the most potent.

France's ally was Spain. This connection constantly threatened to thwart the Americans in the peace negotiations. France claimed no territory on the American continent, but Spain was determined to extend her possessions to the whole of the Mississippi valley and gain control of the Gulf of Mexico. King Charles III, uncle of Louis XVI, was shadowy compared with his bold Premier, Count Floridablanca, who was absolutist, reactionary. Vergennes, the engine of French policy, kept his eye on every European court, but his stated commitment was to Spain, which meant, so far as the Americans were concerned, to Floridablanca. The expectation of several sovereigns, principally Catherine of Russia and Joseph of Austria, that they would mediate the war, had busied Vergennes earlier. However, their insistence faded as the Minister of Spain took the spotlight with demands to which Vergennes was bound to attend.

The roadblocks that Floridablanca placed in the way of a peace satisfactory to the Americans were typical of the habits of mind and action of European courts of the time. Though George III was dogmatic and obtuse in dealings with his colonies, he did have a functioning Parliament, and active in it were outspoken opponents of his policy. The other sovereigns were autocratic in fact as well as in name. They did not comprehend the democratic government that had risen in America and were prepared to repel it or to make it a pawn in their inter-power moves. The Empress of Russia was nominally represented by a succession of favorites of the council chamber (and, by the same token, of the bedchamber), but she was actually the author of their intrigues.

Elsewhere on the continent of Europe, with few exceptions, the Ministers of state devised and executed their own national purposes. The fact of the American Revolution and the physical presence of commissioners from across the Atlantic hardly disturbed their customary behavior. Little did they guess that the world they manipulated was soon to come tumbling about their ears. Vergennes of France, particularly, joining in the American war in order to thrust at England, had unwittingly allied himself with forces that would destroy all he held dear. Revolution was soon to erupt in his own country, and in its career, blessed and baneful, it would tear apart the very fabric he had been weaving. The American negotiators, in the decent garb of the people, did not confront the last of the decorated noblemen; there were still to be Talleyrand and Metternich, in the heyday of the Congress of Vienna. But their tribe would not increase.

Of the four chosen by Congress to make peace with England, Benjamin Franklin and John Adams had had previous experience of the practiced gentry of the chancelleries. John Jay was making his first venture on diplomacy, and Henry Laurens' credentials had gotten him clapped in the Tower of London. His vessel had been intercepted by the enemy off Newfoundland; when capture had loomed, he had tossed his papers overboard, but some were retrieved by the British seamen, and for fifteen months (October

1780–December 1781) Laurens was a state prisoner, suspected of treason. Franklin, a world-celebrated scientist and philosopher, enjoyed a distinction superior to that of the Foreign Ministers with whom he dealt. He returned their admiration with tolerance for their circumlocutions and postponements; had he wished to play their game, he could have done it in style. John Adams eschewed self-indulgent habits, save for nursing his vanity; clear in mind, blunt in speech, there was no foolishness about him. John Jay appeared equally straightforward and even stiffer, especially as his first assignment was to wait upon the inscrutable Floridablanca at Madrid.

Fortunately for the quartet of Americans, their discussions leading to the provisional treaty of peace were held with a number of private citizens who had been named as agents of the British government. These agents acted as go-betweens for the Earl of Shelburne, King George's Prime Minister, at first in effect, then in fact who was responsible for negotiations with America. Three of Shelburne's deputies were notably friendly toward the American commissioners. They were Richard Oswald, a Scots merchant; Benjamin Vaughan, an intellectual, who had edited Franklin's works; and David Hartley, a member of Parliament and a friend of Franklin and of America.

Shelburne himself was not hostile to peace or to America's claims, save for the prime requirement of independence. Short of that, he was for according the Americans greater liberty in trade and territory than any other loyal servant of King George was. Perhaps his conflicts with himself might have been resolved had Franklin and his colleagues been able to converse with him personally. His dignity as chief adviser of his monarch, which held him aloof, might have been waived, especially since two of the American commissioners, Laurens and Jay, had been president of the Congress. As it was, not only did Shelburne have to rely on his agents for messages and reports, but the Earl also quailed at making liberal proposals to the adamant King.

The profoundest embarrassment and handicap of the American peacemakers was their instruction from Congress binding them to the advice and consent of France. The wording was: ". . . you are to make the most candid and confidential communications upon all subjects to the ministers of our generous ally, the King of France; to undertake nothing in the negotiations for peace or truce without their knowledge and concurrence; and ultimately to govern yourselves by their advice and opinion, endeavoring in your whole conduct to make them sensible how much we rely upon his majesty's influence for . . . everything that may be necessary to the peace, security, and future prosperity of the United States of America."

This trusting mandate was cajoled, or wrung, from Congress in the spring of 1781, when that body was particularly apprehensive of war prospects. A new application had just been made to France for large-scale aid in money and ships. The resolution requiring obedience to French policy was pressed through Congress by vehement pro-French spokesmen directed by Luzerne, the Minister from France, who had his instructions from Vergennes. France was paying the piper and so called the tune. At first John Adams had been named the sole peace envoy, but, as Vergennes feared the independent New Englander would jump over the traces, Luzerne persuaded Congress to add four more commissioners, Franklin, Jay, Laurens, and Jefferson, all with equal powers. Actually, Jefferson did not serve, and Laurens, because of his imprisonment, came late into the conferences.

Only after Congress had toed the French line did Luzerne reveal to that body in full the trimming of American war aims that Vergennes might demand. If necessary for Vergennes' comfort, mediation by a concert of European powers must be accepted. That would be delaying and probably alien to American objectives, but did not cut so deep as other projected requirements. France had all along promised that, come what might, the independence of the United States was indispensable. Now it was disclosed that the settlement might have to leave the British in possession of those territories in America which they held when the fighting ceased, with the exception of New York City and Long Island. As of the spring of 1781, this meant the enemy would retain Georgia, the Carolinas, southern Virginia, the Penobscot region of Maine, and the vast area northwest of the Ohio. Such dismemberment flew in the face of independence of the thirteen states. Further, out of deference to Spain, France's ally, America might be obliged to abandon the claim to extend to the Mississippi River, perhaps might be confined east of the Alleghenies.

These obnoxious conditions, if posed in advance of framing instructions to the American peacemakers, would never have been agreed to. They were too high a price to pay for French help. Rather than buy an ignominious peace, America would have won through to victory by her own, or other, means.

For the time being, the outlook for America, military and diplomatic, was dark. However, the war was not over, and the state of affairs at the end was not foreseeable. In any event, the American commissioners were good men and true, and they could be counted on to reject dishonorable terms of peace; rather than that, the Americans would fight on.

If America's fate, come the worst, was to hang on the designs of European powers, particularly France and Spain, what were their aims? Those of France toward America appeared on the surface to be noble, the vindication of this country's rights and ambitions: independence, of course; acknowledgment of the claims of Southern states that, by their original charters, they reached to the Mississippi; in any case, free navigation of that great waterway; and restoration of fishing in the Gulf of St. Lawrence and off Newfoundland. Suspicious minds had reason to fear. France did not want to raise up on the American continent a nation sufficiently powerful to challenge the world domination which France herself coveted. France wanted England to retain Canada as a bulwark against expansion of the United States. France was also tender of Spain, and she would preserve the Spanish empire in the New World, to the hurt of the rebellious British colonies.

What of the demands of Spain herself? These were not nebulous. She must have back Gibraltar. She must own both banks of the Mississippi and command navigation of that stream. For this purpose, and to protect the Gulf of Mexico, she demanded restoration of East and West Florida, which she had lost in the Seven Years' War. To the same end, English settlers cutting logwood and mahogany in Honduras and Campeche, Mexico, must be expelled and Spanish sovereignty in those regions must be conceded.

The year before his engagement on the peace mission, Jay had been appointed Minister Plenipotentiary to Spain, to form an alliance and secure loans. The partial wreck of the vessel on which he and his wife left America, and the fleas and lice that plagued the exhausting journey from Cadiz to Madrid, were forecasts of the painful treatment he was to receive in two years of frustrated petitions to the Spanish court. Floridablanca, the First Minister of the King, refused to recognize Jay as the envoy of the independent United States; his greatest concession was a long-delayed invitation to him to dine with the Minister "as a private gentleman of distinction." Jay at first held out for the Americans' right to navigation of the Mississippi, but even when this was withdrawn on condition that Spain enter into an alliance, the offer was refused. The British capture of Charleston appeared to encourage Spain's contemptuous response to American overtures, and the American capture of Cornwallis' army at Yorktown eighteen months later did not improve Spanish manners. Promises of financial assistance went unfulfilled. Poor Jay, at his wit's end to meet bills of exchange drawn on him by Congress, occasionally received small sums at the eleventh hour, but finally he had to let bills go to protest. For his living expenses, Jay had to spend his own money and to borrow. In the end he was rescued only by remittances from

Franklin, in Paris. By the time Jay left Spain, in May 1782, to join his colleagues of the peace mission, it appeared that the court of Madrid was scarcely less hostile to American pretentions than to British.

The American peacemakers were commanded by Congress to be governed by France. But France was obligated to advance the war aims of Spain. Since Spanish objects were antithetical to American interests, the commissioners of the United States in Paris were in a dilemma. Fortunately, the drastic failure of two joint enterprises of Spain and France had cooled the ardor of the belligerent Vergennes for cooperation with his neighbor to the south. The first, in the summer of 1779, was the attempted invasion of England by 60,000 troops, who were to cross the Channel in 400 transports convoyed by combined French and Spanish warships. The British were comically unprepared for naval and land defense, and they were divided in councils. The opposition in Parliament hinted that the only safety lay in forcing King George to abdicate—which, of course, would sweep out the North ministry—then seizing on effective measures of resistance. Actually, England was well protected by the imbecility of the French-Spanish naval and military leadership, plus smallpox in the crowded holds of the cross-Channel fleets. After months of laughable errors on both sides, the allied Bourbons defeated themselves.

Then, three years later, in September 1782, Spanish and French fleets laid siege to Gibraltar. French floating batteries, boasted to be indestructible, were set aflame by red-hot cannonballs from the Rock, and the garrison was relieved by the nimble fleet of Lord Howe. Spanish warships hung about for despairing months, but the fortress that could not be taken by arms was plainly not to be acquired by argument.

In an early meeting with Oswald, the British agent, Franklin posed America's "necessary" terms of peace, three in number. "Full and compleat independence" was foremost. Second, the bounds of Canada must be pushed back to their earlier limits, giving the Old Northwest to the United States. The last article was the freedom to fish on the Newfoundland Banks. Besides these essential demands, Franklin proposed "desirable" provisions of the treaty. American citizens should be compensated for property losses at the hands of the British during the war, as a means of promoting good relations between the two countries into the future. More important, he urged trade reciprocity between Britain and the United States. This benefit was not included in the treaty as drawn, and commerce between the two nations was vexed by discriminations in the years to come. If Franklin's wish had been pursued, it might have met the approval of Lord Shelburne, to whom free trade was a favorite principle. The resentments of both sides stood in the way of mutual concessions, but experience was to show that economic exchanges bulked large in gains from the peace. In losing colonies, Britain secured customers. American trade, which had been diverted to France during the war, returned to the mother country, and this commerce expanded beyond expectation, to the advantage of both parties, inducing not only economic, but political ties.

America's minimum requirements, with others which the commissioners promptly brought forward, became the basis of discussions. One of Franklin's "desirable" features—the acquisition by the United States of the whole of Canada—was early scrapped. Aside from opposition of the British, the French (read Vergennes) wanted to cramp the United States territorially as severely as possible, a policy in which Spain vehemently concurred.

Worse, it soon developed that Vergennes meant to modify France's pledge to obtain the independence of her American ally. Ironically, he explored means of minimizing the political freedom of the United States, though not as overtly as King George and the British cabinet did. Franklin and Jay, and Adams when he joined them in the conversations, were determined on this score, as Congress was in all of its instructions. John Jay insisted that the perfect independence of his nation must be acknowledged before peace negotiations were formally entered into. This should be done by act of Parliament, or, since Parliament was not in session, by proclamation of the King. Aside from the principle that discussions should proceed between Ministers with equal powers, a mere truce and cease-fire would be perilous to America. Washington's army would substantially disband, leaving British garrisons intact for possible resumption of hostilities.

Franklin was no less firm on independence, but he did not insist that it be acknowledged as a precondition of peace negotiations. He was amenable to having independence stated in an article of the treaty. Jay and Adams, both eminent lawyers, considered prior recognition of the sovereignty of the United States more than a technical precaution. Franklin, with them in spirit, was a publicist and diplomat rather than a legalist. In his approach he was less formal than his colleagues, more tolerant of give and take around the edges, so long as central contentions of his country were satisfied. Moreover, he had been long in France, in intimate connection with the court as interpreter of American war aims and beggar for French assistance. Jay and Adams were new brooms.

Franklin got wind of rumors that Lord Shelburne favored retention of King George's sovereignty over America, granting the colonies a separate parliament. This was an alarming retreat from what Franklin had understood from Shelburne's agents— namely, "that the point of dependence was given up, and that we were to be treated as a free people." In response to Franklin's remonstrance, or request for clarification, Shelburne sought, through Oswald, to reassure the American. The promise of "the most unequivocal acknowledgment of American Independency" seemed explicit, but the Earl knew how to blur the meaning. Oswald's commission empowered him to treat, conclude, etc., with representatives of "the colonies or plantations . . . or any of

[340]

them." Here was no recognition of the new nation, and in fact the plain intention was that some states might be separated from the others. There was more hedging and qualification. Oswald's instructions cautioned that independence was to be admitted as "the price" of peace—that is, would be conceded as an article in the treaty, if a treaty were agreed upon, otherwise, Britain still claimed "the colonies." Also, if the Americans would not enter into a "political league of union or amity" exclusively with Britain, their independence would be invalidated, in British eyes, if they agreed with any other power; they must not continue in alliance with France. The idea was to coax the United States out of the war so His Majesty could concentrate on defeating France, Spain, and Holland.

Jay held talks with the Spanish Ambassador to France, Aranda, who had been deputed by Floridablanca. The question was American boundaries. Language difficulties resulted in both Ministers drawing lines on a map. Jay took in everything east of the Mississippi down to West Florida (31° north latitude) and thence by the borders of the Floridas to the Atlantic. Aranda countered with limits of the United States that coincided pretty much with the old Proclamation Line of 1763, running along the crest of the Appalachians.

The Spanish demand for confining the area of the United States was unacceptable to Franklin and Jay, and they were troubled by Shelbourne's shiftiness on American independence. Vergennes urged it would be enough if Oswald exchanged full powers with the American commissioners; that would be tantamount to acknowledging American sovereignty. Let Britain confirm this in the first article of the treaty. Franklin consented to this procedure, but not Jay. Thenceforth Jay saw Vergennes as intriguing against the interests of the United States. Vergennes would encourage the British to delay recognition of American independence. This would keep America in the war until Spain's objectives were achieved.

Jay guessed the truth—that Vergennes did not want the United States to extend to the Mississippi. In fact, he had proposed setting up a buffer Indian state between the claimants.

The revelation of Vergennes' intent to put restraints on the young republic drove a wedge in the American-French alliance. Thereafter, Jay and Adams were suspicious of French good will, and ready, if necessary, to disregard the instructions of Congress to do nothing without French knowledge and approval. Franklin was similarly distrustful, but he was more communicative with the Court of Versailles. Laurens, though descended, like Jay, from Huguenot refugees, did not lose confidence in America's ally.

The rift was widened by both England and France. Shelburne improved the opportunity to pry America from her ally and make a separate peace. He persuaded the British cabinet to grant all that the Americans demanded as essential. Parliament would acknowledge American independence prior to framing the treaty. The troops would be withdrawn from America. Britain would concede the area north of the Ohio, including a southern portion of Ontario. In the treaty payment of prewar debts, those owed to British merchants would not be claimed, nor would compensation to the loyalists be stipulated, though satisfaction on both counts, it was understood, would be secured otherwise. American fishermen would be given access to the North Atlantic coast fisheries. Since Franklin had omitted to mention rights to dry fish on shore and had not asserted that American territory must extend to the Mississippi, the English cabinet chose to be technical and likewise said nothing on these important points. Oswald was instructed to convey this package offer to the American envoys.

Vergennes, on the part of France, sent his assistant, Reyneval, to be Shelburne's house guest while they discussed terms of peace between their countries. Reyneval's mission was an open secret, and the Americans knew quite well what he was offering to the British. France was content to have the British delay recognizing

American independence. If the British would share the fisheries with France, France would join in excluding the Americans. The British should keep the Old Northwest. In accordance with British demands, the Americans would be kept from the Mississippi. These overtures to the common enemy were made behind the Americans' backs.

Jay was profoundly disquieted by the evidence that France designed to keep America in the war until a general peace was made. For the purpose of that design, Vergennes encouraged the British to postpone acknowledging America's independence; France would do the bargaining for both of them. Jay forthwith sent word to Shelburne, urging him "to cut the cords which tied us to France." To speed this proposal, Jay was willing to negotiate formally if Oswald presented a new commission authorizing him to treat with representatives of "the Thirteen United States of America." That would serve for recognition of independence, and free America from any subordination, in British eyes, to French spokesmen. The British cabinet complied. Franklin was pleased with the result of Jay's compromise solution; the treaty of peace could now go forward.

In response to Jay's appeal, John Adams promised to join his colleagues at Paris as soon as he could finish his business in Holland. Meantime Jay drafted a provisional treaty. Along with the essentials Franklin had declared, he included the right of Americans to dry fish on the Newfoundland coast. He stipulated that there should be reciprocal trade privileges between the two countries. He offered no pardon to Tories who had taken British protection, no payment of debts owing to British merchants.

Jay did more. Irked by the refusals he had had from Spain, and by the willingness of France to subordinate American interests in the peace to Spanish demands, Jay proposed that the British should send troops to seize West Florida. Oswald enthusiastically urged this project on his government. It would give the British direct access to the Mississippi, the navigation of which the Americans agreed to share with them. Oswald sweetened the prospect by suggesting that if Britain acquired West Florida, the Americans, in the treaty, would consent to have the northern boundary moved up three degrees, to the thirty-fourth parallel. If Spain kept West Florida the boundary would remain at 31°. Jay and Franklin consented. Franklin was dissuaded from informing Vergennes of what was afoot, and this engagement became a secret article in the provisional treaty. So far had the cleavage of confidence between America and France widened.

Oswald and Vaughan gladly agreed to Jay's draft of the provisional treaty. They were buoyed by the advantages to Britain from the resumption of commerce with an expanding American nation. In their elevation of spirit, they did not insist on incorporating certain coveted items contained in their instructions.

When the draft was received in London, the cabinet was not so acquiescent. Protests arose that might have been foreseen. The fishing interests wanted to deny Americans the right to dry their catch on Newfoundland shores. Expropriated Tories must be indemnified, if not by the Americans, then by their yielding the area north of the Ohio, which would be used for settlement of refugees or sold for their benefit. Otherwise, Nova Scotia should be enlarged by the addition of Maine. The treaty must stipulate payment of debts due to British merchants. Mutual trading privileges would not be admitted. A rigid Undersecretary of State was sent to Paris with new instructions for the compliant Oswald.

John Adams now joined Jay and Franklin. Franklin was suspected by the others of being too friendly with the French, but he assured them that he would omit visits to Versailles and make common cause against the fresh British resistance.

After haggling, Jay wrote a new draft of a provisional treaty. America's claim to extend to the Mississippi was recognized, the British yielding the Old Northwest. The Americans gave up southern Ontario, and agreed to an enlarged West Florida if that province became British. The maps conflicted on which rivers might be designated to separate Maine from Nova Scotia; America retained most of northern Maine, but defining the line was left to a later, mixed commission. The Americans could fish in the Gulf of St. Lawrence and on the Banks, but were denied drying rights on Newfoundland. The best the Americans could do on debts and loyalists was to promise to recommend just action in state courts and legislatures, which alone had jurisdiction, as Congress did not.

The British cabinet, encouraged by the French to stand out on the issues of Tories and fisheries, made further revisions. These led to tedious, tiring discussion by the commissioners of both parties in Paris. They disputed over the meanings of words; the Americans wanted the "right" to fish, the British preferred to concede only the "liberty" to fish. Henry Laurens then joined his American colleagues at the bargaining table. He was as firm as the others on the issue of loyalists. Franklin revived the counterclaim of reparations for British war destruction and abduction of slaves, if restitution to the loyalists by America was insisted upon.

Finally agreement was reached. The provisional treaty was signed on November 30, 1782. The Americans had violated their instructions to work in concert with their French ally. Vergennes did not know in advance the contents of the preliminary treaty, and, of course, he was kept ignorant of the secret article. Jay could justify this behavior to Congress more easily than Franklin could explain it to Vergennes. Franklin's embarrassment was the greater because in the same breath he was asking Vergennes for the further aid of six million livres.

King George III, with a pang, in his speech from the throne on the opening of Parliament on December 2, 1782, accepted the independence of the United States. Discontent in Parliament with concessions to America in the preliminary treaty led to the fall of Shelburne's ministry in February 1783. In the new coalition ministry, Charles James Fox was Foreign Secretary. David Hartley, who replaced Richard Oswald as Chief British negotiator, urged commercial reciprocity, which would give the Americans their object of direct trade with the British West Indies. Fox and the whole contingent who supported the Navigation Acts refused, whereby hung unhappy consequences which are no part of the present story.

In Congress, the terms of the provisional treaty were welcomed, but the manner of the American commissioners in making it, without knowledge of the French, was censured in debate. Particularly, the secret article designed to give England West Florida with increased area drew sharp condemnation. Then, on March 23, 1783, Congress received the news that the preliminary treaties had all been signed, and that hostilities in America had been ordered ended. West Florida went to Spain, so the secret article, reprehensible or not, was canceled. Robert R. Livingston, Secretary for Foreign Affairs, commended the commissioners for what they had achieved, but scolded them for their concealments from France. The fact was that, 3000 miles away from the scenes of negotiation, Livingston could not know the provocations, French and Spanish, under which the American envoys had acted.

The provisional treaty between Britain and the United States underwent no substantive changes. The definitive treaty was signed September 3, 1783, the same day as corresponding treaties were signed by Britain with France and Spain. As a matter of form, proxies signed for the Empress of Russia and the Emperor of Austria as mediators.

⌐

Eight years of war had accomplished independence, but that did not ensure unity at home. Internal jealousies promoted confusion and weakness under the Confederation in the years 1783–89. Nor did the firmer bond of the new Constitution prevent incipient threats of disobedience in New England in 1804 and again in 1814. These lapses were followed by bold nullification of national authority in South Carolina in 1832, then a generation later came full-scale attempted secession of the Southern states. One may say that the Revolution, or the spirit of revolt of part against the whole, turned inward and persisted for eighty years or more. These unwelcome trials were necessary to complete the promise of the War of Independence.

Selected Bibliography

American Archives

Ethan Allen, *A Narrative of Col. Ethan Allen's Captivity* (Walpole, N.H., 1807).

Thomas Anburey, *Travels through the Interior Parts of America* (2 vols., Boston, 1923).

Thomas Andros, *The Old Jersey Captive* (Boston, 1833).

E. L. Armbruster, *The Wallabout Prison Ships, 1776–1783* (New York, 1920).

P. M. Ashburn, *A History of the Medical Department of the United States Army* (Boston, 1929).

Lucius I. Barber, M.D., *A Record and Documentary History of Simsbury* (Simsbury, Conn., 1931).

Robert W. Barnwell, Jr., "The Migration of Loyalists from South Carolina," *Proc. S.C. Hist. Assn.,* 1937.

Carl Leopold Baurmeister, *Revolution in America,* trans. by B. A. Uhlendorf (New Brunswick, N.J., 1957).

Simeon Baxter, *Tyrannicide Proved Lawful . . . a Discourse Delivered in the Mines of Symsbury . . .* (London, 1782).

Ebenezer Beardsley, M.D., History of a Dysentery . . . ," *Proc. New Haven Co. Med. Soc.,* Vol. I (New Haven, 1788).

SELECTED BIBLIOGRAPHY

Lewis Beebe, M.D., *Journal,* ed. by F. R. Kirkland (Philadelphia, 1935).

Henry Belcher, *The First American Civil War* (London, 1911).

Alfred H. Bill, *Valley Forge* (New York, 1952).

W. H. Blumenthal, *Women Camp Followers of the American Revolution* (Philadelphia, 1952).

Mark Mayo Boatner, III, *Encyclopedia of the American Revolution* (New York, 1966).

Charles K. Bolton, *The Private Soldier under Washington* (New York, 1964).

Arthur G. Bradley, *Colonial Americans in Exile; Founders of British Canada* (New York, 1932).

Henry Bronson, "Historical Account of Connecticut Currency, Continental Money, and the Finances of the Revolution," *New Haven Co. Hist. Soc. Papers,* Vol. I, 1865.

Harvey E. Brown, *The Medical Department of the United States Army, 1775 to 1875* (Washington, D.C., 1873).

Wallace Brown, *The King's Friends* (Providence, 1966).

John M. Buckalew, *The Frontier Forts within the North and West Branches, Susquehanna River* (Wilkes-Barre, 1896).

Charles J. Bullcok, *Essays on the Monetary History of the United States* (New York, 1900).

———, "The Finances of the United States, 1775–1789," *Bulletin Univ. Wis., Economics,* Vol. I, No. 2, pp. 117–272 (Madison, 1895).

Edmund C. Burnett, *The Continental Congress* (New York, 1964).

———, (ed.), *Letters of Members of the Continental Congress,* (7 vols., Washington, D.C., 1921–36).

North Callahan, *Royal Raiders* (Indianapolis, 1963).

———, *Flight from the Republic; the Tories of the American Revolution* (Indianapolis, 1967).

William W. Campbell, *Annals of Tryon County. . . .* (New York, 1831).

Eli W. Caruthers, *Revolutionary Incidents* (Philadelphia, 1954).

Frances M. Caulkins, *The Stone Records of Groton* (Norwich, Conn., 1903).

———, *History of New London, Connecticut* (New London, 1852).

Harvey Chalmers, *Joseph Brant, Mohawk* (East Lansing, Mich., 1955).

SELECTED BIBLIOGRAPHY

Victor S. Clark, *History of Manufactures in the United States,* Vol. I, 1607–1860 (New York, 1929).

Charles H. Clark, "Old Newgate Mine and Prison," *Papers of Soc. of Colonial Wars in State of Connecticut,* Vol. I.

Continental Congress, *Journals, 1774–1789* (Johnson reprint, New York, 1968).

Frederick Cook (comp.), *Journals of the Military Expedition of . . . Sullivan against the Six Nations* (Auburn, N.Y., 1887).

Sir Henry Clinton, *The American Rebellion,* ed. by Wm. B. Willcox (New Haven, 1954).

Edward E. Curtis, *The Organization of the British Army in the American Revolution* (London, 1926).

Danske Dandridge, *American Prisoners of the Revolution* (Baltimore, 1967).

Elsie N. Danenberg, *The Romance of Norwalk* (New York, 1929).

A. W. Davis, "The Indian and the Border Warfare of the Revolution," in Justin Winsor (ed.), *Narrative and Critical History of America,* vol. 6, pp. 605ff., (Boston, 1887).

Malcolm Decker, *Benedict Arnold, Son of the Havens* (Tarrytown, N.Y., 1932).

————— *Ten Days of Infamy. . . .* (New York, 1969).

Davis R. Dewey, *Financial History of the United States* (New York, 1928).

Dictionary of American Biography (New York, 1928).

Thomas Dring, *Recollections of the Jersey Prison Ship,* ed. by Albert Greene (New York, 1961).

Max von. Eelking, *The German Allied Troops in the North American War of Independence,* trans. and abridged by J. G. Rosengarten (Baltimore, 1969).

H. E. Egerton, *The Royal Commission on the Losses and Services of American Loyalists, 1783–85* (New York, 1969).

John E. Ellsworth, *Simsbury . . .* (Hartford, Conn., 1935).

William Feltman, *Journal* (Philadelphia, 1853).

E. J. Ferguson, *The Power of the Purse, A History of Public Finance, 1776–1790* (Chapel Hill, 1961).

William W. Fink, *Valley Forge* (Des Moines, 1870).

Elijah Fisher, *Journal while in the War for Independence* (Augusta, Me., 1880).

SELECTED BIBLIOGRAPHY

James Thomas Flexner, *Mohawk Baronet, Sir William Johnson of New York* (New York, 1959).

————, *The Traitor and the Spy* (New York, 1953).

G. J. M. French, M.D., "The Simsbury Copper Mines," *New England Magazine,* March 1887.

James E. Gibson, *Dr. Bodo Otto and the Medical Background of the American Revolution* (Baltimore, 1937).

George B. Griffenhagen, "Drug Supplies in the American Revolution," *Bulletin U.S. National Museum,* No. 225 (Washington, D.C., 1961). See p. 117 for Dr. Treadwell's surgical instruments.

Nelson Greene, *History of the Mohawk Valley* (Chicago, 1925).

Edwin Hall (comp.), *The Ancient Historical Records of Norwalk, Ct.* (Norwalk, 1865).

F. W. Halsey, *Old New York Frontier* (New York, 1901).

William W. Harris (comp.), *The Battle of Groton Heights* (New London, 1882).

L. C. Hatch, *The Administration of the American Revolutionary Army* (New York, 1904).

William Heath, *Memoirs. . . .* (Boston, 1798).

George L. Heiges, "Letters Relating to Colonial [actually, Revolutionary] Military Hospitals in Lancaster County," *Lancaster Co. Hist. Soc. Papers,* Vol. LII, No. 4, 1948.

Francis B. Heitman, *Historical Register of Officers of the Continental Army during the . . . Revolution* (Baltimore, 1967).

Richard Hildreth, *The History of the United States of America,* Vol. III (New York, 1849).

Merrill Jensen, *The New Nation, A History of the United States during the Confederation, 1781–1789* (New York, 1950).

————, *The Articles of Confederation . . .* (Madison, 1959).

H. P. Johnston, *The Yorktown Campaign* (Yorktown, Va., 1958).

John W. Johnston, *Centennial Celebration of the Minisink Battle* (Barryville, N.Y., 1879?).

John Jones, M.D., *Plain Concise Practical Remarks on the Treatment of Wounds and Fractures* (New York, 1775).

John W. Jordan, "Military Hospitals at Bethlehem and Lititz during the American Revolution," *Pennsylvania Magazine of History,* Vol. XX.

Joseph Joslin, Jr., *Diary, Coll. Conn. Hist. Soc.,* VII, pp. 297ff.)

SELECTED BIBLIOGRAPHY

Howard A. Kelly and W. L. Burrage (eds.), *Dictionary of American Medical Biography* (New York, 1928).

Lester S. King, M.D., *The Medical World of the Eighteenth Century* (Chicago, 1958).

Ernst Kipping, *The Hessian View of America, 1776–1783* (Monmouth Beach, N.J., 1971).

Bernhard Knollenberg, *Washington and the Revolution. . . .* (New York, 1940).

Richard H. Kohn, "The Inside History of the Newburgh Conspiracy . . . ," *William and Mary Quarterly,* 3rd. Ser., Vol. XXVII, No. 21.

John Charles Philip von Krafft, *Journal, 1776–1784* (New York, 1968).

Lee Papers, Coll. New-York Hist. Soc., 1874.

Mrs. William S. Little, *The Story of the Massacre of Cherry Valley* (n.p., 1891?).

B. J. Lossing, *The Pictorial Field-Book of the Revolution* (2 vols., New York, 1859).

Edward J. Lowell, *The Hessians and Other German Auxiliaries . . . in the Revolutionary War* (New York, 1884).

Simeon Lyman, "Journal of 1775," Coll. Conn. Hist. Soc., Vol. 7 (Hartford, 1899).

Joseph Plumb Martin, *Private Yankee Doodle . . . ,* ed. by George F. Scheer (Boston, 1962).

William S. Middleton, "Medicine at Valley Forge," *The Picket Post,* 38th year, No. 77.

Charles Miner, *History of Wyoming* (Philadelphia, 1845).

Lynn Montross, *Rag, Tag and Bobtail, The Story of the Continental Army, 1775–1783* (New York, 1952).

George Henry Moore, *Mr. Lee's Plan, March 29, 1777* (Port Washington, N.Y., 1970).

H. H. Moore, *Life and Services of General Anthony Wayne* (Philadelphia, 1845).

Richard B. Morris, *The Peacemakers* (New York, 1965).

Wilbur A. Myers (ed.), *The Book of the Sesquicentennial . . . of the Battle of Wyoming* (Wilkes-Barre, 1928).

William H. Nelson, *The American Tory* (Boston, 1964).

A. Tiffany Norton, *History of Sullivan's Campaign against the Iroquois* (Lima, N.Y., 1879).

SELECTED BIBLIOGRAPHY

Henry O'Reilly, *Notices of Sullivan's Campaign.* . . . (Rochester, 1842).

William O. Owen, *The Medical Department of the United States Army during the* . . . *Revolution* (New York, 1920).

Francis R. Packard, M.D., *History of Medicine in the United States* (New York, 1962, Vol. I, chap. VIII, "The Medical Profession in the War of Independence").

Samuel W. Patterson, *Knight Errant of Liberty, The Triumph and Tragedy of General Charles Lee* (New York, 1958).

Samuel W. Patterson, *Horatio Gates, Defender of American Liberties* (New York, 1941).

Captain Georg Pausch, *Journal* (Albany, 1886).

Pennsylvania Archives, Ser. 1, Vol. IV (Philadelphia, 1853, material on Yankee-Pennamite wars).

Richard H. Phelps, *Newgate of Connecticut* (Hartford, 1901).

Stephan Popp, *A Hessian Soldier in the American Revolution,* trans. by R. J. Pope (Racine, Wis., 1953).

Sir John Pringle, *Observations on the Diseases of the Army* (London, 1752, 7th ed., 1782.)

———, *Observations on the Nature and Care of Hospital and Jayl Fevers* (London, 1750.)

Baroness Fredericke Riedesel, *Journal and Correspondence* . . . *1776–1783,* trans. by Marvin L. Brown, Jr. (Chapel Hill, 1965).

Erna Risch, *Quartermaster Support of the Army* . . . *1775–1939* (Washington, D.C., 1962).

Oscar E. Rising, *A New Hampshire Lawyer in Washington's Army* . . . (Geneva, N.Y., 1915).

Kenneth Roberts (ed.), *March to Quebec, Journals of the Members of Arnold's Expedition* (New York, 1938).

Benjamin Rush, M.D., *Directions for Preserving the Health of Soldiers* (Lancaster, Pa., 1778).

Lorenzo Sabine, *A Historical Essay on the Loyalists of the American Revolution* (Springfield, Mass., 1957).

Johann D. Schoepff, *Travels in the Confederation,* trans. by Alfred J. Morrison (Philadelphia, 1911).

James E. Seaver, *A Narrative of the Life of Mrs. Mary Jamison* (Canandaigua, N.Y., 23rd printing, 1929).

Andrew Sherman, *Historic Morristown* (Morristown, N.J., 1905).

SELECTED BIBLIOGRAPHY

Richard H. Shryock, *Medicine and Society in America, 1660–1860* (New York, 1960).

C. Hale Sipe, *The Indian Wars of Pennsylvania* (Harrisburg, 1931).

John R. Spears, *Anthony Wayne* (New York, 1903).

Charles R. Stark, *Groton, Conn., 1705–1905* (Stonington, 1922).

Charles J. Stillé, *Major General Anthony Wayne and the Pennsylvania Line in the Continental Army* (Philadelphia, 1893).

William L. Stone, trans., *Letters of Brunswick and Hessian Officers during the American Revolution* (New York, 1970).

———, *Life of Joseph Brant, Thayendanegea* (2 vols., Cooperstown, N.Y., 1847).

William S. Stryker, *The Capture of the Block House at Toms River, N.J.* (Trenton, 1883).

———, *The Battle of Monmouth,* ed. by Wm. Starr Myers (Princeton, 1927).

John Sullivan, *Letters and Papers, 1779–1795,* ed. by Otis G. Hammond, Vol. III (Concord, N.H., 1939).

William Graham Sumner, *Robert Morris* (New York, 1892).

———, *A History of American Currency* (New York, 1884).

———, *The Financier and the Finances of the American Revolution* (2 vols., New York, 1892).

Howard Swiggett, *War Out of Niagara* (New York, 1932).

Banastre Tarleton, *A History of the Campaigns of 1780 and 1781, in the Southern Provinces of North America* (London, 1787).

James Thacher, *Medical Biography . . . to which is prefaced a succinct history of medical science in the United States* (2 vols., Boston, 1828.)

———, *Military Journal, during the American Revolutionary war* (Hartford, 1854.)

Louise Hall Tharp, *The Baroness and the General* (Boston, 1962).

Therapeutic Notes, Vol. 65, No. 4, April 1958 (for cover picture of pocket case of Revolutionary surgical instruments).

James Tilton, M.D., *Economical Observations on Military Hospitals and the Prevention and Cure of Diseases Incident to the Army* (Wilmington, Del., 1813).

James A. Tobey, *The Medical Department of the Army* (Baltimore, 1927).

[355]

SELECTED BIBLIOGRAPHY

Joseph M. Toner, *The Medical Men of the Revolution* (Philadelphia, 1876).

Benjamin Trumbull, "Journal of the Campaign at New York, 1776–7," *Coll. Conn. Hist. Soc.*, VII).

B. A. Uhlendorf, *The Siege of Charleston, from the von Jungkenn Papers* (New York, 1968).

Univ. of State of New York, *The Sullivan-Clinton Campaign in 1779. . . .* (Albany,1929).

Carl Van Doren, *Mutiny in January* (New York, 1943).

——, *Secret History of the American Revolution* (New York, 1941).

Baron Gerard Van Swieten, *The Diseases Incident to Armies . . .* , trans. by John Ranby (Philadelphia, 1776).

Claude H. Van Tyne, *The Loyalists in the American Revolution* (Gloucester, Mass., 1959).

Clarence L. Ver Steeg, *Robert Morris, Revolutionary Financier* (Philadelphia, 1954).

M. H. Volm, *The Hessian Prisoners in the American War of Independence. . . .* (n.p., 1937).

Albegence Waldo, M.D., "Diary," *Annals of Medical History*, Vol. X, pp. 486ff. (New York, 1928).

Alexander J. Wall, "The Story of the Convention Army, 1777–1783," *New-York. Hist. Soc. Quarterly Bulletin*, Oct. 1927).

Willard Wallace, *Traitorous Hero* (New York, 1954).

Christopher Ward, *The War of the Revolution*, ed. by J. R. Alden (2 vols., New York, 1952).

George Washington, *Writings,* ed. by John C. Fitzpatrick (Washington, D.C., 1931).

Bayze Wells, "Journal, May 1775–Feb. 1777," *Coll. Conn. Hist. Soc.*, Vol. 7. He was on the Canadian expedition from Ticonderoga.

Horace White, *Money and Banking* (New York, 1923).

William A. Wilcox, *The Flight from Wyoming* (Wilkes-Barre, 1900).

Henry E. Wildes, *Valley Forge* (New York, 1938).

Murray S. Wildman, *Money Inflation in the United States* (New York, 1905).

Sally Wister, *Journal,* ed. by Albert Cook Myers (Philadelphia, 1902).

SELECTED BIBLIOGRAPHY

Louis A. Wood, *The War Chief of the Six Nations*. . . . (Toronto, 1915).

Henry Woodman, *History of Valley Forge* (Oakes, Pa., 1922).

Albert Hazen Wright, *The Sullivan Expedition of 1779* (Ithaca, N.Y., 1943).

Wyoming Historical Geological Society, *The Sesqui-Centennial of the Battle of Wyoming, 1778–1928* (Wilkes-Barre, 1928).

Index

INDEX

Camden, Battle of, 27, 28, 295
Campbell, Col. William, 29, 31
Canada, 336-37, 339; invasion of, 4-5; failure, 17; refuge for loyalists, 33-34; proposed second attack on, 77, 78; withdrawal from, 163
Canadians with American invasion, 10
Canajoharie, N.Y., 255, 267
Carleton, Gen. Guy, 6, 17, 255; in command of Quebec, 9, 12, 15; paroles prisoners, 16, 246; and Huddy case, 33
Carlisle, F. H., Earl of, 55, 64
Carroll, Charles, of Carrollton, 42
Catherine the Great, 225, 332, 333, 346
Chambly, Canada, 6, 163
Charleston, S.C., 121, 167, 168, 191-92, 249, 295, 301, 317, 337; capture of, 27-28; exodus by loyalists, 33; defense by Lee and Moultrie, 57
Charlotte, N.C., 28
Chastellux, Gen. F. J., 303
Chatham, N.J., 217, 218
Cheraw, S.C., 28
Cherry Valley, N.Y., 27; raid on, 261-64
Chesapeake Bay, 28, 296, 298; French victory in, 308
Church, Dr. Benjamin, 144

Church of England, 19
Cleveland, Col. Benjamin, 29
Clinton, George, 242, 330
Clinton, Gen. Sir Henry, 27-28, 63, 64, 84, 114, 121, 170, 171, 189, 190, 195, 197, 198, 249, 273, 275-76, 283, 305-6; and Huddy case, 32; march across N.J., 65ff; André acts for, 187; agrees to Arnold's terms, 193; forbids André to enter American lines, 194; tries to save André, 202-3; effort to entice American mutineers, 209ff
Clinton, Gen. James, 262, 263, 264, 267ff
Cochran, Dr. John, 145, 151
Colburn, Reuben (boat builder), 6
Concord, Mass., fight at, 20
Confederation, 35, 36, 220, 316, 320, 346; limitations of, 38-39, 48; Articles of, 49ff; ratified, 55
Confiscation of enemy property, 19, 26, 35
Connecticut, 94-95, 97, 115, 257; attacked by Arnold, 275ff; Western Reserve, 288
Constitution of U.S., 37, 330, 346; called a conspiracy, 38, 52
Continentals (troops), 138, 168
Continental Congress, 63, 72, 74, 85, 311-12; abandons Ticonderoga, 4; reinforces Canadian ex-

[361]

Continental Congress (*cont.*)
pedition, 13, 14; and Asgill, 33; and confiscated estates, 34; weakness of, 36ff; poor attendance on, 40ff; rejects Howe's peace overtures, 52; favors to Conway, 75-76; projects second attack on Canada, 77, 79; informed by Washington of Conway's censure, 81; favors Conway and Gates, 82; functions in exile, 84; lacks power to tax, 92, 93-94; praises, then repudiates paper money, 92ff; assurances on paper money doubted, 99; resorts to revenue in kind, 103-5; administration by committees inefficient, 107-9; finally appoints Supt. of Finance, 109-10; drafts on envoys, 111-12; recruiting by, 115; establishes medical service, 144; incompetent to help hospitals, 152; and Morristown mutiny, 210; and mutineers in Philadelphia, 220ff; moves to Princeton, 223; dishonors Saratoga agreement, 241; thanks victorious officers, 243; and surrendered matériel, 244; suspends embarkation of Saratoga prisoners, 249; blamed for breaking convention, 249-50; often fails to discharge responsibilities, 289, 301; compliant to foreign officers, 290; officers' petition to, 313ff

Contributions in kind, 86, 103-4

Conway, Gen. Charles, 76, as rival of Washington, 72-73; taken to task by Washington, 75; Inspector General, 75; name given to cabal, 76ff; Lafayette will not accept, 78; resigns, 79

Cornwallis, Gen. Lord Charles, 21, 27-28, 67, 113, 220, 240, 249, 276, 295, 297, 301, 303, 306ff; and Negroes with his army, 25; punishes patriots, 26; captures Fort Lee, 58; at Fort Washington, 294; surrenders, 311

Coryell's Ferry, 64

Counterfeit currency, 32, 91-92, 247

Cowpens, S.C., 29

Craik, Dr. James, 154

Crown Point (on Champlain), 15, 16; sickness at, 164

Cunningham, Capt. William, 168, 169-70

Danbury, Conn., 134, 141, 275, 276

Dayton, Col. Elias, 217

Deane, Silas, 109, 289-91

Declaration of Independence, 20, 38; reluctantly adopted, 48, 49

INDEX

INDEX

Frederick the Great, 57, 77, 127, 224, 225, 332
French alliance, 17, 23, 49, 54, 55, 186, 208, 300, 302-3; American peace commissioners hampered by, 335; rift in, 342ff
French fleet, 296, 297

Gadsden, Christopher, 26
Gage, Gen. Thomas, 169
Galloway, Joseph, 120
Gardiner's Island, N.Y., 296, 298
Gates, Gen. Horatio, 15, 27, 57, 61, 62, 76, 77, 84, 120, 241ff, 327-28; champion of Washington's critics, 72ff, 322; does not report Saratoga surrender to Washington, 74-75, 82; and slurs by Conway, 80 ff; gold medal for, 243; head of War Board, 245
Georgia, 28, 45, 319
Germain, Lord George, 63, 118
German mercenaries, 14, 20, 224ff, 251, 276, 278, 280, 294, 311; officers' professional pride, 56; in N.J. retreat, 65; punishments among, 122; homesick, 231; Americans' hatred of, 231-32; thousands remain in America, 232-33
Germantown, Battle of, 73, 150

Gerry, Elbridge, 95, 245
Gibraltar, 112, 337
Gloucester Point, Va., 310
Grayson, William, 42
Great Britain, 46, 48
Greene, Gen. Nathanael, 75, 113, 201, 291, 293, 295, 297, 299, 326; on Whig-Tory strife, 18; and Monmouth attack, 65ff; becomes Quartermaster General, 133, 140; notifies Congress Charleston is evacuated, 317
Groton, Conn., 94; Arnold's attack on, 276ff
Gunpowder, 125-26

Hackensack, N.J., 58, 59, 235, 292, 293, 294
Hamilton, Lt. Col. Alexander, 65, 67, 68, 109, 185, 200ff, 300, 317, 320, 321; accused by Gates, 80-81; critical of war finance, 87, 95-96; and Philadelphia mutiny, 221ff
Hand, Gen. Edward, 120, 268
Harmar, Col. Josiah, 46
Harnett, Cornelius, 94
Hartley, David, 334ff
Haverstraw, N.Y., 60, 194
Hazen, Col. Moses, 78
Head of Elk (Elkton, Md.), 134, 307

[364]

INDEX

Heath, Gen. William, 59, 244, 246, 247, 292

Von Heister, Gen. Leopold, 233-34

Henry, Patrick, 48, 79

Henry, William, 221

Herkimer, Gen. Nicholas, 255ff

Hesse-Cassel, 225, 227-28

Hesse-Hanau, 228

Hopewell, N.J., 65

Hospitals, 143; general vs. regimental, 146, 148ff; lack supplies, 150-53; for prisoners, 173, 178

Howe, Lord Richard, 52, 64, 338

Howe, Gen. Robert, 193, 194, 218

Howe, Gen. Sir William, 15, 52, 58, 61, 62, 71, 73, 84, 169, 170, 171, 233, 246, 250-51, 297; blamed by Washington for mistreatment of prisoners, 179

Huddy, Capt. Joshua, 32-33

Hudson River, 4, 15, 31, 62, 194, 255, 291ff, 303, 308

Ile aux Noir, 6; sickness at, 14, 164

Import duties for Congress, 319, 329-30

Impressment, 86, 134, 246, 299

Indians: employed by Americans, 273; proposed use by British, 274

Indians of Canada, 3, 4; join forces with loyalists, 27; as allies of British, 118-19, 165; employed by Congress, 120

Jay, John: defends paper money, 95; envoy to Spain, 112; peace commissioner, 333ff

Jameson, Lt. Col. John, 199

James River, 309, 311

Jefferson, Thomas, 89-90, 240, 335

Jersey (prison ship), 175ff

Johnson, Sir Guy, 27, 255, 258ff; at Newtown battle, 269

Johnson, Sir John, 253, 254, 269

Johnson, Sir William, 254, 255

Jones, Dr. John, 147, 148, 159, 160, 161

Jones, Joseph, 246, 320, 321, 324

Kanadaseago, 263, 268

King George III, 19, 22, 23, 39, 48, 106, 118, 171, 189, 211, 249, 254, 255, 266, 333, 334, 338, 339, 345; hires German auxiliaries, 224ff

King Louis XVI, 331, 332, 335

King's Bridge, 157, 234

King's College, 146, 168

King's Ferry, 194ff

Knox, Gen. Henry, 15, 75, 114, 200, 212, 290, 291, 313, 321, 326, 327

INDEX